The Ascendancy of Taste

*Ideas and Forms
in English Literature*

Edited by John Lawlor
Professor of English, University of Keele

The English Georgic
John Chalker

Number Symbolism
Christopher Butler

Ideas of Greatness
Eugene M. Waith

Voices of Melancholy
Bridget Gellert Lyons

The Grand Design of God
C. A. Patrides

The Ascendancy of Taste

The achievement of Joseph and Thomas Warton

Joan Pittock

Department of English, University of Aberdeen

Routledge and Kegan Paul
London

First published 1973
by Routledge & Kegan Paul Ltd
Broadway House, 68–74 Carter Lane,
London EC4V 5EL
Printed in Great Britain by
The Camelot Press Ltd, London and Southampton

ISBN 0 7100 7535 9

Library of Congress Catalog Card No. 72–97948

to

Malcolm and Murray

General Editor's Introduction

This series aims to explore two main aspects of literary tradition in English. First, the role of particular literary forms, with due emphasis on the distinctive sorts of application they receive at English hands; second, the nature and function of influential ideas, varying from large general conceptions evident over long periods to those concepts which are peculiar to a given age.

Each book attempts an account of the form or idea, and treats in detail particular authors and works rather than offering a general survey. The aim throughout is evaluative and critical rather than descriptive and merely historical.

J. L.

Contents

Acknowledgments

My obligations to so many friends and colleagues for their help and encouragement are too numerous to detail but are deeply felt. The editorial keenness, generosity and patience of Professor John Lawlor, and the lucid good sense of my colleague, Dr Thomas Craik, have eliminated many mistakes: for those which remain I am solely responsible. To W. S. Watt, Professor of Humanity in the University of Aberdeen, I am particularly indebted for translations of Thomas Warton's Latin criticism; to J. M. G. Blakiston, Fellows' Librarian of Winchester College, and John Cooper, Librarian of Trinity College, Oxford, I am grateful for their assisting my researches among the Warton MSS. over many years. I am grateful, too, to the Trustees of the British Museum, the Warden and Fellows of Winchester College and the President and Fellows of Trinity College for permission to reproduce parts of the Warton MSS.

It is due to the grants for research allotted me by the Trustees of the Carnegie Travelling Research Fund that I have been able to extend my researches into the writings of the mid-eighteenth century while employed at the University of Aberdeen. The completion of this work, as of others, is due to the devoted and painstaking typing of my mother which has been generously assisted by the secretarial staff of the English Department, Miss Lily Hay and Miss Ida Blacklaws. To my husband's rigorous critical sense and reformulations of half-thought-out ideas I owe a great deal: for my small son's patience I can now only express my gratitude.

J. P.

. . . genius, fancy, judgement, goût,
Whim, caprice, je-ne-sçai-quoi, virtù,
Which appellations all describe
Taste, and the modern tasteful tribe.

Robert Lloyd, 1757

The man, the nation, must therefore be good, whose
chiefest luxuries consist in the refinement of reason,
and reason can never be universally cultivated unless
guided by Taste, which may be considered as the link
between science and common-sense, the medium through
which learning should ever be seen by society.

Oliver Goldsmith, 1759

Taste . . . intermingles with, directs, even anticipates
execution . . . directs and animates the observation of
Nature, giving thus the initial impetus to creative
imagination; and . . . by forming the habits of fancy,
it gives regularity and correctness to creation. The
relative predominance and the degree of development of
different ingredients of taste – judgment and the inter-
nal senses – determine the varieties of artistic genius.

Alexander Gerard, 1758

One

Taste and Augustanism

I

The tendency to polarise the Augustans and the Romantics has usually been accompanied by a neglect of the period of transition between the two – the mid-eighteenth century. Its historical importance has, of course, always been recognised; but the intrinsic interest of its taste and criticism has been virtually ignored. It is forty years since David Nichol Smith complained of the 'sense of contention' with which critics approached this period, and of their predilection for seeing it either as, 'from one point of view, a period of decadence, and, from another, a period of preparation', – rather than as a period with its own distinctive preoccupations.[1] But the complex patterns of its literary concerns remain simplified while writers classified 'pre-romantic' or 'transitional' – according to the bias of the enquirer – receive little attention so far as their individual achievement is concerned. So, for example, Joseph and Thomas Warton were in the nineteenth century generally regarded as being precursors of Romanticism, though to their contemporaries there had seemed little that was startlingly new in their work, while modern scholarship has largely occupied itself with identifying the nature of their indebtedness to their predecessors. No large-scale assessment of Joseph Warton's work has been published; and there has been no full examination of Thomas's since Clarissa Rinaker published her study in 1916.[2]

Yet the critical writings of the Wartons are of particular interest. Joseph Warton's reaction against the didactic and satiric poetry of Pope in his *Essay on the Genius and Writings of Pope* (1756–82) – 'What is there very sublime or very Pathetic in Pope?' – seems to be an attempt to identify the distinctive features of poetry as affective rather than formal. Thomas Warton, in his *Observations on the Faerie Queene* (1754), applied historical and comparative criteria, quoting romance material, to show that Spenser was trying to write an epic radically different from those of Homer and Virgil. And his *History of English Poetry* (1774–81) is the first attempt to examine English poetry as a diversified yet coherent tradition.

To appreciate their achievement for its own sake, as well as historically, it is first of all necessary to look more closely at the ways in which the permanent questions of criticism are posed at this time – those questions which concern the role of art, the nature of the artist's gifts, and the kind of relationship which the current vocabulary of critical terms presupposes to exist between the work of art and the audience. This involves a consideration of the criticism of the early eighteenth century; then – to see what developments have taken place – of the mid-eighteenth century. It should be possible to go on from this point to see how far the work of the Wartons reflects the prevailing assumptions of their time; to discover what is of historical significance in their work, and what is the permanent nature of their achievement as critics.

II

The word 'taste' in the early eighteenth century provides a common ground for the reinterpretation of existing standards and the formulation of new ones. It acquires an unprecedented importance from being a key term in the presentation of the Augustan social image; in the new developments in philosophical speculation; and in those trends in criticism which were movements away from a predominantly formal approach. 'Taste' is, of course, a word susceptible of large interpretations: always inherent in them, however, is the suggestion of its subjective and individual origin.

In a social context 'taste' indicates a cultivated response, an educated and consciously selective preference for a certain kind of aesthetic experience. So when changes in social structure effect a reaction against the traditional values of a dominant cultural group the word takes on a special significance, as those trained to the appreciation of one kind of art or literature recognise a threat to their standards. At this point the defence of taste becomes confused with the preservation of a whole way of life. Then there is always the danger that subsequent writers on the period will take the dominant cultural group at its own valuation: and this has been largely the case with the twentieth-century view of Augustanism.

III

The vicissitudes, political and religious, of the seventeenth century might seem to have been due to an indulgence in enthusiasm and dissent to the point of endangering the whole social fabric. As Dryden had put it in 'Religio Laici' (1682):

> In doubtfull questions 'tis the safest way
> To learn what unsuspected Ancients say:
> For 'tis not likely *we* shou'd higher Soar
> In search of Heav'n, than *all the Church before* . . .
> 'Tis some Relief, that points not clearly known,
> Without much hazard may be let alone . . .
> That private Reason 'tis more just to curb,
> Than by Disputes the publick Peace disturb.
> For points obscure are of small use to learn:
> But *Common quiet* is *Mankind's concern.*
>
> (435–8, 443–4 and 447–50)

Written before the 1688 Revolution, these sentiments were even more generally acceptable after it. Pope makes a similar point with a specifically political application in his 'Essay on Man' (1734):

> For Forms of Government let fools contest;
> Whate'er is best administer'd is best.
>
> (iii, 303–4)

A strong sense of social duty, based on moderation and good sense, would help to counterbalance dissident tendencies which might at any moment of unrest rouse the city mobs. And these qualities were exemplified in the writings of one of the classical models whose work had already been widely admired and imitated in France, the country which held the lead in literary experiment and speculation. The urbane wittiness of Horace, his concern for formal perfection and ease and lucidity of statement, were desirable in the sphere of polite literature. And in a period threatening to break out in different types of unrest the educated upper classes of the eighteenth century could prize in addition Horace's celebration of the virtues of the golden mean – stoical good sense, moderation, tolerance, politeness and the cultivation of the civilised and social virtues. The Latin poet had stressed the importance of decorum, of an accepted decent standard of normal feelings and behaviour: departures from these he had exposed to ridicule for correction. His example was followed by Pope; but it fell in, too, with the satire of manners in the drama, to establish in the periodicals of the day what was to become a traditional preoccupation with social satire of a lighter kind – of manners rather than politics or other issues of serious concern which might arouse strong feelings.

The claims to civilised and social behaviour which the Augustans made for their society were supported during the first decades of the century by the national pride in a recently established political settlement and in an expanding economy. The development of a measure of political stability and religious toleration and the increasing wealth and importance of the middle classes engendered a pride and self-confidence in the nation which might mask for the time being the extent of its social ills – infant mortality and drunkenness in particular – ills which were to demand some public attention and agitation for redress when they increased sharply between 1720 and 1750.[3] Poets could continue, however, to extol the nation and society as Britannia, the home of liberty. In 1727 Thomson celebrated 'Happy Britannia'

> . . . where the Queen of Arts
> Inspiring vigour, Liberty, abroad
> Walks unconfined even to thy farthest cots,
> And scatters plenty with unsparing hand.
>
> Thy country teems with wealth;
> And Property assures it to the Swain,
> Pleased, and unwearied, in his guarded toil.
>
> ('Summer', 1442–5 and 1454–6)

The literary conventionality of the diction smoothes the rural scene to one of universal harmony. Nor do Thomson's cities reveal the filth and poverty of Hogarth's:

4

> Full are thy cities with the sons of art;
> And trade and joy, in every busy street,
> Mingling are heard: even Drudgery himself,
> As at the car he sweats, or, dusty, hews
> The palace-stone, looks gay . . .
>
> ('Summer', 1457–61)

For a nobility which had become respectable, a landed gentry, and an aspiring middle class, increasingly wealthier through trade and commerce, an attractive social ideal was that of the man of taste – the educated, well-bred, witty *arbiter elegantiarum* – the descendant of the Restoration wit, reformed to all outward appearances. It was he whom Pope invoked in Horatian terms when complimenting his noble acquaintance in the 'Epilogue to the Satires':

> How can I PULT'NEY, CHESTERFIELD, forget,
> While *Roman* Spirit charms, and *Attic* Wit?
>
> ('Dialogue ii', 1738, 84–5)

To have taste was a fashionable pursuit. The increase in wealth was applied to the conspicuous manifestation of an ability to purchase cultural superiority:

> For what has Virro painted, built, and planted?
> Only to show how many Tastes he wanted.
> What brought Sir Visto's ill-got wealth to waste?
> Some Daemon whisper'd, 'Visto! have a Taste'.
>
> ('Epistle to Burlington', 1731, 13–16)

It was for these as well as for Burlington, Bathurst, and Boyle, whose discrimination Pope praised in the 'Moral Essays', that eighteenth-century achievements in the various architectural and decorative arts were effected. The pursuit of taste enabled the newly wealthy to feel closer to the interests of the aristocracy. Such a union was attempted in the *Spectator*, where character-types – Sir Roger de Coverley and Sir Andrew Freeport are the obvious examples – are presented, not as realistically delineated individuals, but as exhibiting the idealised attributes of members of the gentry and middle classes.

It is interesting in view of the relationship between society and the state of the nation as a whole that Johnson in his 'Life of Addison' should imply that the foundation of the *Spectator* was connected with the manipulation of public feeling away from urgent national concern towards the domestic and social:[4]

> It has been suggested that the Royal Society was instituted soon after the Restoration, to divert the attention of people from publick discontent. *The Tatler* and *Spectator* had the same tendency; they were published at a time when two parties, loud, restless, and violent, each with plausible declarations, and each perhaps without any distinct termination of its views, were agitating the nation; to minds heated with political contest they supplied cooler and more inoffensive reflections; and it is said by Addison in a subsequent work, that they had a perceptible influence upon the conversation of that time, and taught the frolic and the gay to unite merriment with decency – an effect which they can never wholly lose, while they continue to be among the first books by which both sexes are initiated in the elegances of knowledge.

In his 'Letter Concerning Enthusiasm' (1708) the third Earl of Shaftesbury had advocated the use of wit and ridicule as the best means of combating such anti-social qualities as vanity, laziness and fanaticism: so in the tenth number of the *Spectator* Addison announced his intention of enlivening morality with wit and tempering wit with morality,

> that my readers may, if possible, both Ways find their Account in the Speculation of the Day. And to the End that their Virtue and Discretion may not be short transient intermitting Starts of Thought, I have resolved to refresh their Memories from Day to Day, till I have recovered them out of the desperate State of Vice and Folly into which the Age has fallen. The Mind that lies fallow but a single Day, sprouts up in Follies that are only to be killed by a constant and assiduous Culture. It was said of *Socrates*, that he brought Philosophy down from Heaven, to inhabit among Men; and I shall be ambitious to have it said of me, that I have brought Philosophy out of Closets and Libraries, Schools and Colleges, to dwell in Clubs and Assemblies, at Tea-Tables and in Coffee-Houses.

IV

It was likely, of course, that this impulse would lead to the simplification of issues of morality and taste in the interests of satire and didacticism, and thereby distort the traditional humane values which Addison was trying to uphold. The attempt to popularise tends to result in a superficiality of treatment and a coarsening of what are frequently venerable traditions of thought. So in the 'Essay on Man' (1733–4) Pope huddled together notions from Platonic thought, from Leibniz, Spinoza, Pascal and Shaftesbury, to give a scientific account of human nature

> reduced to a *few, clear points*; There are not *many certain truths* in this world. It is therefore in the Anatomy of the Mind as in that of the Body; more good will accrue to mankind by attending to the large, open, and perceptible parts, than by studying too much such finer nerves and vessels, the conformations and uses of which will forever escape our observation. The *disputes* are all upon these last, and, I will venture to say, they have less sharpened the *wits* than the *hearts* of men against each other, and have diminished the practice, more than advanced the theory, of Morality. If I could flatter myself that this Essay has any merit, it is in steering betwixt the extremes of doctrines seemingly opposite, in passing over terms utterly unintelligible, and in forming a *temperate* yet not *inconsistent*, and a *short* yet not *imperfect* system of Ethics.   ('The Design')

The smoothing out of differences, the assimilation of different wisdoms to a universal good sense is typically Augustan. Inherent in the ethics which Pope versified is the traditional body of wisdom, which his age had inherited, concerning man in relation to the universe. His contemporaries' awareness of this encouraged a stoical view of mankind as subject to the vicissitudes of the human condition. Man, his reason beguiled by his will and his passions, could be at one and the same time 'the glory, jest, and riddle of the world'. Like the races of the past he was doomed to depart from life's scene. On the one hand this engenders in the Augustan literary mode the sense of the transitoriness of human existence. It enables the Augustan poet with his dexterous use of classical literary allusion to give expression to a sense of long perspectives of generalised wisdom; though he is often, of course, in danger of falling into glib sententiousness. But presented, as it often is, in terms of the social tones and idioms of contemporary polite conversation to achieve effects of satire and irony, Augustan poetry eschews a straightforward treatment of man in his universal setting, relying rather on sophisticated wit to ridicule mankind's pretentiousness and folly. So even when Pope is addressing Bolingbroke on the theme of man's place in the universe at the beginning of the 'Essay on Man' he announces '(since Life can little more supply/Than just to look about us, and to die)' that his purpose is to:

> Eye Nature's walks, shoot Folly as it flies,
> And catch the Manners living as they rise;
>
> (13–14)

– an odd way to approach so serious a theme.

The Augustan technique of presenting human experience is inherently a narrowing and simplifying one, though it may appear attractively assured and civilised. Occasionally it can, in Swift for example, break out into an assertion of the claims of ordinary humanity on man's benevolence – as in *A Modest Proposal* (1729) – but this humane note tends to be incidental to the main thrust of the satire. The way in which it was possible for the mingling of the inherited ideas of the past, enunciated with classical poise and wit, to oust the realities and complexities of contemporary life is shown in the empty pretentiousness of the conclusion to the 'Essay on Man' with its exaltation of the poet and his noble friend – Bolingbroke, of course – above terrestrial concerns:

> Oh, while along the stream of Time thy name
> Expanded flies, and gathers all its fame,
> Say, shall my little bark attendant sail,
> Pursue the triumph, and partake the gale?
> When statesmen, heroes, kings in dust repose,
> Whose sons shall blush their fathers were thy foes,
> Shall then this verse to future age pretend

Thou wert my guide, philosopher, and friend?
That urg'd by thee, I turn'd the tuneful art
From sounds to things, from fancy to the heart;
For Wit's false mirror held up Nature's light;
Shew'd erring Pride, WHATEVER IS, IS RIGHT;
That REASON, PASSION, answer one great aim;
That true SELF-LOVE and SOCIAL are the same;
That VIRTUE only makes our Bliss below;
And all our Knowledge is, OURSELVES TO KNOW.

The succinctness with which Pope voiced such precepts was especially agreeable to those in political and social control; and it is not remarkable that the 'Essay on Man' achieved popularity in translation throughout Europe. But however acceptable Pope's ideas may have been to the ruling and upper classes, they appeared to the unprejudiced a couple of decades later flagrantly simple and naive. So Johnson found them in his review of Soame Jenyns's *Enquiry into the Nature and Origins of Evil* (1756); and he condemned them later in his 'Life of Pope'. Writing long after, Dickens observed of 'Whatever is, is right', that it is 'an aphorism that would be as final as it is lazy, did it not include the troublesome consequence, that nothing that ever was, was wrong' (*A Tale of Two Cities*, pt II, ch. 2).

The coarsening of standards of culture was well described by Eliot. Of the pleasure of taste Addison had observed:

A man of a Polite Imagination is let into a great many
Pleasures that the Vulgar are not capable of receiving.
He can converse with a Picture, and find an agreeable
Companion in a Statue. He meets with secret
Refreshment in a Description, and often finds a greater
Satisfaction in the Prospect of Fields and Meadows
than another does in the Possession.

(*Spectator*, no. 411)

Eliot comments:[5]

The eighteenth century emphases are illuminating. . . .
I suppose that Addison is what one would describe as
a gentleman, as, one might say, no better than a
gentleman. . . . And, gentleman as he is, he has a very
low opinion of those who are not genteel.

V

Augustan standards could hold good only so long as the importance of polite conduct could usurp the place of a moral code; so
long as good sense was regarded as the equivalent of wisdom, and
literature was preoccupied with the formal and didactic, and so
long as these standards were voiced by men prominent in the
intellectual society of a metropolis which had as yet surrendered
little of its importance to provincial centres, and whose attitudes
towards literature were, for one reason or another, remarkably
homogeneous. The members of the Scriblerus Club – Pope, Swift,
Arbuthnot, Garth and Gay – satirised the vanity and hypocrisy of
polite society in a polite way, exalting as they did so the good sense
and good taste of their acquaintance.

But the reliance on a classically educated minority for the
preservation of standards of taste – Dryden had referred to them in
the preface to his translation of the *Aeneid* as the 'iudices natos',
'These *born* to Judge' (Pope, 'An Essay on Criticism', 1711, 14) –
seemed to be endangered by the state of affairs in which pro-
fessional writers and journalists wrote to meet the demands of the
public at large for the informative, the edifying, the marvellous
and affecting. The *Adventurer* had observed that 'there never was a
time, in which men of all degrees of ability, of every kind of education, of every profession and employment, were posting with
ardour so general to the press' (no. 115). The expanding appetites
for reading matter which the Grub Street writers and their publishers catered for were not oriented towards the culture of the
arbiters of taste but towards the zest for the sensational and marvellous in life and literature. The popular taste was caught, as
Shaftesbury complained in 1710, by[6]

> Captains and trusty Travellers, (who) pass for
> authentic Records . . . They have far more Pleasure in
> hearing the Monstrous Accounts of monstrous Men,
> and Manners; than the politest and best Narrations of
> the Affairs, the Governments, and Lives, of the wisest,
> and most polish'd People.

Accounts such as these abounded, from the serialisation of the
Arabian Nights in Parker's *London News* and *Penny Post* in 1724–5,

and the monthly publication by instalment of travels, histories, biographies and novels, to Defoe's accounts of the adventures of Robinson Crusoe, Colonel Jack and Moll Flanders. To Shaftesbury traditional standards might well seem in danger of being swamped, so that the view in 'The Dunciad' of the Empire of Chaos being restored passed for a relevant, if comic, observation on the contemporary state of affairs. What I have suggested so far in this chapter, however, is that it has been misleading in dealing with the early eighteenth century to accept the dominant cultural group at its own valuation.

VI

Twentieth-century discrimination between good and bad taste has resolved round issues strikingly similar to those which confronted the writers and critics of the Augustan era. For the Augustan, good taste as the purlieu of a select minority in a mass civilisation was thought to be endangered by the practice of writers who had not been trained by education or upbringing to appreciate the best models. In this context the single-minded pursuit of scholarship to the possible detriment of good manners might be as damaging as lack of education. So in 'The Dunciad' Pope ridiculed both Bentley and Defoe – the one for his pedantry, the other for his ignorance. In *After Strange Gods* (1934) Eliot attacked Lawrence for his inability to respect the cultural values of his society because of his lack of the right kind of cultural training. That cultural responsibility was associated with training of a special kind was maintained by F. R. Leavis in 'The Idea of a University'; and that the Augustan dilemma seemed particularly relevant to the twentieth-century scene was made clear by Q. D. Leavis's special commendation of Gissing's *New Grub Street* on the ground that it exposed the corruption of literary standards by popular journalism.[7]

Cultural minorities assume, of course, the desirability of educating others to a higher pitch of perceptiveness and refinement within their own tradition. It follows too easily that the tastes of the mass of the population are to be condemned, and that the reformation of taste is to be a reformation in accordance with the cultural interests of a minority group, and that group one which is specially privileged, whether by wealth or education. So the impulse towards reform has tended to involve – whether for Pope and Addison or Arnold and Leavis – an unduly narrow sensitivity to humanity in general, characterised by a lack of actual grasp on the realities of political and social existence. And much of the writing which has associated itself with the safeguarding of cultural standards has tended to confuse the state of public taste with the well-being of the nation. So Pope's jettisoning of most of the distinguished scholarship of his time, his distrust of his contemporaries' enthusiasm for scientific and antiquarian investigation, is subsumed for Dr Leavis in the poet's alarm at the threat to his cultural standards presented by those hacks who catered for the tastes of the masses. The conclusion to 'The Dunciad', therefore, evokes a special admiration from Dr Leavis, not merely because of its superb exploitation of mock-heroic effects in the grand finale, but as a genuine and serious projection of a cultural dilemma in terms of the survival of civilisation itself. This tendency to take the Augustan writers at their own valuation continues, and has been further sophisticated, for example, in Paul Fussell's *Rhetorical Basis of Augustan Humanism* (1965) where Pope joins Swift, Gibbon and Burke in a group which is considered to 'largely redeem the period' from its faults of grandiosity, sentimentality, self-satisfaction and archness. This it does for Fussell, as one might anticipate, by upholding 'a serious humanist orthodoxy' in an 'ethically involved style'.

VII

But apart from the question of the Augustan social image – though of course connected with it – the idea of taste had a special significance in both the philosophy and criticism of the early eighteenth century. Ideas of the social importance of good taste were given a basis in philosophical speculation which strengthened their role and extended it to the moral realm. The seriousness with which 'taste' could be used in a social context and the relevance with which standards of taste might be invoked was due chiefly to the importance of the term in the writings of the third Earl of Shaftesbury.

In his *Characteristics of Men, Manners, Opinions, Times* (1711) Shaftesbury, postulating the existence of an innate moral sense, reacted against the materialistic influence of his former tutor, Locke. The popularity of Shaftesbury's work and its widespread influence was sufficient testimony to the acceptability of his ideas.[8] On these Francis Hutcheson based his *Essay on the Nature and Conduct of the Passions and Affections* (1728): this in turn was the basis for much of the work of the empirical philosophers of the mid-eighteenth century whose characteristic preoccupation was with the nature of the aesthetic response – the problem of taste.

Shaftesbury describes his moral sense as a 'reflex sense', and his account of its operations associates the aesthetic with the moral: the awareness of right and wrong is, at one and the same time, an awareness of the beautiful and the ugly:[9]

> The Case is the same in the *mental* or *moral* Subjects, as in the ordinary *Bodys*, or common Subjects of *Sense.* The Shapes, Motions, Colours and Proportions of these latter being presented to our Eye; there necessarily results a Beauty or Deformity, according to the different Measure, Arrangement, and Disposition of their several Parts. So in *Behaviour* and *Actions*, when presented to our Understanding, there must be found, of necessity, an apparent Difference, according to the Regularity or Irregularity of the Subjects.

This capacity in man having been identified as taste, it follows that a correct training will enable him to choose the reasonable and the natural, the true and the beautiful. Hence that part of man's nature which enabled him to appreciate the wisdom he had inherited from the past was identified more closely with his psychological fabric – that sense which could appreciate beauty and truth – than with his reason.

Shaftesbury's ethical and aesthetic positive is, then, an expression of the desire for an ordered, social, reasonable and natural harmony, so often celebrated by the Augustan humanists:

> What Mortal being once convinc'd of a difference in *inward Character*, and of a Preference due to *one* Kind

above *another*; wou'd not be concern'd to make *his own*
the best? If *Civility* and *Humanity* be a TASTE; If
Brutality, Insolence, Riot be in the same manner a TASTE;
who, if he cou'd reflect, wou'd not chuse to form
himself on the amiable and agreeable, rather than the
odious and perverse Model? Who wou'd not endeavour
to *force* NATURE as well in this respect, as in what
relates to a *Taste* or *Judgment* in other Arts and
Sciences? For in each place the *Force* on Nature is us'd
only for its Redress. If a natural *good* TASTE be not
already form'd in us; why shou'd not we endeavour to
form it, and become *natural*?

The impulse to strive towards the perfection of a higher nature,
to man's ideal potential, has its antecedents in Plato: now the key
to man's realisation of his true nature is proclaimed as his taste.
And for Shaftesbury the general standards of contemporary taste
seemed to make reform imperative. The means of doing so, of
course, lay in an acquaintance with the classical authors. By reading them, the taste 'which makes us prefer a *Turkish* History to a
Grecian or a *Roman*; an ARIOSTO to a VIRGIL; and a Romance or
Novel to an Iliad' will be improved. The distinctive feature of an
uneducated taste is its addiction to sensational subject-matter: so,
among the vulgar, '*he* is ever compleatest, and of the first Rank,
who is able to speak of Things the most *unnatural* and *monstrous*.'[10]
This is the taste which Addison condemned as 'Gothic' in his
sixty-second *Spectator*: 'I look upon these Writers as *Goths* in
Poetry, who, like those in Architecture, not being able to come up
to the Simplicity of the old *Greeks* and *Romans*, have endeavoured
to supply its Place with all the Extravagances of an irregular
Fancy.' And he quotes Dryden, in support of his contention 'that
the Taste of most of our *English* Poets, as well as Readers, is
extremely *Gothick*'.

This kind of taste did not, that is, find the strict formal organisation of material according to classical precedent as congenial as
variety of subject-matter for its own sake. For Dryden, correctness
and formal perfection did not march with imaginative exuberance.
After the Restoration the imitation of French and classical models
focused the attention of writers on formal requirements of art:
movements in scientific and philosophical thought reinforced the

dominant cultural group's view of itself as enlightened, sceptical and empirical. This could be strengthened merely by a lack of historical awareness. In his *History of the Royal Society* (1667), Sprat attacked the poet's use of allegorical and supernatural figures as fantastic and irresponsible fabrications by expounding the current myth of progressive enlightenment:[11]

> The *Poets* began of old to impose the *Deceit*. They, to make all Things look more venerable than they were, devis'd a thousand false *Chimaeras*; on every *Field*, *River*, *Grove* and *Cave*, they bestow'd a Fantasm of their own making. With these they amaz'd the World; these they cloth'd with what Shapes they pleas'd; by these they pretended, that all Wars and Counsels, and Actions of Men were administered. And in the modern *Ages* these *Fantastical Forms* were reviv'd and possess'd Christendom, in the very height of the *Schoolemens* time: an infinite Number of *Fairies* haunted every House; all Churches were fill'd with *Apparitions*; Men began to be frightened from their *Cradles*, which Fright continu'd to their *Graves*, and their Names also made the Causes of scaring others. . . . But from the time in which the *Real Philosophy* has appear'd there is scarce any whisper remaining of such *Horrors*: every man is unshaken at those Tales at which his *Ancestors* trembl'd: The Course of Things goes quietly along, in its own true Channel of *Natural Causes* and *Effects*.

The dominant influence of Dryden, and later Pope, in expressing this point of view established the interpretation of the native literary tradition as that of a movement towards correctness, or formal perfection. This view received encouragement from arguments in favour of modern as against earlier writers. So Atterbury described Waller in 1690 as[12]

> the Parent of English Verse, and the first that shew'd our Tongue had beauty and numbers in it. I question whether in Charles the Second's Reign English did not come into its first perfection; and whether it has not had its Augustan Age as well as the Latin.

VIII

But for some time the need had been felt for a vocabulary to denote appreciation of that quality in art – greatness or sublimity – which could not be accounted for in terms of formal criteria. It was to meet this need that 'taste' acquired authority in literary criticism. Descending from the mid-seventeenth-century concept of '*le bon goût*', it gained force from the critical practice of Boileau and Saint Evrémond, among others, who stressed the importance of that power of moving the audience which was to be variously attributed to the effects of beauty, novelty, pathos, grandeur and sublimity. It was a convenient term for men of refinement to assert their perception and the importance of their own subjective response to art in face of the frequently authoritarian spirit of the rules and the growing tendency among the increasing numbers of critics to employ them mechanically. A knowledge of the formal requirements of each kind of writing was clearly important, but it was even more important to know when to rise above them:[13]

> In *Poets* as true *Genius* is but rare,
> True *Taste* as seldom is the *Critick's* share;
> Both must alike from Heav'n derive their Light,
> These *born* to Judge, as well as those to Write.

The man of taste was the superior type of critic: the 'School of Taste' among critics insisted on the importance of the appreciation of beauties rather than the enumeration of faults. Classical authority for this point of view was to be found in the treatise, reputedly by Longinus, *On the Sublime*, which Boileau had translated in 1674. Its author analysed the emotional impact of great literature, including the Bible; of the sublime in subject-matter as well as in style; and asserted the superiority of an original, inspired author with faults to a mechanical but faultless one. In this way the treatise encouraged the reliance on a subjective response – though, given the social context, on a special kind of individual taste, one trained and educated – as a valid criterion. The treatise became perhaps the most popular critical work of the early eighteenth century. Swift warned his would-be author,

> A forward critick often dupes us
> With sham Quotations *Peri Hupsous*:

And if we have not read *Longinus*,
Will magisterially outshine us.
Then, lest with Greek he over-run ye,
Procure the Book for Love or Money.
                    ('On Poetry, a Rhapsody', 1733)

Already, then, the importance of the term as expressive of a subjective response to art shows the way in which the emphasis may shift from a cognitive and formal view to an interpretation of art as affective, a vehicle for the expression of emotion by the author to affect the sensibility of the reader. With this went the slower decline of decorum as the essential organising principle. That art should recall the experience of life and give the illusion of it was essential. That this experience should be shaped in accordance with traditional practice of different kinds of writing – as Aristotle had outlined in his comments on epic, tragedy and comedy – was basic to the criticism of Dryden and Pope and to many of their successors. The relevance of such craftsmanship is permanent; but the insistence on this aspect of art in the late seventeenth and early eighteenth centuries was accompanied by other factors in the nature of the creative writing of the time which made formal considerations pre-eminent. The wider appeal of recognisably ordinary human feelings in the novel, however, and the difficulty of establishing a final model of decorum in this mode; the increasing reliance on subject-matter whose attraction lay in presentation of feeling or novelty, rather than on the artist's display of skill in handling a traditional literary form: both of these weakened the significance of formal criticism. Increasingly, then, in the description of art as an 'imitation of nature' the term 'imitation' lost its wider significance, and 'nature' acquired a bewildering complexity of literary uses. Its part in eighteenth-century thought in general has been examined at length by A. O. Lovejoy in *The Great Chain of Being* (1936) and by Basil Willey in *The Eighteenth Century Background* (1939). I shall consider briefly its specifically literary critical uses.

IX

'Nature' was, at its highest level, the merely ideal nature of Platonic and neo-Platonic thought. It could easily in this connection take on suggestions of the divine, which became confused with the manifestation of the divine in the real world:

> All Nature is but Art, unknown to thee;
> All Chance, Direction, which thou canst not see;
> All Discord, Harmony, not understood;
> All partial Evil, universal Good:

or 'Nature well known, no prodigies remain'.[14] It is an easy transition in this context from philosophical to specifically aesthetic thought.

For Aristotle the nature of a work had been its kind – those features which were peculiar to it and not shared by other art forms. In this connection 'nature' was of specific relevance to literature, and with the emergence of national literatures and the establishing of vernacular literary traditions, comparisons between contemporary achievements in critical and creative writing and those of antiquity were inevitable. So the corpus of classical criticism which had been inherited by Renaissance critics – chiefly from Aristotle and Horace – was amplified by them and their French successors to assist contemporary writers in composing according to the best models available. The motive behind the influential writings of Rapin, Boileau and Le Bossu was voiced in England by Milton when he described criticism as:[15]

> the sublime art which in Aristotle's Poetics, in
> Horace, and the Italian commentaries of Castelvetro,
> Tasso, Manzoni and others, teaches what the laws are
> of a true epic poem, what of a dramatic, what decorum
> is, which is the grand masterpiece to observe.

But the rules of writing began to usurp the authority of the best models. It was clear to practising dramatists like Corneille and Dryden, for example, that consideration of the rules did not adequately explain the nature of a work's appeal to the audience – that other factors would have to be taken into account besides artistry – and that works like Shadwell's *Sullen Lovers* (1668), composed in strict accordance with the rules, promoted nothing but boredom in reader or audience. Pope, therefore in his 'Essay on Criticism', whilst treating the rules with respect –

Those RULES of old, *discover'd*, not devis'd,
Are *Nature* still, but *Nature Methodiz'd* . . .
The *Rules* a Nation born to serve, obeys,
And *Boileau* still in Right of *Horace* sways.
But *we* brave *Britons, Foreign Laws* despis'd,
And kept *unconquer'd*, and *unciviliz'd*.

(88–9 and 713–16)

– recommended an adherence to the ancient authors as models:

Learn hence for Ancient *Rules* a just Esteem:
To copy Nature is to copy *Them*.

(139–40)

Nature could also be interpreted, then, as that organisation of subject-matter which appeared in the writings of classical times – a view expressed by Dryden when he wrote:[16]

Homer and Virgil are to be our guides in the epic;
Sophocles and Euripides in tragedy: in all things we
are to imitate the customs and times of those persons
and things we represent . . . to be content to follow
our masters, who understand nature better than we.
But if the story we treat be modern, we are to vary the
customs according to the time and country where the
scene of the action lies; for this is still to imitate
nature, which is always the same, though in a different
dress.

External everyday reality was regarded, then, as merely a clothing for nature: nature itself is the general and typical in human experience throughout the ages. Dryden takes it for granted that human nature is always and everywhere the same; and this assumption is central to the literary and critical theories of his time. The chief concerns of literature, human actions and passions – even manners – had to all intents and purposes been explored and mapped out already, either by classical writers or by the earlier moderns. In the *Essay of Dramatic Poesy* (1668) Dryden laments that the only province of drama which has not been exhausted by earlier writers is that of heroic tragedy. As for excelling the ancients, this has been done in satire. Satire was the natural expression of a sophisticated self-consciousness, in which the standards of a refined and correct society could be enunciated in the fresh treatment of contemporary material after the manner of Persius, Horace or Juvenal – with the help of a more subtle wit and ridicule through skilled exploitation of the wide range of contemporary linguistic usage.

In a scheme of literature dominated by the ideal of decorum any eccentricity or unnaturalness of subject-matter would be bound to destroy the homogeneous illusion of reality created by the work of art – a point Horace had urged in his *Ars Poetica*. In this regard the requirements of the general public are at odds with the conscious artistry demanded by the culturally sophisticated among the audience. Dryden comments on this difficulty from the point of view of the practising dramatist in his preface to *An Evening's Love* (1671):

> There is the same difference between farce and comedy
> as betwixt an empiric and a true physician: both of
> them may attain their ends; but what the one performs
> by hazard, the other does by skill. And as the artist is
> often unsuccessful while the mountebank succeeds; so
> farces more commonly take people than comedies. For
> to write unnatural things is the most probable way of
> pleasing them, who understand not nature. (i, 146)

As the validity of the subjective response to art became increasingly recognised, critical standards would naturally be called into question, and the relationship between the work of art or aspect of nature evoking the emotional response and the response itself would seem to be the necessary focal point of theoretical speculation.

X

The greatest exception to the neoclassical interpretation of the literary tradition which Dryden attempts is, of course, Shakespeare. The terms in which he is described in the *Essay of Dramatic Poesy* are significant. He appears as:

> the man who of all modern and perhaps ancient poets
> had the largest and most comprehensive soul. All the

images of nature were still present to him, and he
drew them not laboriously but luckily; when he
describes anything, you more than see it, you feel it
too. Those who accuse him to have wanted learning
give him the greater commendation; he was naturally
learned; he needed not the spectacles of books to read
nature; he looked inwards and found her there. (p. 67)

Here Dryden moves from the acceptance of nature as having
fixed series of permanent shapes, to the understanding of nature as
the protean quality of human consciousness. Johnson was to carry
this further in his commendation of Shakespeare as the poet of
nature, in all its psychological and social manifestations.

At the same time the importance of external nature as a stimulus
to the imagination – the Lockian stress on sight as the sense most
easily impressed was popularised by Addison in his papers on 'The
Pleasures of Imagination' (*Spectator*, nos 411–21) – and the impact
of Newtonian thought, increasingly associated nature with the
external universe, depriving the word of some of its earlier associations. The widespread deistic tendency to see in nature evidence of
God's handiwork assisted these shifts in meaning.

XI

Traditionally the process of imitation involved the creative
rendering – by means of the *acer spiritus ac vis* (that 'creative and
glowing imagination') as Quintilian had described it – of the
artist's experience. And in doing this the poet could seem to
transcend the limitations of normal existence in representing life
as better than it could ever be. Indeed, only by doing this could he
perform his true and highest role in society. In his *Apology for
Poetry* (1581), Sidney defined poetry as:

an art of imitation, for so Aristotle termeth it in his
word *Mimesis*, that is to say, a representing,
counterfeiting, or figuring forth – to speak
metaphorically, a speaking picture; with this end; to
teach and delight.

Puttenham had observed in his *Arte of English Poesie* (1589) that:

> It is therefore of Poets thus to be conceived . . . that if
> they be able to devise and make all things of
> themselves, without any subject of veritie, that they be
> (by maner of Speech) as creating gods.

Sidney presents an amplification of this aspect of the poet's role:

> Nature never set forth the earth in so rich tapestry as
> divers poets have done – neither with pleasant rivers,
> fruitful trees, sweetsmelling flowers, nor whatsoever
> else may make the too much loved earth more lovely.
> Her world is brazen, the poets only deliver a golden
> . . . (the poet) yieldeth to the powers of the mind an
> image of that whereof the philosopher bestoweth but a
> wordish description: which doth neither strike, pierce,
> nor possess the sight of the soul as much as that other
> doth.

In this context there is an essential ambiguity in ideal nature. Sidney bases his defence of poetry on the highest type of poetry – the epic – in which characters may be seen as exemplars. This could encourage a didactic view of art in which imitation should not merely invoke moral standards, by representing nature as it ought to be, but should confine itself to beautiful subject-matter. So Dryden approved of the sentiment that painting and poetry

> are not only true imitations of nature, but of the best
> nature, of that which is wrought up to a nobler pitch.
> They present us with images more perfect than life in
> any individual; and we have the pleasure to see all the
> scattered beauties of nature united by a happy
> chemistry, without its deformities or faults.

The popular Horatian parallel with painting, *ut pictura poesis* (as in a painting, so in a poem), for which Du Fresnoy's treatise *De Arte Graphica*, translated by Dryden in 1695, gained widespread acceptance, encouraged the emphasis on the beautiful as the proper subject for representation:

> to take every lineament and feature is not to make an
> excellent piece, but to take so much only as will make
> a beautiful resemblance of the whole: and, with an

ingenious flattery of nature, to heighten the beauties of some parts, and hide the deformities of the rest. (ii, 194)

In such a range the identification of art with an ideal beauty – 'the poet delivers a golden' – is complete. It was only by representing the ideal world that art could instruct and please: here the tension in art between truth as beauty and truth as reality, its decorum and verisimilitude, have been lost sight of in the parallel with painting.

XII

It was possible to make a further distinction between methods of imitation. Since the importance of classical authors as models was contested by those who preferred the moderns, or earlier writers in their own tradition – the three points of view were expressed by Lisideius, Eugenius and Crites in Dryden's *Essay of Dramatic Poesy* – the division between the principle of imitation and originality developed. Artistic creativity seemed with the Augustan period to have become indissolubly linked to the study and emulation of past authors – and those of the classical past were still regarded as providing, on the whole, the best guidance. Imitation had by this time acquired a narrower significance, until with Dryden it became chiefly associated with that sort of translation which aimed to preserve the spirit of the original (as distinct from mere transliteration). So an opposition developed between two modes of creative writing and this was encouraged by the obvious inadequacy of the rules to provide a wholly satisfactory account of the effectiveness of a work of art. It was clear that breaches in artistic decorum could to a large extent be disregarded should an author excel in creative gifts – should he, like Shakespeare, have the inventive powers of genius. The distinction between two kinds of poets was therefore expressed by Addison in terms of those who have the 'natural Fire and Impetuosity' of genius and those who 'have formed themselves by Rules, and submitted the Greatness of their natural Talents to the Corrections and Restraints of Art' (*Spectator*, no. 160).

The narrower meaning of imitation inherent in this description of the lesser type of author is given wider application in the opposition between originality and imitation made by, among others,

Leonard Welsted – an opposition which carries with it the repudiation of the principle of imitation of classical authors:

> Works of Imitation differ from Originals, as Fruits
> brought to Maturity, by artificial fires, differ from
> those that are ripen'd by the natural Heat of the Sun,
> and the Indulgence of a kindly Climate.

The metaphorical appeal of nature has a persuasive energy which
deprives imitation of its traditional significance as a creative
process: the emphasis falls inevitably on originality. So, great poets
and philosophers have been[17]

> men, who have struck out their Discoveries by the
> mere Strength of a Great Genius, without treading in
> the Steps of any who went before 'em; without being
> much oblig'd to the Assistance of Learning.

XIII

The various tendencies outlined above were reflected in contemporary poetry: poets were conscious, as novelists did not need to
be, of the demands of criticism and taste. The improvement of
taste among the literate population is attempted in an abundance
of didactic verse from Blackmore's epics to Armstrong's 'Art of
Preserving Health' (1744). The *Spectator* encouraged this type of
writing by acclaiming Blackmore's 'Creation' as deserving

> to be looked upon as one of the most useful and noble
> creations of our *English* verse. The Reader cannot but
> be pleased to find the depths of Philosophy enlivened
> with all the Charms of Poetry, and to see so great a
> Strength of Reason, amidst so beautiful a Redundancy
> of the Imagination. (no. 339)

But it is the tradition of 'meditative-Miltonising' which has
attracted the contempt of the twentieth-century critics:[18]

> since unconvinced and undistinguished verse in
> Augustan modes – verse offering the virtues of polite
> civilisation – is pretty obviously uninteresting, minor
> talents took largely to the meditative-Miltonising
> poetical modes. . . . The tradition that associated

poetry with the central interests of the civilised mind
having (for them) failed, they naturally sought poetry
in the poetical – in specialised (and conventional)
sentiments and attitudes representing, as it were, a
solemn holiday or Sabbath from the everyday serious.

The implication that it succeeded the Augustan modes is, of
course, misleading; the two existed side by side. These minor
talents might equally well have been interpreted as a reaction
against the limitations of the Augustan tradition in its deliberate
and conscious narrowing of the interests of the civilised mind to
social concerns which bore only a superficial relevance to the life
of the times. The deistic effusions of Addison, for example, are
only one aspect of an age which produced the hymns of Watts and
Wesley. In his Preface to *Horae Lyricae* (1709) Watts asserts that the
true source of poetry is religious experience – as John Dennis had
done in his *Grounds of Criticism in Poetry* (1704). And Milton's
popularity, as great as that of Pope, is in part at least due to the
taste for edification which could relapse on the one hand into
the didacticism of Watts's 'How doth the Little Busy Bee', and on
the other into the sentimental religiosity and charnel-house gusto
of Young's 'Last Day' (1713) where:

> Fragments of bodies in confusion fly
> To distant regions journeying, there to claim
> Deserted members and complete the frame.
>
> (28–30)

This elicited Steele's enthusiastic acclaim:

> All other poetry must be dropped at the gate of death,
> this alone can enter with us into immortality . . . . It
> shall not be forgotten, when the sun and the moon are
> remembered no more; it shall never die, but be the
> measure of eternity, and the laudable ambition of
> heaven. How can any other poesy come into
> competition with it? (*Guardian*, no. 5)

XIV

The work of one writer above all epitomised those qualities of
good sense, lucidity, elegance and wit in the service of morality of

which the age approved. The poetry of Pope reflects the literary preoccupations of this time and, while it presents no arresting development in subject-matter, reveals a perfection of statement which it would seem impossible to go beyond. The imitations of classical writers in the Pastorals and the 'Essay on Criticism', in the 'Imitations of Horace', and 'The Dunciad' and of Denham's 'Cooper's Hill' in 'Windsor Forest', emphasise his concern with craftsmanship. The 'Elegy to the Memory of an Unfortunate Lady' and 'Eloisa to Abelard' reflect the popularity of poetic gloom and introspective melancholy which was beginning to reveal its association with a pride in cultivated sensitivity of soul. The 'Essay on Man' is Pope's philosophical justification of the contemporary social structure, showing the indebtedness of Augustanism to a traditional valuation of man's place in the universe, as well as the glib superficiality with which it could be voiced; while the 'Moral Essays', if narrow in scope, reveal as solid a grasp of strictly social virtues as the age, taken as a whole, could offer. 'The Rape of the Lock' – for all its indebtedness to Boileau's 'Lutrin' – and 'The Dunciad', display Pope's quint-essential gifts of delicate ridicule, raillery and satire.

It was, however, as Pope declared in the 'Epistle to Arbuthnot', the true vocation of the poet to be didactic rather than inventive:

> . . . not in Fancy's maze he wander'd long,
> But stoop'd to Truth and moralised his song.
>
> (340–1)

His devotion to the ideals of precision and lucidity, to truth to nature in its general aspect – which for him was associated with imitation of earlier writers as a basic requirement of composition – placed him firmly for his contemporaries in the main neoclassic tradition of imitation. His easy subordination of the satiric impulse to the dominant social and cultural temper of his time (in a way which marks him off from Swift); his reliance on the accepted ethical code as a satiric norm, might – despite the wit and exuberance of metaphorical life with which his themes are treated – seem to a later public, attracted by a different mood from that of the social, and valuing above all the emotions of the individual, to indicate an absence of originality in thought and a dearth of feeling for everyday humanity.

The centrality of the culture to which Pope belonged, and

whose standards of taste and morality he voiced with such persistence and skill, could not last; and as the influence of other poets, especially Milton, increased, and the horizons of taste widened under the pressure of philosophical speculation and scholarship – as, eventually, a deeper awareness of the real predicaments of individual men crept into poetry, the reaction against the earlier literary tradition would inevitably focus itself on that author who had given it its most consistent expression.

The emphasis on poetry as a predominantly social utterance, the importance of the hierarchy of the kinds, and the dominance of the rules in criticism – all these ran counter to the older national achievement in poetry. The current demand for the social, lucid, and rational in style might readily provoke the assumption that the poetry of the Augustan era was essentially lacking in the qualities of true poetry; that, in short, it was written from the judgment rather than from the imagination, from the head rather than the heart.

XV

The cultivation of taste, of a sensibility to art as a means of appraisal which could function alongside the framework of the rules, readily associated itself with the Lockian emphasis on the senses as the foundation of knowledge, in a new kind of concern with the effect of the work of art on the reader. On the level of serious speculation this moved within the English and Scottish empirical tradition towards an attempt to ground criticism more firmly in psychological enquiry. 'Within a period of twenty years', one critic observes, 'several of the ablest minds in England and Scotland, including Burke, Hume, Hogarth, Reynolds, Kames and Gerard – most of them interested in literary criticism – were focused upon the problem of taste.'[19] The preoccupation with abstract and rational ideas of literary excellence in art evinced in the greater part of criticism in the late seventeenth and early eighteenth century was to shift to a concern with the effect of the work of art on the emotions conceived in terms of taste and the vocabulary of taste. The terms available for the description of these effects – the beautiful, the pathetic, the sublime, and, later, the picturesque – were to be analysed and commented on over and over again.

Connected with the interest in terms descriptive of the subjective response was the reaction against the insistence on the more formal attributes of poetry. This reaction took the form of discussions concerning the permanent problems of the nature of the artist's inspiration, of the faculties which are most highly developed in the poet. These were largely reinterpretations of the traditional critical assumptions about literary creativity, but the concern springs into prominence in the 'fifties and 'sixties in works chiefly devoted to considering the qualities which distinguish the poet – invention, originality, genius, imagination, judgment and so on. Joseph Warton's *Essay upon the Writings and Genius of Pope* (1756), Edward Young's *Conjectures upon Original Composition* (1759) and Duff's *Essay on Original Genius* (1767) all reflected on Pope's achievement in the light of traditional poetic creativity. Wood in his *Essay on the Original Genius and Writings of Homer* (1769) and Blair in the *Critical Dissertation on the Poems of Ossian* (1763) examined what characteristics geniuses of the past had in common. The poet's quest for inspiration turned from the social world of Pope and the main neoclassical tradition to that of natural scenery and solitude in Blair's 'Grave' (1743), Akenside's 'Pleasures of Imagination' (1744) and Young's 'Night Thoughts' (1742–5).

Developments in historical and comparative studies of literature were related to contemporary taste by writers who were conscious of the neglect among their contemporaries of the native literary tradition. Thomas Warton, Richard Hurd and Thomas Percy, in their efforts to stress the relevance to the national heritage of the poetry of Spenser, Milton and the ballads had as their incentive a felt need[20]

> of overcoming prejudices against certain productions of the past which had been conceived in an idiom different from the prevailing mode, or of doing fuller justice to esteemed poets or artists who, when viewed apart from circumstances of time and place, had been blamed for faults not properly theirs.

The issues inherent in the Ancients and Moderns controversy (as they had arisen in seventeenth-century France) involved the recognition of a superior refinement in the work of the moderns as against the primitive simplicities of ancient writers, and had naturally aroused critics' interest in comparing different types of literature from different countries and different periods. The criterion of refinement became irrelevant where truth to nature clearly involved such infinite variety in its literary manifestations. Comparative and historical studies began to supersede critical quibbles over the different achievements of classical and modern writers in the various kinds of composition. Blackwell, Lowth and Wood related the Hebrew and Greek ways of life to their literatures. Lowth traced the relationship of the Bible to its Hebrew background and origins in his *Praelectiones De Sacra Poesi Hebraeorum* delivered in 1741, though not published until 1753; Blackwell had already performed a similar service for Homer in his *Enquiry into the Life and Writings of Homer* (1735). The trend was to expand alongside the revival of interest in the ballads and the collections of old songs already begun by Ramsay and continued in the work of Percy, Ritson and many others. Probably the most complete expression of the historical and comparative approach to literature was Thomas Warton's *History of English Poetry* (1774–81): he had already given an outline of the subject earlier in his *Observations on the Faerie Queene* of 1754.

It is within these areas of speculation and scholarship that the existing English tradition in poetry and criticism was to move towards a change more fundamental than anything it had experienced for centuries. In the following chapters I shall look at the ways in which a critical vocabulary based on sensibility to art and nature – that is, on taste – evolved; and at the difficulties which confronted the creative artist. How these circumstances affected the attempt to introduce a new valuation of poetry, and influenced the interpretation of literary history will be considered in relation to two dominant figures, Joseph and Thomas Warton.

Notes

1 Preface to *Oxford Book of Eighteenth Century Verse* (Oxford, 1926), pp. viii–ix. Nichol Smith's comments on the poetry of the period are equally applicable to the criticism.

2 'Thomas Warton', *University of Illinois Studies in Language and Literature*, ii, no. 1 (1916), 9–241.

3 M. Dorothy George, *London Life in the Eighteenth Century* (London, 1965), ch. i, 'Life and Death in London'.

4 'Life of Addison', *Lives of the English Poets*, ed. G. Birkbeck Hill, 3 vols (Oxford, 1935), ii, 94–5.

5 *The Use of Poetry and the Use of Criticism* (London, 1948), 60–1.

6 'Advice to an Author', *Characteristics of Men, Manners, Opinions, Times*, 3 vols (London, 1773), i, 345.

7 *Education and the University* (1943); Q. D. Leavis, 'The Novels of George Gissing', *Scrutiny*, 1936.

8 See R. L. Brett, *The Third Earl of Shaftesbury* (London, 1951), ch. ix.

9 'An Inquiry Concerning Virtue', *op. cit.*, ii, 28–9.

10 'Advice to an Author', *ibid.*, i, 339, 346, 347.

11 London, 1734, p. 340.

12 *Preface to The Second Part of Waller's Poems* (1690) reprinted in *Essays in Criticism*, xv (1965).

13 Pope, 'An Essay on Criticism' (1711), 11–14.

14 'An Essay on Man', Epistle I, 289–92. 'Epistle to Cobham' *Moral Essays* I. 208.

15 'Of Education: Letter to Hartlib' (1664), ed. C. E. Vaughan (London, 1927), 50.

16 'Preface of the Translator, with a Parallel of Poetry and Painting Prefixed to *De Arte Graphica*' (1695); *Of Dramatic Poetry and other Critical Essays* ed. G. Watson (2 vols, London, 1962), ii, 195.

17 Leonard Welsted, 'Dissertation Concerning the Perfection of the English Tongue and the State of Poetry' (1724), *Critical Essays of the Eighteenth Century*, ed. W. H. Durham (New Haven, 1915), 378.

18 F. R. Leavis, *Revaluation* (London 1949), 115–16.

19 E. N. Hooker, 'The Discussion of Taste from 1750 to 1770, and the New Trends in Literary Criticism', *P.M.L.A.*, xliv, 577.

20 R. S. Crane, 'English Neo-classical Criticism: an Outline Sketch', *Critics and Criticism Ancient and Modern* (Chicago, 1952), 385.

Two

Towards a Rationale of Feeling

I

From Addison's *Spectator* to Burke's *Reflections on the Revolution in France* (1790) the relationship of man to society is one of the most characteristic preoccupations of the eighteenth century. But between Addison, Swift and Defoe on the one hand, and Burke, Paine and Godwin on the other, there is a marked change in the way this relationship is formulated. Man as a component part of a divinely organised whole could be type-cast in accordance with his social rank, his religion, or his occupation. Men, however, were – it became increasingly obvious – creatures of needs, if not of desires, and did not necessarily accommodate themselves to the requirements of the politically and socially dominant groups. Thus the body politic is envisaged less in terms of a civilised and sophisticated *status quo*, and more as an evolutionary product – possibly perfectible – of historical, social and economic forces.

In England Priestley seizes with an enlightened impartiality on a preoccupation of his contemporaries in asserting that 'the happiness of the majority is the best in every political question'. From Europe comes the familiar paradoxical epigram of Rousseau: 'Man is born free, but is everywhere in chains.' The wider implications of such statements are not relevant here; but in the recognition of man as a creature of varied sensibilities which is a major theme of this chapter there is reflected a growing impulse to recognise and explore not merely the individual's relationship to society but the position of man – as the title of a recent collection of essays puts it – 'versus society in the eighteenth century'.[1]

As the individual complexity – and value – of each and every human being gains acknowledgment, existing assumptions are inevitably called into question. What rights has the individual in society? To what extent are the claims of subjective feeling, of man's response to his environment, reconcilable to the prevailing

31

social ethos? It is in this context that the recognition and exploration of human feelings – feelings common to all men, yet differing
from individual to individual, according to circumstances, education and sensibilities – can be located as a distinctively mid-
eighteenth-century phenomenon. It was acknowledged as such by
contemporary writers, and as an issue requiring urgent philosophical and critical investigation. And this is manifested in the
attention paid to the concept of taste as the agent of the subjective
response, and to genius as the hallmark of a highly individual
creative activity. How far should an inherited cultural tradition
take account of the pressures of popular taste? How might an
original imagination best give expression to a subjective awareness of an increasingly complex environment?

In the next two chapters I shall explore the attempts to establish
different rapprochements between individual feelings and the
social and public demands to which they are subjected. My
immediate concern is to consider the relationship between the
emotions and the imagination – that essentially psychological
responsiveness which is identified with taste – as it is dealt with by
philosophers and critics writing chiefly in the fifth and sixth
decades of the century. They are attempting to provide a rationale
for a new kind of vocabulary – the vocabulary of feeling. Always,
however, the modes of social, public analysis tend to lag behind
developments in the everyday world; to impose on art and literature a simplified image which might be identified with a distinctively British cultural tradition; and consequently to obscure the
various tensions between the personal and the social on the one
hand, and life and art on the other.

II

The growth of a literate public had become more widely diversified.[2] There was a rising demand for self-culture among those to
whom culture was far from being a traditional inheritance. The
demand for culture as identifiable with refinement, encouraged by
the continuing importance of taste as a civilising and social factor,
came not only from the wealthy upper and middle classes, nor
from those citizens who aped the gentry, but from the buyers of

monthly part issues of histories, dictionaries, voyages of discovery, and romances – aspiring minds like that of Gray's poet (with whose epitaph the 'Elegy' concludes), or of the youthful Crabbe, gleaning a poetical education from the 'Poet's Corner' of newspapers. Allan Ramsay, the Edinburgh wig-maker who founded the first circulating library, celebrated education as making 'the genius bright': for him books were 'thae silent friends that ever please'.[3] Self-improvement of this kind had already opened avenues to success. Robert Dodsley, for example, had risen from footman to highly respected bookseller. And a literary culture became associated with spiritual edification among those of John Wesley's followers who read the versions of Bunyan's *Pilgrim's Progress* (1743), Milton's 'Paradise Lost' (1763) and Young's 'Night Thoughts' (1769), which he had simplified for their benefit.

The gap between the classically educated, generally aristocratic, minority and readers of broadside ballads and chapbooks had been narrowed in the previous century. Men had become habituated to the language of the Bible as well as to the prose of sectarian controversy, while the political pamphleteering of the age of Anne had accustomed audiences from all but the lowest levels of society to plain and vigorous polemic. An increasingly wide and indeterminate public awaited with omnivorous rather than discriminating appetites the edification, information and entertainment which a growing industry of booksellers and their hacks – Johnson of course among them – provided. The classical orientation of culture had already begun to give ground to the new claims of religious and didactic material: it had been radically affected by the pressures of middle-class values. It was to be further eroded by the extension of elementary education, however inadequate many of its provisions might be.

The veneration for antiquity and for traditional literary forms gave place to a wider variety of subject-matter – often contemporary; the novel emerged as the dominant literary mode. 'Nature' was no longer identified with ideal representation on the classical model, but with what was natural – everyday human emotions. The ancients are now accused not only of lacking natural sensitivity – true human feeling – but even of corrupting through encouraging false ideals. As such they are attacked in *Sir Charles Grandison*:[4]

Are they not inflamers of the worst passions? With
regard to *epics*, would Alexander, madman as he was,
have been so *much* a madman, had it not been for
Homer? Of what violences, murders, depredations,
have not the epic poets been the occasion, by
propagating false honours, false glory, and false
religion?

For Richardson Pamela's attempts at self-government were
meant to be associated with her moral superiority to her gentle-
manly would-be seducer, and Clarissa's bourgeois origins do not
impair her capacity for delicacy and refinement in moral sensibility, nor her consequent superiority to the aristocratic Lovelace.

III

Nor was cultural activity centred so exclusively on London.
There was a quickening of the whole nation as the century
advanced: theatres were established in provincial towns; and
literary and philosophical societies began to spread. In Scotland
especially the patriotic reaction sparked off by the Union of 1707
and revived by the impact of the Jacobite risings in '15 and '45
encouraged the growth of large numbers of clubs and societies to
encourage improvements in science and medicine on the one
hand, and on the other to further the study of literature and to
give opportunities for debate. With intelligibility (not to say
eloquence) at a premium, the art of rhetoric flourished. Sheridan's
triumphant series of lecture courses in Edinburgh in the 'sixties
indicates how fashionable a study it was: the popularity of such
courses was responsible too for the development of a larger
audience for 'polite literature'. As early as 1742 Adam Smith had
delivered lectures on rhetoric and belles lettres in the University
of Edinburgh. Matthew Bramble in *Humphry Clinker* (1771) describes Edinburgh as a 'hot-bed of genius' (Everyman ed., p. 221).
It was the scene of much philosophical speculation by the 'Common-sense School' headed by Reid and Stewart, who consolidated
the empirical bent of British philosophy. In the Scottish Renaissance of the mid-eighteenth century the philosophers – Hume,
Gerard and Kames; historians – Hume again and Robertson;

the economist Adam Smith, and Ferguson (pioneering sociological thought) contributed to a European culture in this age of enlightenment which extended the mental horizons of what had now become Great Britain, its economic as well as its political boundaries having been expanded by the Act of Union.

The prosperity which trade with the American colonies had augmented, to the benefit of Defoe's Colonel Jack among others, was extended abroad by trade with the West Indies and Africa – the slave-trade being a profitable side-line – and later, of course, with India. The conquest of Canada which came at the end of George II's reign in 1759 encouraged a latent sense of empire so that Britannia becomes more than the guardian of liberty, the ruler of the waves. Cowper's bard prophesies to Boadicea that

> Regions Caesar never knew
> Thy Posterity shall sway.

> (29–30)

Internally the organisation of agriculture, industry, commerce and transport became increasingly efficient through the efforts of a numerous band – Townshend, Metcalf, the Denbys of Coalbrook-dale, Roebuck, Wedgwood, and Brindley, to name a few at random. The presence of a high standard of culture had never made itself more obvious than in the architecture, landscape gardening, furniture, music and painting where Vanbrugh, the Adam brothers, Brown, Chippendale, Kent, Gibbons, Arne, Boyce, Handel, Stanley, Hogarth, Ramsay, Gainsborough, Stubbs and Reynolds flourished. Before the end of the 'fifties the British Museum had assembled the finest collection of antiquities in the world, and in 1768 came the founding of the Royal Academy with Reynolds as its first president.

IV

In contrast, starvation, disease, overcrowding in big cities, and insecurity of livelihood threatened the working classes. There was widespread rioting against the price of food; looting in order to sell food at a price realistically adjusted to wages became more frequent throughout the country. In *Methodism and the Common People of England in the XVIII Century* (1957) Wearmouth cites innumerable reports of such riots from the State Papers and local newspapers of the time:

> Writing on April 26 1751 to the State Secretary, a correspondent at Ross-on-Wye maintained that the inhabitants in that place were 'so poorly supplied with wheat that there has not been for a long time a Quantity Sufficient to furnish half the necessary Wants of the Labouring Poor'. . . . A petition from Leeds signed by the Mayor, Aldermen, and others, comprising altogether one hundred and forty-eight names, admitted that 'the Corn and Grain grown in that part of the Country is by no means sufficient to maintain the numbers of People there inhabiting the land.' 'The poor manufacturer', they contended, 'cannot out of his present wages provide himself with Bread for the ordinary Support of himself and Family.' . . . On Monday, August 30 (1756), the *Public Advertiser* announced that 'the Price of Bread has rose no less than six times since the beginning of May, viz. a Penny per Peck each Time.' (pp. 57–8)

The distress increased in the new decade as the export of wheat continued and low wages kept workers in a state of starvation. Wearmouth quotes from the *London Chronicle* of 11 September 1762:

> They did not desire to see their children 'weep for bread and none to give them', shouted the rioters from Rossendale, Rochdale, and Saddleworth, as they raided the premises of certain 'obnoxious employers' at Manchester in the autumn of 1762; vengeance was vowed on all the 'canables' and 'men slayers'. Seeking to justify their lawless conduct, they cried out: 'We may as well all be hanged as starve to death.' (pp. 59–60)

The overall sense of political and social well-being might still succeed in masking for the majority an increasingly articulated unrest, but as Plumb comments:

> by the 1760s there existed, in effect, two political nations in England, one growing, the other shrinking,

with little contact between them. Had there been more
the grosser follies of handling both Wilkes and America
could scarcely have taken place. The formal electorate
was dwindling and called to execute its judgement less
and less. Those who by education and interest might
reasonably expect a political voice but were denied it
were steadily increasing. There were other factors, too,
at work to help widen this cleavage.

Chief among these were the dissenters:

> Much of the aggressive criticism of parliament in the
> second half of the century came from dissent. . . . It
> was the exclusion from political power which they felt
> was rightly theirs because of their social and economic
> activity that led men such as Josiah Wedgwood to
> support annual parliaments, universal suffrage and the
> control of a member's actions by his constituents. . . .
> Historians, I feel, never give sufficient emphasis to the
> prevalence of bitter anti-monarchical, pro-republican
> sentiment of the 1760's and 1770's . . . conflict existed
> between the political establishment and the political
> nation . . . the growth of the political nation was
> always far faster than the spread of representative
> government. ('Political Man', pp. 14–16)

I have quoted at some length because I think it is important to
remember the complexity of social realities which urged themselves on the attention of contemporaries. One of the most vital
sources of communication was that agent whose civic usefulness
has been so frequently debated and which now emerges for the
first time in a significant role. In 1758 Johnson observed:

> Not many years ago the nation was content with one
> gazette, but now we have not only in the metropolis
> papers for every morning and every evening, but
> almost every large town has its weekly historian who
> regularly circulates his periodical intelligence.
> (*Idler*, no. 30)

R. M. Wiles has established that by 1760 provincial newspapers
were not only being produced 'in all the major towns in England',

but in some places different newspapers competed for readers, and itinerant pedlars and stage coaches assisted in the distribution of metropolitan and provincial news alike. By these means social news – local as well as national – of crimes, riots, executions, as well as of regional events were brought to the notice of the majority of the population. It follows that the effect of this on men's awareness of the kind of society they were living in was far-reaching.

Although the earlier complacency of 'Whatever is, is right' is acceptable – as ever – to the majority of the socially privileged (the number of editions of the 'Essay on Man' and Soame Jenyns's *Enquiry into the Nature and Origin of Evil* provide enough evidence of this) it is being eroded by a growing awareness of the conditions under which one's fellow human beings try to exist. There is not by any means a developed sense of social responsibility, but something approaching it is increasingly common among individuals and occasionally compels even the government to act. There is, then, an increase in private philanthropy – Captain Coram's establishing a Foundling Hospital in 1753, for example, which Hogarth and Handel supported; or individuals exert their influence to eradicate social abuses – as the brothers Fielding did in their capacity as magistrates; or the government might introduce measures to control abuses, and – as it was enabled by the public impact of Hogarth's 'Gin Lane' (1751) – to legislate against the interests of a prosperous minority on behalf of the welfare of the lowest classes of society. Both Johnson and Voltaire attack the belief in any religious and philosophical justification for human misery: Voltaire in his lines on the Lisbon Earthquake (1755) and Johnson in his review of Jenyns's *Enquiry* (1756) emphasise the need for a more realistic understanding of the conditions of all men alike. Johnson expounds the need for education to offer a means of providing an equal opportunity for all:[5]

> That hope and fear are inseparably or very frequently
> connected with poverty, and riches, my surveys of life
> have not informed me. The milder degrees of poverty
> are sometimes supported by hope, but the more
> severe often sink down in motionless despondence. Life
> must be seen before it can be known. This author and
> *Pope* perhaps never saw the miseries which they

imagine thus easy to be born . . . Those who
communicate literature to the son of a poor man,
consider him as one not born to poverty, but to the
necessity of deriving a better future for himself. In
this attempt, as in others, many fail, and many
succeed. Those that fail will feel their misery more
acutely; but since poverty is now confessed to be such a
calamity as cannot be born without the opiate of
insensibility, I hope the happiness of those whom
education enables to escape from it, may turn the
balance against that exacerbation which the others
suffer.

The fashionable interpretation of the development of society as
deteriorating through over-refinement and luxury, however, is
typified in Goldsmith's *Enquiry into the State of Polite Learning in
Europe* (1759). Current attitudes oscillate between satisfaction in
the progress of civilisation and refinement and the newly apprehended attractions (stimulated by voyages of discovery) of simple,
primitive existence, untrammelled by the vitiating luxuries of a
commercial and industrial civilisation with its attendant problems.
It was fashionable to condemn the effects of luxury on society,
and it was a fashion which Johnson attacked. Boswell writes:[6]

Goldsmith expatiated on the common topick, that the
race of our people was degenerated, and that this was
owing to luxury. JOHNSON . . . Consider to how very
small a proportion of our people luxury can reach . . .
Luxury, so far as it reaches the poor, will do good to
the race of people; it will strengthen and multiply
them. Sir, no nation was ever hurt by luxury; for, as I
said before, it can reach but to a very few. I admit
that the great increase in commerce and manufactures
hurts the military spirit of a people; because it
produces a competition for something else than martial
honours, – a competition for riches. It also hurts the
bodies of the people; for you will observe, there is no
man who works at any particular trade, but you may
know him from his appearance to do so. One part of
his body being more used than the rest, he is in some

degree deformed; but, Sir, that is not luxury. A tailor
sits cross-legged; but that is not luxury.

It is a rare and disinterested attitude. It is one reflecting a
strong moral sensibility, and, voiced at a time when the cultivation
of moral sensibility was in vogue, it could be received with nothing
else than that respect which enshrined its author as the Grand
Cham of English letters.

V

It was an age in which there was a widespread demand for the
expression of moral sentiments. The social and ethical drive of
Augustanism coincided with the wider reading public's demand
for the strong in feeling and the improving in theme. Besides the
insistence on practical advice in the novels of Defoe, and – of a
different kind – in those of Richardson (in *Pamela* morality – as
Fielding saw – conveniently and attractively combines with
expediency), there is an increasing number of periodicals which
also meet these requirements. Emotions are presented in terms of
mood and sentiment, rather than passion, for sentiment is capable
of carrying a burden of moral reflection which may be highly subjective or social as the talents and mood of the author dictate.
Sterne, alarmed by some reactions to *Tristram Shandy*, designed in
its successor, he wrote, 'to teach us to love the world and our
fellow creatures better than we do – so it runs most upon those
gentle passions and affections, which aid so much to it' (*A Sentimental Journey*, Penguin ed., p. 11).

Johnson's commendation of Gray's 'Elegy' – that it 'abounds
with sentiments to which every bosom returns an echo' – suggests
a potential association of feeling with morality, in which the
former often takes precedence to encourage sentiment. At its
finest there is established an authentic personal note of true feeling
for an actual predicament – spiritual or social. It was this which
Johnson sought and did not find in Milton's 'Lycidas'. He notes
the poem's deficiency in natural human feeling, its artificiality,
just as Wordsworth in the preface to the *Lyrical Ballads* (1800)
was to remark on what seemed to him the same defect in Gray's
sonnet on the death of Richard West. What is interesting, how-

ever, is that if one compares Gray's 'Elegy' with Pope's 'Elegy to the Memory of an Unfortunate Lady' the later poet has found the note of a personally apprehended and deeply felt common human experience. The extraordinary success of the 'Elegy' is due to the way in which sentiments of universal weight are associated with rich and poor and with the author himself as involved in the pathos of a common human condition. It is a pathos which does not now take on Pope's voice of generalised stoicism:

> Poets themselves must fall, like those they sung;
> Deaf the praised ear, and mute the tuneful tongue
>
> ('Elegy', 75–6)

but instead offers a moving evocation of the bonds of human feeling and of human interdependence from the standpoint of the isolated solitary observer:

> On some fond breast the parting soul relies,
> Some pious drops the closing eye requires;
> Ev'n from the tomb the voice of Nature cries.
>
> (89–91)

But a cult of feeling could serve as a substitute – and often a fairly coarse one – alongside the moral reflections which were also desired for the achievement of that genuine and highly cultivated sensibility which had been Shaftesbury's ideal. Since education and feeling are socially desirable and fashionable they are to be catered for. In his account of *The English Novel in the Magazines, 1740–1815* (1962), Mayo remarks:

> The fact that there was so much fiction published in
> eighteenth-century magazines, at the same time that it
> was so bloodless, is a phenomenon in the history of
> taste. It is largely the result of the rapid growth of a
> new reading audience which was naive, sentimental,
> and eager for airs of gentility. . . . In the very years
> when the critics of mass culture celebrate the union of
> popular and cultivated taste, new magazines, addressed
> to the sentimental taste and genteel aspirations of a
> numerous class of readers, were already circulating on
> a large scale. Few of these readers, if the common

miscellany is any evidence, showed much interest in
the works of Defoe or Smollett. (pp. 2–3)

The 'gentle passions' were to be cultivated. Habits of feeling
were encouraged, not merely finding expression in traditional
reflections on the passing of time, the vicissitudes of love, and the
inevitability of death, but in a specific cultivation of sensibility for
its own sake. A taste for sentiments might naturally give rise to
sentimentality.

Among dissenters melancholy was cultivated as a state proper
to the soul and as a proof of exquisite sensibility. 'Blair and Young
accepted it as the norm of religious experience and as a proof of
superior refinement, and so keyed their whole mental life to a
higher pitch.'[7] Sophia Western, of course, 'loved a tender sensation, and would gladly pay the price of a tear for it at any time'.
The fluctuations in fortune of the hero of *The Vicar of Wakefield*
(1766) afforded Goldsmith the opportunity of combining moral
reflection with range of feeling, while Henry Mackenzie's *Man of
Feeling* (1771) offers even more copious fare (one editor provides a
separate index for the incidence of tears), and from earlier in the
century the popularity of Scots songs and ballads had aroused a
Jacobitism too sentimental, as events proved, to bear practical
fruit.

Writing in a Victorian context George Meredith categorises the
sentimentalist as a spiritual snob who supposes himself to be
possessed of insights and emotions rarer than the ordinary. 'The
snob is concerned about his valuation in the social world, the
sentimentalist about his valuation in the world of feeling.'[8] But the
bogus quality Meredith sees as inseparable from the word was less
obvious in Johnson's time, for it was still associated with those
sentiments engendered by the genuine pleasure gained from
exploring the inward self and with a real capacity for formulating
responses to one's environment. So in his introduction to the
Penguin edition of *A Sentimental Journey* Alvarez enlarges on
Sterne's intention:

> Sterne had always written from his nerve-ends, with a
> quivering, edgy liveliness; the new novel was to show
> that this was genuinely the product of an intensity of
> emotion, not of mere nerviness. On the surface there

was something almost didactic in its purpose: it
would teach people how to react, show them that the
simplest incident – an innocent exchange with a
mendicant monk, a peasant with his dead donkey –
swarmed with high feeling. It would show them that
the value of travelling was not in . . . exquisite views
exquisitely rendered back into prose; it was, instead,
the traveller's receptiveness to feelings, and the flair
and subtlety with which he expressed them. (p. 11)

Not that this is an adequate account of the work as a whole, but it
is undoubtedly a major part of its effect.

In what is one of the greatest novels of the eighteenth century,
Richardson's *Clarissa*, it is the author's exploration of the inner
workings of a delicate moral sensibility which weighs every motive
and action with scrupulous care that makes it a major influence
not only in the English but in the European tradition of novel-
writing. And in poetry the growing preference for blank verse,
which so irked Dr Johnson, provided its writers with that very
opportunity which both Dryden and Johnson had seen as an
inevitable consequence of abandoning the disciplined form of the
couplet. Young's 'Night Thoughts' (1742–5) and Akenside's
'Pleasures of Imagination' (1744) reveal a sensitive melancholy
in their reflections on human life and their own feelings. In these
lengthy works the sententiousness mutes, without (as it had done
in Pope's work) transforming, the expression of individual
emotion. The themes of death, solitude and human transitoriness
are explored, not so much to draw a moral as to articulate varieties
of mood and feeling. So Goldsmith's 'Deserted Village' employs
the traditional material of pastoral – as Crabbe observed in his
attack on the mode in the opening sections of 'The Village' – but
with a range of personal feeling and with a modern social application which merges at the end into direct expression of the personal
predicament of the poet in his society. It was, however, after the
appearance of the Ossianic poems in 1760 that this insistent preoccupation with moods and feelings associated with melancholy
reflections contingent on the passing of time and – probably more
important – with other ways of life, swept into European prominence, and both Goldsmith and Ossian play their part in accentu-
ating the *Sorrows of Werther*.

VI

As a general term used to signify all kinds of subjective response involving some kind of choice or selection 'taste' had moral as well as cultural, social, educational and philosophical connotations. The socially fashionable appetite for objects of *virtu*, for instance, was ridiculed by Samuel Foote for the benefit of his Haymarket audience. In the prologue to *Taste* (1752) Peter Puff, the auctioneer, announces:

> My best antiquities are made at home.
> I've *Romans, Greeks, Italians,* near at hand
> True Britons all – and living in the Strand.

The home manufacture of 'classical' antiques might cater for the socially aspiring, but more exotic tastes were developing. The *World* (no. 117) satirised the prevailing taste for Chinese furniture and ornamentation; the authors of the 120th number of the *Connoisseur* commented:

> Taste is at present the darling idol of the polite
> world. . . . The fine ladies and gentlemen dress with
> taste; the architects, whether Gothic or Chinese, build
> with taste; the painters paint with taste; and, in short,
> fiddlers, players, singers, dancers, and mechanics
> themselves are all the sons and daughters of taste. Yet
> in this amazing superabundancy of taste, few can say
> what it really is, or what the word itself signifies.

As taste operated with increasing diversity in a prosperous nation, the whims, fancies and aspirations of individuals and groups alike seemed to confirm the proverb that 'tastes are not to be disputed'. But there were those to whom by this time there was more or less a social obligation to dispute tastes, especially in literature. To accompany the proliferation of culture had emerged, of course, a proliferation of critics. Dodsley, who as a bookseller spoke with authority, lamented the widespread addiction to criticism: 'It is not more true that man is born in SIN than that he is born in criticism' (*World*, no. 32).

There was no longer any accepted standard of values which was clear enough to employ in critical discrimination. Whereas it was easy for critics to make use of the traditional genre requirements relating to each piece of writing, epic, tragic or lyric, as the case might be, they had become patently inadequate – as Johnson tried to demonstrate in the preface to his edition of Shakespeare – in a world in which shifting conceptions of 'nature' were undermining the classical ideal. Most influential French criticism, too, had insisted on the necessity for an emotional response to art as well as an appreciation of its technique. In his preface to his translation of the 'Longinus' treatise in 1674 Boileau had emphasised the importance of the feelings which the word aroused; and Du Bos analysed this approach more closely, associating it with the effects of painting and poetry in his *Réflexions* of 1719. The popularity of Longinus increased, and with it the use of affective terms, the sublime and the pathetic. To these were added the beautiful and the picturesque as the parallel between poetry and painting was examined – notably by Spence in his *Polymetis* (1747) ('Each from each contract new strength and light') – in relation to the feelings which each aroused.

The faculty which responded to these effects had been identified with 'taste'. Invoked to cover so many fields of experience and such different levels of response – even equated with the imaginative faculty itself – it becomes manifestly overworked and its significance tends to crumble beneath the lack of discrimination with which it is employed. Mid-century writers lamented the impossibility of finding an adequate definition for the 'Poor monosyllable TASTE'. The insistence on the need for defining standards of taste had become so marked by 1759 that Johnson satirised it in Dick Minim, his canting critic, who: 'often wishes for some standard of taste, some tribunal, to which merit may appeal from caprice, prejudice and malignity' (*Idler*, no. 61).

It is in the work of philosophers, however, that the new consciousness which the term covers, that of an innate, individual responsiveness and sensitivity, is seriously explored and its different implications given shape and substance. In 1755 the Edinburgh Society for the Encouragement of Arts (as well as Sciences, Manufactures and Agriculture) proposed to award a gold medal to the best essay on the subject of taste. The medal was won in the following year by Alexander Gerard, at that time Professor of Moral Philosophy in the University of Aberdeen, and one of a group of Scottish empiricists who were preoccupied with the operations of taste in its social as well as in its individual contexts.

VII

Imagination and taste had become easily identifiable in so far as they were both concerned with the creation of art and the response to it. In his introduction to the facsimile reproduction of the 1780 edition of Gerard's *Essay on Taste* (1963) Walter Hipple comments on the connection between this and Gerard's other major work, the *Essay on Genius*, written in 1758 but not published until 1774:

> The imagination is, for Gerard as for Hume, the fundamental faculty of the mind. Hume, of course, takes both memory and the various modes of reason to be special modifications of the imagination. Gerard allows memory a more independent status, and he asserts a variety of intuitive principles which account for some of the phenomena of reason independently of the habits of the imagination. Yet imagination still swallows up almost all the mind. The internal sources of taste are special modes of imagination; even the judgment of taste turns out to depend upon habits of fancy; and the workings of genius turn out to be imaginative as well. (p. xvii)

The energy inherent in the subjective response had naturally identified the operation of the imagination with the energy of the emotions. In his 'Essay on Taste' John Gilbert Cooper describes the response of the perfect reader as:[9]

> that instantaneous glow of Pleasure which thrills thro' our whole Frame and Seizes upon the Applause of the Heart before the intellectual Power, Reason, can descend from the Throne of the Mind to ratify it's Approbation.

'No man', John Dennis had written, 'can judge of a Beautiful Imagination in another without some degree of it in himself.'[10] And Shaftesbury's distinction between true and false enthusiasm in part III of *The Moralists* involves the idea of man's awareness of his own identity being achieved through his exploration of his different faculties. As he does so his apprehension of Beauty, for example, takes on a creative energy of its own and becomes aware of its supernatural source: 'that which fashions even Minds themselves, contains in itself all the Beauty's fashion'd by those Minds; and is consequently the Principle, Source, and Fountain of all *Beauty*.'

Shaftesbury's Platonism conceives of the mind as essentially creative whether in invention or in response. The operation of taste is in itself active and energetic:[11]

> [Theocles] . . . setting aside those Productions which just now you excepted against as Master-pieces *of another Hand*; think what there are which more immediately proceed from us, and may more truly be term'd our *Issue*. . . . Wou'd you have me be conscious for you, of that which is immediately *your own*, and is solely in and from *yourself*? You mean my *Sentiments*, said I. Certainly, reply'd he: and together with your *Sentiments*, your *Resolutions*, *Principles*, *Determinations*, *Actions*; whatsoever is handsom and noble in the mind; whatever flows from your good *Understanding*, *Sense*, *Knowledge*, and *Will*; whatever is ingender'd in your *Heart* (good Philocles!) or derives it-self from your *Parent*-MIND, which, unlike to other *Parents*, is never spent or exhausted, but gains Strength and Vigour by producing.

The last clause throws into relief that self-perpetuating energy which goes into the cultivating and refining of subjective responses, and which is the product of that source of emotion, the heart, as well as of the mind. This is a reaffirmation of man's potentialities in terms of the creative vigour, the spark of the divine, in the workings of the imagination. For Shaftesbury, the imagination is intuitive and grounded in the emotions, apprehending the workings of the underlying principles of human existence. It is not yet articulated as a theory of perception as in itself creative, nor is it that power to which Coleridge refers in his first 'Lay Sermon' as uniting 'clearness with depth, and plenitude of sense with the comprehensibility of the understanding, so that, impregnated with the imagination the understanding itself becomes a living power'. But it insists on the importance of the feeling heart in the recognition that the emotions are actively operating both in response and in creation.

Hutcheson, following Shaftesbury, had postulated the existence of a number of reflective senses which would operate on the raw material of sense impressions, and which were responsive to certain qualities – order, beauty, harmony and so on. Commenting on Hutcheson's work in the introduction to his *Essay on Taste* (1759) Alexander Gerard writes:

> Taste consists chiefly in the improvement of those principles which are commonly called the *powers of imagination* and are considered by modern philosophers as *internal* or *reflex* senses supplying us with finer and more delicate perceptions, than any which can be referred to our external organs. These are reducible to the following principles: the senses of novelty, of sublimity, of beauty, of imitation, of harmony, of ridicule, and of virtue.

But there is another essential factor – that of feeling, and feeling not expressed in terms of passion, but of sensibility, with all the range of mood that word implies. Gerard adds later:

> We may here take occasion to mention a principle distinct from all the internal senses from which taste will, in many instances, receive assistance. It is such a *sensibility of heart*, as fits a man for being easily moved, and for readily catching, as by infection, any passion that a work is fitted to excite . . . Since . . . the pathetic is a word of so great moment in works of taste, a man who is destitute of sensibility of heart must be a very imperfect judge of them. He is a stranger to those feelings which are of greatest importance to direct his judgment. If a person possessed all the internal senses in perfection, he could estimate works of genius only by their inferior qualities . . . he can have no relish for any thing that is addressed to the heart. (pp. 86–9)

The influence of Du Bos is acknowledged here:

> It is so much the business of painting and poetry to affect us, by infusing passions, that a very ingenious critic has mistaken it for the *only* business of those arts . . . even [descriptive poetry] will soon grow

languid and unentertaining, if it does not support
itself by introducing subjects of an affecting nature.
(pp. 87–8)

The standpoint is at least half a century old by now; yet the
reason for Gerard's re-statement of the theme lies not only in the
new context of literary preoccupation with sensibility, nor –
though we shall consider it shortly as of greatest importance – in the
articulation of different principles of response and areas of feeling;
but in the responsibility which he felt with his fellow teachers and
philosophers for establishing a standard of taste.

The attempts made by Hobbes and Locke to break down artistic
creativity into its component parts had fostered a narrowing and
circumscribing of the faculty of imagination, making it a relatively
commonplace and pedestrian affair. If all mental activity has its
source in the experience of the senses, memory and imagination –
'but one thing which for divers considerations hath divers names'
– are merely 'decaying sense',[12] but set in motion and shaped anew
by desires and appetites, feelings and passions. Johnson can
emphasise this aspect of the faculty as in his 125th *Rambler* where
he refers to it as a licentious and vagrant faculty. Day-dreaming,
fabling, illusion, fantasy, can be dismissed as a deviation from
reality and from the business and bosoms of men: it does not
satisfy those to whose insights Keats feels he should have aspired:

> . . . those to whom the miseries of the world
> Are misery and will not let them rest.
>
> ('The Fall of Hyperion')

Coleridge was to bridge the gap between imagination as per-
ceiving ideal nature, and as re-creating reality. The gulf between
the object to be admired and its observer was spanned by an
emotional response, grounded in associations drawn from memory,
though fired by warmth of feeling into a vital responsiveness, until
Coleridge formulated the whole operation in terms of the creative
perception which, for him, is that of the imagination. Alongside
the virtual devaluation of the imagination which preceded this,
however, persisted the traditional idea of the imagination as the
creative faculty. Young and Hurd in different ways – the first in
his *Conjectures on Original Composition* (1759) and the second in his
Letters on Chivalry and Romance (1762) – advocate creation un-
impeded by the intervention of either judgment or tradition, but

both are concerned with the poet rather than the reader. The tradition of empirical inquiry into the faculties of man, begun by Hobbes and Locke, was carried further. In the discussions of taste the questions of social as against individual preferences and the nature of subjective feelings concentrate on what seems investigable in the mind of man.

VIII

In his early essay 'Of the Standard of Taste' (1742) David Hume finds it natural that his contemporaries should seek a 'Standard of Taste; a rule, by which the various sentiments of men may be reconciled, at least, a division afforded, confirming one sentiment and condemning another'. He proceeds to explore the consequences of this explicit recognition of feeling as the basis of taste: 'All sentiment is right; because sentiment has reference to nothing beyond itself, and is always real, wherever a man is conscious of it.' So

> a thousand different sentiments excited by the same object are all right: because no sentiment represents what is really in the object. It only marks a certain conformity or relation between the object and the organs or faculties of the mind; and if that conformity did not exist, the sentiment could never possibly have being. Beauty is no quality in things themselves. It exists merely in the mind which contemplates them; and each mind perceives a different beauty.

Taste is in its very nature subjective. It would seem in consequence impossible to establish any standard – 'the proverb has justly determined it to be fruitless to dispute concerning taste'. Here the distinction is made between the public relevance of taste, and the problems which arise from a clash between individual tastes and an inherited body of culture, with all its historical and social importance. And Hume's awareness of the creative potentiality of feeling – it 'is always real, wherever a man is conscious of it . . . each mind perceives a different beauty'[13] – suggests a new interpretation of the role of the imagination. Hume, however, is not attracted to the part played by feeling or intuition in the art of preference or discrimination. The imagination is for him as it had been for Hobbes, mischievous when uncontrolled in its deviations from the truth.

In an age of empirical enquiry, the opposition between the subjectivity of taste and the standards which, in the interests of society, it was essential to establish, would naturally encourage an increasing recognition that it was important to explore the nature of those feelings involved in the operation of taste. The impetus to such enquiries is given by Hume himself. He concludes – empirically – that although the tastes of individuals cannot be disputed, yet experience seems to demand certain qualities in all great art, 'qualities which have been universally found to please in all countries and in all ages'. There must, he deduces from this, be 'certain general principles of approbation or blame, whose influence a careful eye may trace in all operations of the mind'. The 'careful eye' of most of the outstanding philosophers and teachers of rhetoric for the greater part of the century were applied to tracing these very operations of the mind as they are set in motion by objects in nature or art.

IX

In the essay 'On Taste' with which he prefaced the second edition of his *Enquiry Concerning the Origins of our Ideas of the Sublime and Beautiful* (1759) Burke declares:

> if taste has no fixed principles, if the imagination is not
> affected according to some invariable and certain laws,
> our labour is like to be employed to very little purpose;
> as it must be judged an useless, if not an absurd
> undertaking, to lay down rules for caprice and to set
> up for a legislator of whims and fancies. . . .

So, having observed that

> ideas of the sublime and beautiful were frequently
> confounded, and . . . both indiscriminately applied to

things greatly differing, and sometimes of natures
directly opposite,

he sets himself to remedy the situation,

from a diligent survey of the passions in our own
breasts, from a careful survey of the properties of
things which we find by experience to influence those
passions, and from a sober and attentive investigation
of the laws of nature, by which those properties are
capable of affecting the body and thus of exciting our
passions.

Gerard entitled the second part of his *Essay on Taste*: 'The
Formation of Taste by the union and improvement of its simple
principles'; while Kames announced the aim of his *Elements of
Criticism* as the unfolding of 'Principles that ought to govern the
taste of every individual.'

In the conclusion to his book Kames shows that his concern is
overwhelmingly with the defence of standards of taste against the
demand for fashionable novelties – Gothic, Chinese or whatever –
which seemed to threaten cultural anarchy. Given the Augustan
equation of ethical with social there is also the implication that
cultural anarchy would result in the collapse of moral standards
too. In attacking the proverb, that there is no disputing about
taste, he appeals to common sense and reason, and asserts:

One thing, even at first view is evident, that if the
proverb hold true with respect to taste in its proper
meaning, it must hold equally true with respect to our
other external senses: if the pleasures of the palate
disdain a comparative trial, and reject all criticism,
the pleasures of touch, of smell, of sound, and even of
sight, must be equally privileged. At that rate, a man
is not within reach of censure, even when he prefers
the Saracen's head upon a signpost to the best
tablature of Raphael, or a rude Gothic tower before
the finest Grecian building; or where he prefers the
smell of a rotten carcass before that of the most
odoriferous flower, or discords before the most
exquisite harmony.

But we cannot stop here. If the pleasures of external sense be exempted from criticism, why not every one of our pleasures, from whatever source derived? If taste in its proper sense cannot be disputed, there is as little room for disputing it in its figurative sense. The proverb accordingly comprehends both; and in that large sense may be resolved into the following general proposition, That with respect to the perceptions of sense, by which some objects appear agreeable, some disagreeable, there is not such a thing as a *good* or *bad*, a *right* or a *wrong*; that every man's taste is to himself an ultimate standard without appeal; and consequently that there is no ground of censure against anyone, if such a one there be, who prefers Blackmore before Homer, selfishness before benevolence, or cowardice before magnanimity. (ii, 488–9)

The taste which Kames himself displays here was by this time out of date – the success of Ossian and of Walpole's *Castle of Otranto* undermine the assurance of his references to Gothic and Grecian. But, as Richards remarks in his *Philosophy of Rhetoric*, Kames asks the right questions if not in the right way.[14] He is aware that traditional values are threatened, not so much by popular or hack writing as by the repudiation of an inherited cultural tradition in the interests of relative and subjective values. It is still a major social problem.

Burke's approach is more tentative. His method, like that of Kames, is empirical ('to ascend gradually to principles from facts and experiments'), but he admits that, in attempting to dogmatise on matters of taste, 'we seem in danger of circumscribing nature within the bounds of our own notions, which we often take up by hazard or embrace on trust, or form out of limited and partial consideration of the object before us, instead of extending our ideas to take in all that nature comprehends, according to her means of combining' (p. 96).

These enquirers show a continuing awareness of the complexity and validity of actual experience – so much so that Burke, attempting to define taste in terms of the sensory and mental processes, finally rests his argument on the primacy of sensation itself: 'When we go but one step beyond the immediate sensible quality of things, we go out of our depth. All we do after is but a faint struggle, that shows we are in an element which does not belong to us' (p. 256).

X

Within their characteristic range – the investigation of the workings of taste and the ways in which it is affected by different objects – eighteenth-century associationist writers voiced questions in terms of a flexible and comprehensive approach to the operations of the mind. These still occupy modern critical speculation. For Richards, Kames's *Elements* was still a valuable and instructive book, offering a model, not of misconceptions to be avoided so much as problems to be taken up, articulated and carried forward:[15] 'Turning his pages you will again and again find points raised, which, if his treatment of them is unsatisfactory, are none the less points that no serious study of language should neglect.'

As Richards recedes in contemporary significance the preoccupation with standards and traditions seems to be an issue less easy to refer to in terms of foregone conclusions. Apart from this wider question, however, these writers attempt to deal with the nature of the aesthetic response with a fresh relevance and a recourse to detailed discussion of sense experience so that their descriptions take on a scientific clarity of tone which adds a persuasive force to their arguments and establishes the possibility of a different, psychological approach in criticism. Their articulation of questions of response extends the whole area of human awareness in this field.

So Gerard, explaining Hutcheson's description of senses as '*subsequent* or *reflex*' comments:

> *Subsequent* because they always suppose some previous
> perception of the objects, about which they are
> employed; thus a perception of harmony presupposes
> our hearing certain sounds, and is totally distinct from
> merely hearing them, since many, who enjoy the
> external sense of hearing in the greatest perfection,
> have no musical ear; *reflex*, because in order to their
> exertion, the mind reflects upon and takes notice of
> some circumstance or mode of that object which was

perceived, besides those qualities which offered themselves to his attention at first view. Thus the perception of any object does not give us the pleasant sense of novelty, till we have reflected on this circumstance, that we never perceived it formerly. (pp. 1–2n.)

Which is, after all, analogous to the experience reflected in the opening section of 'Tintern Abbey'.

Kames too observes that emotions are occasioned in us, not by the original sight of an object, but also when it is recalled to memory as an idea, fainter than an original perception in proportion as the perception itself is fainter (a notion related to Hobbes's 'decaying sense', as well as to Shelley's 'fading coal'), but he later makes a distinction between ideal presence and reflective remembrance – it is interesting that at this point he regrets the imperfections of language except where it concerns the external senses. He finds a want of proper words to describe ideal presence. Inaccuracies in distinguishing ideal from real presence are therefore unavoidable. Ideal presence, he says, supplies the want of real presence; whereas a general or reflective remembrance cannot warm us into any emotion. He selects theatrical representation of course as the most powerful vehicle of ideal presence (i, 90, 92–6).

Subsequently – and this has a special relevance (as we shall see in chapter 3) to the literature of the mid-eighteenth century – Archibald Alison, in his *Essays on the Nature and Principles of Taste* (1790) distinguishes between two ways of regarding objects. The first is to have merely an awareness of the object, the perception of which may be followed by a train of closely associated ideas that are somehow analogous to the objects themselves; the second involving the imagination, so that 'Trains of pleasing or of solemn thought arise spontaneously within our minds', and the difference between the two consists in the latter being accompanied by a pleasurable emotion. This emotion, then, is identified with the operation of the imagination, and for Alison this second kind of awareness is to experience 'Ideas of Emotion' – an aesthetic experience where thought connections are joined by a pervading mood or feeling (pp. 3, 53).

The attempts to define the various bounds of imaginative activity – whether in terms of the passions of 'self-love and social' or in terms of straightforward associationism – skirt the inevitability of the shift to the mind's own complexities. To attempt exploration of its operations in terms of the senses of beauty, sublimity, novelty, harmony and the rest; to relate its activities to outward forms and appearances was to establish an apparatus of feeling in philosophical and aesthetic terms. But it could not be pursued with profit. The paraphernalia of interpretation of sense impressions which dominate philosophical speculation had to be cleared by an examination of the very nature of the judgment of taste and by the reintroduction of the necessity of *a priori* knowledge. Although Kant accomplishes this the tradition of British empiricism had served its purpose in establishing the aesthetic response as of permanent and universal human concern.

XI

René Wellek attacks these philosophers for their 'slovenly habit of shirking difficult analysis' which had in Britain 'reduced philosophy to mere psychology and empirical ethics' in an atmosphere of 'immutable complacency'.[16] But mistrust and uncertainty are clearly discernible behind their conventional generalisations about nature and taste. Their insistence on the knowledge of the senses as the only knowledge available to man was not presented with complete conviction as to its ultimate truth. For the frame-work of their enquiries they tended to rely on accepted generalisations – though these were modified, as Kames shows, by an awareness of much wider issues. Within their speculations a different attitude clearly makes itself felt. Blake's is the most powerful statement of their shortcomings:

> Thus the terrible race of Los & Enitharmon gave
> Laws & Religions to the Sons of Har, binding them more
> And more to Earth, closing and restraining;
> Till a Philosophy of Five Senses was complete:
> Urizen wept, & gave it into the hands of Newton and Lock.
>
> ('The Song of Los', 44–8)

Establishing the importance of the subjective sensibility they explored avenues of enquiry radiating out of that central preoccupation in such a way that the role of the imagination was enhanced: it was in terms of this faculty that the compound pleasures of the senses and hence of the feelings were described, while its traditional role remained that of heightening experience by combining the evidence of the senses. It was natural that analyses of its responses in terms of strong emotions, evoked by certain kinds of objects – which was the principal concern of most of the empiricists, especially Burke – should result in a heightened awareness of the possibilities of imaginative activity, and in a self-awareness which would bring subjective emotions to the fore. Different passions excited by different kinds of objects could be seen to energise the imagination so that the excitement of strong feeling became a focal point of interest. This becomes clear in the analysis of the effects of the sublime in particular.

XII

With this central term are often associated the 'beautiful', the 'pathetic', and the 'picturesque'. The 'beautiful' tended on the whole to excite less comment than the 'sublime', whether because it was associated with a weaker emotional response, or because it had been coupled so frequently with harmony in Augustan contexts that its importance deriving from its widespread use in philosophical and ethical contexts was more easily to be taken for granted. Hogarth in his *Analysis* had tried to associate it specifically with beauty of nature, infinitely complex and varied, rather than that of ideal form. It is habitually compared and contrasted with the sublime; and its range of significance on one level is conveniently shown by Reynolds: 'The terms beauty, or nature, which are general ideas, are but different modes of expressing the same thing . . . there is but one presiding principle, which regulates and gives stability to every art. The works, whether of poets, painters, moralists, or historians, which are built upon general nature, live forever.'[17]

Thus, comments Hipple, contrasting Reynolds and Burke with Gerard, Kames, and the rest of their group,[18]

the True, the Good, and the Beautiful become, when perfected, equivalent: all are Nature. The theoretic, the practical, and the productive sciences, which

Aristotle carefully separated, are here, however
tentatively, merged: and these easy analogies are not
found among the literal writers of the century, however
fond many of them are of paralleling ethics and
aesthetics.

But the concern with beauty was shifting from its attributes to
the formal responses it aroused and to its manifestations in the
created world. The principles of variety rather than harmony, of
sensuous qualities rather than proportion, are reflected in
Hogarth's demands that representation of beauty shall be based on
principles of beauty to be discerned in the material world; and in
the third part of his *Enquiry* Burke even rejects fitness as a quality
essential to beauty, insisting rather on smoothness, smallness, and
delicacy of texture (sections xiii–xviii).

Similarly, the pathos of art had traditionally been regarded as
the way in which the writer affected the emotions of the reader so
that instruction might follow. The effect of the 'pathos' should
therefore be virtually co-extensive with that of the whole work.
But it is, naturally enough, in terms of the adjective derived from
it that the shift in taste from the sophisticated and classically
informed towards the deliberate cultivation of sensibility for its
own sake is mirrored. What is of particular interest is that it conditions many of Johnson's critical opinions. He adheres to the
necessity of truth to general nature for the inculcation of virtue,
and is aware of the dangers of an indulgence of an uncontrolled
imagination – hence his rebuke to Boswell rhapsodising on the
effects of music: 'Sir, (said he) I should never hear it, if it made me
such a fool' (*Life*, 1953, p. 874). But he frequently places reliance
on the pathetic in its newer and non-classical sense as he stresses
the importance of ordinary everyday human feelings. So the
power of Otway's *Orphan* 'is upon the affections. . . . But if the
heart is interested, many other beauties may be wanting, yet not
be missed' (*Lives*, i, 245).

The pathetic, too, is associated with general nature in terms
again of human nature. Virgil's best pastorals are those which
portray actual occurrences: 'We can always feel more than we can
imagine' (*Adventurer*, no. 92); while in the 'Life of Cowley' he
found that the metaphysicals, as they did not share common
human feelings, were not successful in representing or moving the

affections. It is in this connection that he praises the work of his friend Reynolds: 'I should grieve to see Reynolds transfer to Heroes and Goddesses, to empty splendor and to airy fiction, that art which is now employed in diffusing friendship, in reviving tenderness, in quickening the affection of the absent, and continuing the presence of the dead' (*Idler*, no. 45).

Johnson can even verge on sentimentality in interpreting the force of common sympathy wholly in terms of the emotions: *Jane Shore*, consisting 'chiefly of domestick scenes and private distress . . . lays hold upon the heart', and he comments on Catherine in *Henry VIII*: her 'meek sorrows and virtuous distresses may be justly numbered among the greatest effects of tragedy'. With her character 'the genius of *Shakespeare* comes in and goes out'. So it was that Ossian could by many of Johnson's contemporaries be found more pathetic than Homer. The Reverend Hugh Blair, for example, in his 'Critical Dissertation on the *Poems of Ossian*', enthusiastically remarks that 'The meeting of the lovers . . . the sentiments and the behaviour of Oithona . . . are described with such tender and exquisite propriety, as does the greatest honour both to the art and delicacy of our author; and would have been admired in any poet of the most refined age.'[19]

XIII

Characteristically coupled with the pathetic in the more fashionable criticism of the mid-eighteenth century – that of Dick Minim, for example, as well as of many authentic commentators on literary reputations – was the sublime.

It had emerged in Boileau's translation and preface as a criterion which might supplement genres' requirements, chiefly in terms of style, but also in terms of those flights in writing which achieve the most moving literary effects. Some reference has already been made to its popularity in eighteenth-century criticism; but the reason for its widespread and increasing influence lies deep in the state of religious and philosophical thought; in the changing attitudes towards external nature; and in the way in which the human imagination had to come to terms not merely with new discoveries in science and geography, but with whole new perspectives in history and religion.

In the early eighteenth century the Newtonian universe had itself manifested reason; the interest in natural phenomena shown in the fashionable profusion of scientific enquiries coincided with a religious conception of the universe as the revelation of the existence of an Omnipotent being. Nature was seen as the mirror of divine reason and order:

> The Spacious Firmament on high
> Above the blue ethereal sky
> And spangled Heav'ns, a shining Frame
> Their Great Original proclaim,

as Addison's paraphrase of Psalm 19 attempts to bring home to the reader the necessity for meditation on the divine handiwork for the benefit of the soul (*Spectator*, no. 465). Professor Tuveson describes this as akin to pantheism, and in illustration quotes Bishop Burnet's confession of pleasure in looking upon 'the great concave of the heavens and those boundless regions where the stars inhabit' as well as upon the oceans and mountains of the earth:[20]

> There is something august and stately in the air of
> these things that impress the mind with great thoughts
> and passions. We do so naturally upon such occasions
> think of God and his greatness, and whatsoever hath
> but the shadow and appearance of INFINITE, as all
> things have that are too big for our comprehension,
> they fill and overbear the mind with their Excess, and
> cast it into a pleasing kind of stupor and admiration.

This view of the impact of external nature on the mind, the evocation of depth of feeling, only loosely associated the Divine Maker with the emotional experience; the subsequent rise of deism on the one hand and dissent on the other focused the source of supranormal feeling in the mind's emotional response to certain kinds of objects.

XIV

The tendency to look for manifestations of the divinity in nature became entangled with the influence of Longinus in criticism, since

Longinus had dealt with the sublimity of such natural objects as evoke a response similar to that of sublimity in art – rivers and mountains for example. At this point the subjective consciousness of an individuality of being is again awakened. Locke's psychological approach to the operations of the mind, which had been popularised by Addison and given a visual interpretation specifically in the papers 'On the Pleasures of Imagination', mingled with these threads of thought and feeling so that it came to be believed that:[21]

the greater the size of the object contemplated or recalled, the greater . . . the feeling or thought which results. By the view, said Addison, of a 'vast uncultivated desert . . . of huge heaps of mountains, high rocks and precipices, or a wide expanse of waters', the imagination is flung into 'a pleasing astonishment', for 'The mind of man naturally hates everything that looks like a restraint upon it, and is apt to fancy itself under a sort of confinement, when the sight is pent up in a narrow compass'. . . . Greatness, in other words, by challenging the capacity of the mind and the emotions, frees them for their fullest possible exercise. This general attitude . . . is indicative of a gradual tendency which encourages the romantic stress on subjective 'suggestiveness' as an end in itself – a 'suggestiveness' which gives pleasure by the very action it forces the imagination to undergo.

So speculation concerning the sublime in literature became identifiable with that concerning the sublime of natural objects. We do not need to go far on into the century to find Gray writing in a celebrated letter to West in November 1739 that not a cliff on his journey up the Grande Chartreuse 'but was pregnant with religion and poetry'. John Baillie, in 1747, begins his consideration of the sublime with the declaration that[22]

As the *Sublime* in *writing* is not more than a description of the *Sublime* in *Nature*, and as it were painting to the *imagination* what *Nature* herself offers to the *Senses*, I shall begin with an Inquiry into the *Sublime* of *Natural Objects*, which I shall afterwards apply to *Writing*.

In this way the older interpretation of the sublime as a special
kind of rhetorical effectiveness was associated with a newer kind
of subject-matter by the common constituent, grandeur. The
emotion associated with sublimity at this point is that of awe or
wonder – often equivalent to a religious sense, like that expressed
by Wordsworth in his journey through the Simplon Pass when he
feels that the

> Tumult and peace, the darkness and the light –
> Were all like workings of one mind, the features
> Of the same face, blossoms upon one tree;
> Characters of the great Apocalypse,
> The types and symbols of Eternity,
> Of first, and last, and midst, and without end.
>
> ('Prelude', vi, 635–40)

Baillie's attempt earlier had involved a distinction between the
effects of the sublime and those of the pathetic:

> The *Sublime*, when it exists *simple* and unmixed, by
> filling the Mind with one *vast and uniform* Idea affects
> it with a solemn *Sedateness*; by this means the soul
> itself becomes, as it were, one *simple*, grand, *Sensation*.
> Thus the Sublime not hurrying us from *Object* to
> *Object*, rather *composes* than *agitates*, whilst the very
> *Essence* of the *Pathetick* consists in the *Agitation* of the
> *Passions*, which is ever affected by crouding into the
> Thoughts a thousand different Objects, and hurrying
> the Mind into various Scenes.

But for Baillie uniformity, the grandeur of generality and overall
simplicity of effect (associated with classical requirements of art),
is the keynote of the sublime as it permits the mind to run 'out
into Infinity, continually creating, as it were, from the Pattern'.[23]
There is no sense for him in which the mind animates the scene
with its own associations and reflections as a means of apprehending the divine. Johnson shares Baillie's attitude when he denies
sublimity to the metaphysical poets:

> they never attempted that comprehension and expanse
> of thought which at once fills the whole mind, and of
> which the first effect is sudden astonishment, and the

second rational admiration. Sublimity is produced by aggregation and littleness by dispersion. Great thoughts are always general, and consist in positions not limited by exceptions, and in descriptions not descending to minuteness. (*Lives*, i, 20)

XV

An increased appreciation of Milton's reliance on the Bible as a source of inspiration is part of this taste for the sublime. The virtuous Harriet Byrom gives her views on Milton's debt to the ancients:[24]

His knowledge of their mythology, sir! His own subject so greatly, so nobly, so divinely, above that mythology! I have been taught to think, by a very learned man, that it was a condescension in Milton to the taste of persons of more reading than genius in the age in which he wrote, to introduce, as often as he does, his allusions to the pagan mythology; and that he neither raised his sacred subject, nor did credit to his vast genius, by it.

And so 'the gentleman went away convinced, that the English poet as much excelled the Grecian in the grandeur of his sentiments, as his subject, founded on the Christian system, surpasses the Pagan.'

Lowth recognised in the Bible a kind of poetry which depended on recurrent stresses, not on rhyme – a precedent which increased the dignity of the hymns of nonconformity with their expression of individual communion with God and his works – 'Jesu, Lover of my soul/Let me to thy bosom fly' – and encouraged a new subjectivity of response to the external universe. Nature is not merely a manifestation of divine order but in itself the source of religious experience.

In a letter of 1802 Coleridge contrasts the two cultures:

[In ancient Greece] All natural Objects were *dead*, – mere hollow Statues – but there was a Godkin or Goddessling *included* in each. . . . At best, it is but

Fancy, or the aggregating Faculty of the mind – not *Imagination*, or the *modifying* and *coadunating* Faculty. This the Hebrew Poets appear to me to have possessed beyond all others & next to them the English. In the Hebrew Poets each Thing has a Life of it's own, & yet they are all one life.

In the course of defining a poet in his *Biographia Literaria* he recalls Isaiah, and modifies his definition to read: 'The poet described *in ideal* perfection, brings the whole soul of man into activity.'[25]

The changes in poetic inspiration and in poetic modes of utterance which are touched on here will be considered in my next chapter. But the sublime – its associations with Milton's landscapes in his minor poems, especially in 'L'Allegro' and 'Il Penseroso', as well as with the religious sublimity of style and subject of his epic, go beyond the notion of the grandeur of simplicity as the chief effect of the sublime. The movement outward into a sense of infinity might not yet be a sense of union with the cosmos: it could however be seen as a development towards a tentative recognition of the fascination exercised by the indefinite and obscure, above all of the suggestive and remote.

So Burke sees its effectiveness – again in relation to Milton – to reside in its obscurity. Of the description of Satan he remarks: 'We do not any where meet a more sublime description than this justly celebrated one . . . wherein [Milton] gives the portrait of Satan with a dignity so suitable to the subject'; quoting the passage at length, he continues:

Here is a very noble picture; and in what does this poetical picture consist? In images of a tower, an archangel, the sun rising through the mist, or in an eclipse, the ruin of monarchs, and the revolution of kingdoms. The mind is hurried out of itself, by a crowd of great and confused images; which affect because they are crowded and confused. For separate them, and you lose much of the greatness; and join them, and you infallibly lose much of the clearness. The images raised by poetry are always of this kind; though in general the effects of poetry are by no means to be attributed to the images it raises. (pp. 164–5)

The sublimity of the picture exists in terms of its poetical associations. Metaphorical complexity in terms of epic simile could be subdued to an overall grandeur of suggestion. From a similar starting point Reynolds deduced that: 'We will allow a poet to express his meaning, when his meaning is not well known to himself, with a certain degree of obscurity, as it is one source of the sublime.' The weakness of this critical assumption was remarked on by Blake when he commented: 'Obscurity is Neither the Source of the Sublime nor of any thing else.'[26]

More characteristic of the age, however, is the insistence on sublimity of subject-matter rather than that of style. The sublimity of external nature has already been remarked on as it suggests the presence of the Creator, the ultimate source of the sublime, and a source which falls in too with the pietistic strain dominant in eighteenth-century thought and society. It is a train of thought of course ultimately deriving from Plato, but now receiving special encouragement from religious and class interests. So Lowth observes that sacred poetry 'appears to have been the original office and destination of poetry', and that the Hebrew poetry is superior to the Greek in sublimity, which was 'equalled by the energy of the language and the dignity of the style';[27] while Burke concludes that 'the Scripture alone can supply ideas answerable to the subject [of the Creator]' (pp. 175–6).

XVI

It is clear that the heterogeneity of impulses from which the concept of sublimity springs would substantially weaken its usefulness as a critical term. The deistic, scientific, religious, social, rhetorical and literary strains made it capable of only vague and suggestively general interpretations.

Burke's is the most significant of the empirically based analyses of the aesthetic response. He goes further than most of his contemporaries in emphasising the intensity of the emotional impact of the sublime, a response felt with such vigour and vitality that it seems to proceed less from the workings of sensation alone than from the uninhibited release of imaginative energy. His idea of the sublime goes far beyond the grandeur which others associate with it. He insists on the apprehension of overwhelming power, of darkness, obscurity and horror affecting man's primal instinct of self-preservation as they make their impact on the senses without the intervention of reflection. So he writes of the passion evoked by the sublime, introducing the horror of the experience and its numbing effect on the workings of the mind: 'Astonishment is that state of the soul, in which all its motions are suspended, with some degree of horror. In this case the mind is so entirely filled with its object, that it cannot entertain any other, nor by consequence reason on that object which employs it' (p. 157). This is in contrast to Baillie and Dennis who presuppose some intervention by the learning and reflective powers on sense impressions. They assume as an essential part of the response a realisation of the order, beauty, harmony and proportion of the universe, and this prevents an apprehension of the sublime as Burke presupposes it, concerned as he is with the effects of power and terrifying objects at a more elemental and purely emotional level.

Burke is, of course, ostensibly within the humanist tradition when he asserts that 'The elevation of the mind ought to be the principal end of all our studies, which if they do not in some measure expect, they are of very little service to us.' He continues, however:

> But, besides this great purpose, a consideration of the rationale of our passions seems to me very necessary for all who would affect them upon solid and sure principles. It is not enough to know them in general: to affect them after a delicate manner, or to judge properly of any work designed to affect them. We should know the exact boundaries of their several jurisdictions; we should pursue them through all their variety of operations, and pierce into the innermost, and what might appear inaccessible parts of our nature. (p. 153)

Although, then, Burke relates his exploration of the passions aroused by the sublime in nature and art to the traditional ethical framework of his day, this is essentially a directing of the artist's attention to the most elemental, and hence subconscious working of men's minds as material to be made use of.

But as there were so many more writers, and so much larger and less discriminating a public than heretofore, this emphasis on certain subjects as arousing strong emotions of a traditionally exciting and pleasurable kind – the tales of horror and the super-natural, the satisfactions of romance – fell increasingly into more sensational projections of the artist's – particularly the minor artist's – experience and feelings. Commenting on this develop-ment with disapprobation R. S. Crane remarks:[28]

> The eighteenth-century Longinians themselves did not escape the contagion of the new psychological aesthetics. Of what sort are the elevated conceptions and emotions in the poet which constitute the most important sources of the sublime in writing? Longinus did not say, and it is one of his merits that he left the matter vague. But many of his modern disciples, from Dennis on, had no such scruples about definition. The great writer is one who thinks about 'great things' – 'Gods, Daemons, Hell, Spirits and Souls of Man, Miracles, Prodigies, Enchantments, Witchcrafts, Thunder, Tempests, raging Seas, Inundations, Torrents, Earthquakes, Volcanoes, Monsters, Serpents, Lions, Tygers, Fire, Water, Pestilence, Famine, etc.' – feels the pleasing terror which such objects inspire, and imparts his thoughts and emotions in words. For how much bad criticism – and poetry – this degraded kind of Longinianism was responsible in the eighteenth century and after I need not say.

Mrs Barbauld affirms that 'The Old Gothic Romance and Eastern Tale, however a refined critic may censure them as absurd and extravagant, will ever retain a most powerful influence on the mind.' Dante's popularity rose in this cultural atmosphere. Sherlock wrote in 1781, 'Longinus who would have condemned to the flames that "monstrum horrendum, informe, ingens", the Divinia Commedia, would have read some of its verses with transport.' And showing how the taste of the century has become more sensational he adds, 'On pursuing the canto of Count Ugolino, the sentimental soul of Longinus would have exclaimed "Homer has nothing so sublime".' Walpole lamented that: 'The cast of the age (I mean in its compositions) is too sombre. The giantry of Ossian has introduced mountainous horrors. The exhibitions at Somerset House are crowded with Brobdingnagian ghosts.'

It was 'Monk' Lewis who therefore caught the 'taste' of the last decades of the century; so that Wordsworth observed after seeing *The Castle Spectre* in 1798 that 'It fitted the taste of the audience like a glove.'[29] The scenic grandeur of nature; the supernatural stimulation of horror and terror; the projection of deeply felt emotions in terms of a recognisable area of subject-matter, and often of style as well, mark the apprehension of sublimity. In addition religious, historical and philosophical reflections imbue the texture of the literary work of authors of varying levels of achievement.

XVII

The discussion of the nature of sublimity and of the objects producing deeply felt emotional responses subsequently provoked discussion of its companion term, the picturesque – though this had for a long time been a major consideration in gardening (Shenstone's 'Leasowes', for example), art and poetry. There had, of course, been a wealth of speculation concerning the relationships between the sister arts throughout the century. Exploration of the *ut pictura poesis* tag, elaborated by Du Fresnoy, and popularised by Dryden's translation of the *De Arte Graphica*, re-translated (after many editions) by Defoe in 1720, becomes more explicit and its implications are explored in comparative and historical studies of the development of the different arts; and in aesthetic speculation it is built into the literature and art of the century by such writers as Spence, Harris, Mason, Reynolds, Price, Gilpin, Knight and Alison.

Addison had firmly established the dependence on the sense of sight of most of the pleasures of the imagination; and there is in consequence a further and more powerful emphasis given to the old parallel between poetry and painting which, voiced by Horace, compared different art forms and their respective effects on the audience. Spence's *Polymetis* (1747) is an example of this approach which Lessing was to counter as a pernicious confusion in the *Laokoon* (1766).

The parallel, however, is important, first, for the formal

criteria it provides – history paintings and epic poems are of greater significance than landscapes and descriptive poetry. It is important too in that it reflects the current recourse to allegory in poetry as an obvious manifestation of the inventiveness of the poet in the particularity of detail with which the abstract idea could be made concrete and lifelike. And, more relevant still to the insistence on emotional and reflective response to natural scenery, it associates the landscapes of favourite painters with the depth of thought and reflection they arouse.

The taste in art which spread with the habit of the Continental tour earlier in the century, and which with the increase and wider dispersal of wealth had cultivated native talent in domestic and landscape as well as portrait painting, encouraged in literature a dependence on scenic effects of well-known painters in order to bolster the emotional response of the reader. This was true in particular of the popular Claude, Poussin and Salvator Rosa. A passage from *The Man of Feeling* strikes a note which was becoming increasingly familiar to novel readers towards the end of the century, and which, later still, formed part of the apparatus of the writer of the Waverley novels:[30]

> He was one of those figures which Salvator would have drawn; nor was the surrounding scenery unlike the wildness of that painter's backgrounds. The banks on each side were covered with fantastic scrubwood and at a little distance, on the top of one of them stood a finger-post to mark the direction of the two roads. . . . A rock, with some dangling wild flowers, jutted out above where the soldier lay, in which grew the stump of a large tree, white with age, and a single twisted branch shaded his face as he slept. 'Father,' said Harley (who by this time found the romantic temper rising within him) . . .

In addition to these factors, of course, the pleasure of vision was regarded as foremost among those of the imagination which it was the business of art to affect. So it followed that the most poetical kind of description was to be sufficiently particularised. Warton censured Pope's 'Windsor Forest' on the grounds that it lacked original, detailed description.[31] Gray praised Joseph

Warton's 'Enthusiast, or Lover of Nature' as 'all pure description', though he observed later to Beattie: 'As to description, I have always thought that it made the most graceful ornament of poetry, but never ought to make the subject. Your ideas are new, and borrowed from a mountainous country, the only one that can furnish truly picturesque scenery.'[32] Ideas, traditionally associated with landscape poetry, are now to emanate from a vivid realisation of a particular scene by a more subjective and individual process of association than that which characterises Denham's 'Cooper's Hill' or Pope's 'Windsor Forest'. Here Blair's observations on the poetry which combined Highland scenery with biblical, epic with supernatural grandeur in strains predominantly pathetic – that of Macpherson's *Ossian* – are significant:[33]

> A poet of original genius is always distinguished by his talent for description. A second-rate writer discerns nothing new or peculiar in the object he means to describe. His conceptions of it are vague and loose; his expressions feeble; and of course, the object is presented to us indistinctly, and thus through a cloud. But a true poet makes us imagine that we see it before our eyes; he catches the distinguishing features; he gives it the colours of life and reality; he places it in such a light that a painter could copy after him.

Granted that the description should be so presented as to place a picture before the eye of the reader, there should then follow an evocation of the impression made by those objects, not only on memory but on the senses. Blair continues:

> That Ossian possesses this descriptive power in a high degree, we have clear proofs, from the effect which descriptions produce upon the imaginations of those who read him with any degree of imagination and taste . . . whilst reading him we are transported into a new region, and dwell among his objects as if they were all real.

For Gray as for Goethe, the landscapes against which were set the misfortunes of Tamora or the laments of Ossian liberated repressed feeling; just as for Cowper the 'Atlantic billows' in which his castaway perished were the physical counterpart of his own spiritual torment, and the 'happy shades' of the shrubbery intensified by contrast his own 'fixed unalterable case'. Where the picturesque is concerned, then, the portrayal of objects is subordinated to the idea of a composition which orchestrates feeling or mood. So Alison writes in his *Essay on the Nature and Principles of Taste* (i, 42–3) that:

> the effect produced by association, in increasing the
> emotions of sublimity or beauty, is produced also,
> either in nature, or in description by what are
> generally termed Picturesque Objects. An old tower in
> the middle of a deep wood, a bridge flung across a
> chasm between rock, a cottage on a precipice . . .
> suggest an additional train of conceptions.

XVIII

I shall move on in my next chapter to discuss the problems of the creative writer. They are related to the problem of the current interpretation of literary history and to a rapidly changing society with the painful difficulties it imposed on the poet in particular of working out some modification of the existing assumptions about the importance of individuals, alone, and in society and the wider world. But here it is perhaps fitting to conclude with a few generalisations.

There is in mid-century a loosening and a decentralisation of cultural authority. Attempts to resist too swift changes of taste and the validity of subjective judgment are accompanied by a repudiation of outworn and (in the light of new philosophical methods of enquiry) apparently over-simplified criteria in the interests of an empirical grounding of standards of taste on the senses and emotions of mankind as a whole. This exploration of a new dimension of man's existence is accompanied by an awareness of the potentialities of his individual consciousness – which had for a long time in a dissenting context been identifiable with conscience.

The vocabulary evolved for the description of states of emotion is a focal concern of philosophers and critics. Meantime there is among authors a delight in cultivating sensibility of heart very much, on the whole, for its own sake. The hero of Beattie's 'Minstrel' (1771) is, as we might now expect,

> . . . a strange and wayward wight,
> Fond of each gentle and each dreadful scene:
> In darkness and in storm he found delight; . . .
> Ev'n sad vicissitude amused his soul:
> And if a sigh would sometimes intervene,
> And down his cheek a tear of pity roll,
> A sigh, a tear so sweet, he wish'd not to controul . . .
>
> There would he dream of graves and corses pale;
> And ghosts that to the charnel-dungeon throng,
> And drag a length of clanking chain, and wail
> Till silenced by the owl's terrific song
> Or blast that shrieks by fits the shuddering isles along . . .
>
> Ah what is mirth but turbulence unholy
> When with the charm compared of heavenly melancholy?
>
> (stanzas xxii, xxxii, lv)

But it is intended that the expression of sensibility shall be modified by the presence of reflection: as Beattie remarks in his preface, the Spenserian stanza 'allows the sententiousness of the couplet, as well as the more complex modulation of blank verse'.[34]

We are a long way from the conception of the poet as a man speaking to men: 'a man, it is true, endowed with more lively sensibility, more enthusiasm and tenderness, who has a greater knowledge of human nature, and a more comprehensive soul, than are supposed to be common among mankind' (Wordsworth, 1800 Preface). Human sympathy of this social kind is not the only aspect of human nature which requires expression in the work of its artists. Poets of any period are faced with problems of individual human concern which are not necessarily, except in the widest sense, social; and it is their special task to express in terms of illusion the dilemmas of reality.

Notes

1 James L. Clifford (ed.), *Man versus Society in Eighteenth Century Britain* (Cambridge, 1968).

2 See pp. 10–11; J. H. Plumb, 'Political Man' in Clifford, *op. cit.*, 11; R. Altick, *The English Common Reader, a Social History of the Mass Reading Public* (Illinois, 1957), 33.

3 Allan Ramsay, 'The Gentle Shepherd', *Poems*, selected and arranged by J. Logie Robertson (London, 1887), 51, 60.

4 *Sir Charles Grandison*, quoted by Ian Watt, *The Rise of the Novel* (London, 1963), 254.

5 *Works*, ed. A Murphy, 12 vols (London, 1806), viii, 33 and 35–6.

6 *Life of Johnson*, ed. R. W. Chapman (Oxford Standard Authors; London, 1965), 513–14.

7 J. W. Draper, *The Funeral Elegy and English Romanticism* (New York, 1929), 16.

8 J. W. Beach, *The Comic Spirit in George Meredith* (New York, 1911), 87.

9 'Letters Concerning Taste' (1755); *Augustan Reprint Society Publication no. 30* (Los Angeles, 1951), Letter i, pp. 2–3.

10 'A Large Account of the State of Taste in Poetry' (1702), *Critical Works*, ed. E. N. Hooker, 2 vols (Baltimore, 1939), i, 336.

11 *Characteristicks*, 'The Moralists', ii, 409.

12 *Leviathan* (London, 1885), 7.

13 David Hume, *Essays Moral, Political and Literary*, ed. T. H. Green and T. H. Grose, 2 vols (London, 1875), i, 268 and 269.

14 *Philosophy of Rhetoric* (Galaxy paperback; New York, 1965), 104.

15 *Ibid.*

16 René Wellek, *Immanuel Kant in England, 1793–1838* (Princeton, 1931), 4.

17 Sir Joshua Reynolds, *Discourses* (Everyman; London, 1906), Seventh Discourse (1776), 107.

18 W. J. Hipple, *The Beautiful, the Sublime and the Picturesque in Eighteenth-Century British Aesthetic Theory* (Carbondale, 1957), 138.

19 *The Poems of Ossian translated by James Macpherson, Esq., with Dissertations on the Era and Poems of Ossian and Dr. Blair's Critical Dissertation*, 2 vols (Glasgow, 1821), ii, 212.

20 E. L. Tuveson, *The Imagination as a Means of Grace* (Berkeley, 1960), 69–70.

21 W. J. Bate, *From Classic to Romantic* (Harvard, 1949), 99–100.

22 'On the Sublime', *Augustan Reprint Society Publication, no. 43* (Los Angeles, 1953), 3.

23 *Ibid.*, 33, 9.

24 *The History of Sir Charles Grandison; The Novels of Samuel Richardson*, with introduction by Ethel M. M. McKenna, 20 vols (London, 1902), xiv, 76–7.

25 *Collected Letters of Samuel Taylor Coleridge*, ed. Earl Leslie Griggs, 4 vols (Oxford, 1956), ii, 457–8; *Biographia Literaria*, ed. J. Shawcross, 2 vols (Oxford, 1907), ii, 12.

26 *Seventh Discourse* (1776), 101; *The Works of William Blake*, ed. E. J. Ellis and W. B. Yeats, 3 vols (London, 1893), ii, 339.

27 R. Lowth, *Lectures on the Sacred Poetry of the Hebrews*, tr. G. Gregory (London, 1847), 30.

28 *English Literature 1660–1800. A Bibliography of Modern Studies compiled*

for Philological Quarterly, ed. Louis A. Landa and others, 2 vols (Princeton 1950–2), i, 436–7.

29 E. F. Carritt, *A Calendar of British Taste, 1600–1800* (London, 1948), 345, 376, 371, 440.

30 *The Works of Henry Mackenzie*, 8 vols (Edinburgh, 1808), i, 156–7.

31 *An Essay on the Writings and Genius of Pope* (London, 1756), 20.

32 *The Correspondence of Thomas Gray*, ed. Paget Toynbee and Leonard Whibley, 3 vols (Oxford, 1935), i, 224.

33 *Op. cit.*, 215.

34 *The Minstrel* (London, 1819).

Three

The Creative Impasse: Imitation and Originality

I

As the social and economic structure of the country changed, existing standards in culture and criticism could no longer remain unquestioned: there developed a gradual reorientation of the role of the imagination. Attempts to rationalise criticism in terms of a vocabulary of taste and feeling were considered in chapter 2: here I shall look at the new awareness of individuality and its expression in literature.

The over-riding interest in a rationale of sensibilities expressed by contemporary philosophers was paralleled by a spate of mid-century works on genius and originality. And those who discoursed on genius often associated its operations with the value of fiction and fable, of pure poetry, as against that of reality and truth to nature. At this time there is a new and urgent apprehension of a difficulty inherent in artistic expression – how to establish new but acceptable modes of statement (for a reading public wider and less homogeneous than ever before) so that the communication of personal emotions and reflections might stimulate and engage the responsiveness of an audience. For the novelist, who was to all intents and purposes shaping his own mode of expression, having inherited little or no awareness of the conventions of his medium, the potentialities of man as an individual being caught up in different kinds of social relationships presented an untapped source of invention. For the poet on the other hand, working within a highly sophisticated literary tradition, and succeeding to the achievement of the most technically brilliant and consummately skilled of modern English poets, the problem of finding new modes of expression was acutely difficult. Probably the most characteristic aspect of mid-eighteenth-century poetry as a whole is the way in which it reveals in its different aspects a quest for new yet acceptable fictions and forms through which the poet can convey his responses to his environment in terms of his own feelings.

II

Discussion of the contemporary artist's difficulties centres in two main issues. Firstly, it had for a long time seemed inevitable that invention would become increasingly stultified as society grew more educated and refined. All that seemed to be left to modern writers was to embellish the themes, plots and characters which earlier authors had virtually exhausted. The term 'imitation' suffered a narrowing in significance throughout the Augustan period: Dryden's use of it to denote translation conveying the spirit of an original goes with his strong feeling that his predecessors exhausted the common stock of literary materials:[1]

> There is scarce an humour, a character, or any kind of
> plot which they have not blown upon; all comes
> sullied or wasted to us: and were they to entertain this
> age, they could not make so plenteous treatment out of
> so decayed fortunes. This therefore will be a good
> argument to us either not to write at all, or to
> attempt some other way.

In Pope's mature work the technical and thematic brilliance of his juxtapositioning of different literary modes to achieve effects of irony or paradox, places a stranglehold on creation through imitation, as it inhibits that expression of direct feeling which might seem naturally to lie at the heart of originality.

Next, as historical and comparative studies flourished, theories of literary history developed. It was widely held that earlier writers might have enjoyed conditions of existence in which the state of religion, or superstition, the manners of the times and its language were especially conducive to the production of works of genius. Writers, in short, needed only in these circumstances to imitate the life of their times. The dilemma of the modern poet is meditated upon by Imlac:

> it fills me with wonder, that, in almost all countries,
> the most ancient poets are considered as the best:
> whether it be . . . the poetry is a gift conferred at once;
> or that the first poetry of every nation surprised them
> as a novelty, and retained the credit by consent which
> it received by accident at first: or whether, as the

province of poetry is to describe Nature and Passion,
which are always the same, the first writers took
possession of the most striking objects for description,
and left nothing to those that followed them, but
transcriptions of the same events, and new
combinations of the same images. Whatever be the
reason, it is commonly observed that the early writers
are in possession of nature, and their followers of art:
that the first excel in strength and invention, and the
latter in elegance and refinement. (*Rasselas*, ch. x)

With the preferred critical currency insisting on an emotional
response in terms of 'sublime', 'pathetic', and 'sentimental' it was
clear that the meaning of 'nature and passion' – as we have seen –
could be shifted to an inward emphasis, so that the expression of
individual feelings might itself become a guarantee of originality.
So far as imitation is concerned, two lines of thought were possible:
on the one hand it could be maintained that authors had merely
imitated the manners and customs of their own age and society;
on the other, that it was in fact the lack of learning and sophistication of the writer in earlier periods that allowed him free scope for
the exercise of his imaginative invention, or – to use the language
of the day – his original genius.

III

In his *Conjectures on Original Composition* (1759) Edward Young
makes a distinction between two kinds of artist:[2]

Imitations are of two kinds; one of nature, one of
authors. The first we call originals, and confine the
term imitation to the second. . . . An original may be
said to be of a vegetable nature; it rises spontaneously
from the vital root of genius; it grows, it is not made:
Imitations are often a sort of manufacture wrought by
those mechanics, art, and labour, out of pre-existent
materials not their own.

Addison had made a similar point in the *Spectator* (no. 160). His
distinction, however, was between two kinds of genius, the first,

like Shakespeare, natural, wild, irregular; the second, like Milton, formed by the rules and the 'restraints of art'. Young's opposition degrades the second and attributes an organic quality to the first. Johnson, comprehending the traditional significance of the word in his references to representations of general nature, employs it with precision and weight in his dictum: 'No man ever yet became great by imitation' (*Rambler*, no. 154).

The artistic roles of invention and imaginative originality exemplified in Shakespeare (as Logan Pearsall Smith showed in *Words and Idioms*, 1925) acquired transcendental overtones in their association with genius. So Robert Lloyd describes Shakespeare:[3]

> True Genius, like Armida's wand,
> Can raise the spring from barren land:
> While all the art of Imitation,
> Is pilf'ring from the first creation;
> Transplanting flowers, with useless toil,
> Which wither in a foreign soil.

The message is the same as Young's, and it is associated with the diffused climate of religious dissent, which, contrasting with the spiritual poverty and obvious self-seeking of the established church, stressed the existence of the inner light of the soul – or (in more sophisticated circles) the operations of a superior sensibility. So Lloyd continues:

> As conscience often sets us right
> By its interior active light,
> Without th'assistance of the laws
> To combat in the moral cause;
> So Genius, of itself discerning,
> Without the mystic rules of learning,
> Can, from its present intuition,
> Strike at the truth of composition.

In the same way Young abstracts from the traditional concept of genius all but the diversity of the gift, the supernatural attributes of the writer:

> what, for the most part, mean we by genius, but the
> power of accomplishing great things without the means
> generally reputed necessary to that end? A genius

differs from a good understanding, as a magician from
a good architect: that raises his structure by means
invisible; this by the skilful use of common tools.
Hence genius has ever been supposed to partake of
something Divine . . . *Sacer nobis inest Deus*, says Seneca.
With regard to the moral world, conscience, with
regard to the intellectual, genius is the God within.
(pp. 279–80)

Wellek comments on the *Conjectures* that they assert that all men
are born 'originals', no two faces or minds are alike. 'The process
of creation', he writes:[4]

not being easily observed or measurable, was
conceived as something fundamentally irrational, a
result of the subconscious forces of the human mind,
a product of feeling and volition, even of enthusiasm,
passion and inspiration. Such a process of creation was
considered ideal; it was projected into the past as the
process by which original genuine poetry was
produced, in contrast to the mechanical, cerebral way
of composing recent poetry.

While an analysis of the powers of genius by Young, or Duff, for
example, depended on accepted views of the workings of the
imagination, the phrasing of Young's 'Reverence thyself. . . . For
nothing original can rise, nothing immortal can ripen in any other
sun' suggests a kind of supernatural energy released in creativity
which explains the relatively sudden impact of the *Conjectures* and
their wide European influence. For in England Welsted had made
the same kind of observation a quarter of a century before.[5]

IV

The growing importance attributed to genius in England had
been encouraged by the widespread concern that Shakespeare
and other great writers in the native tradition – especially Spenser
and Milton – should be vindicated from the charge that they
violated the rules of drama and of the epic. So Hurd, arguing in
his *Letters on Chivalry and Romance* (1762) for an imaginative if not

a formal epic unity for the *Faerie Queene*, complains that French criticism[6]

> supposes that the poets, who are lyers by profession,
> expect to have their lyes believed. Surely they are not
> so unreasonable. They think it enough, if they can but
> bring you to *imagine* the possibility of them. . . . So
> little account does this wicked poetry make of
> philosophical or historical truth: all she allows us to
> look for is *poetical truth*; a very slender thing, indeed,
> and which the poet's eye, when rolling in *a fine frenzy*,
> can but just lay hold of.

Hurd proceeds to re-interpret Hobbes: 'To speak in the philosophic language of Mr. Hobbes, it is something *much beyond the actual bounds, and only within the conceived possibility of nature.*' And 'by nature we are to suppose can only be meant the known and experienced course of affairs in the world, where experience has less to do than consistent imagination.' The proper business of the poet is to create a world of illusion, rather than a formal structure on epic, dramatic or didactic lines. And there naturally developed from this the assumption that the true poet, the original creative genius, is distinguished by his capacity for creating pure fiction.

Hence the appreciation of Shakespeare's magic received critical validation; hence the absence of learning – of the classical kind – from the education of the Bard, was hotly disputed in a debate which is characteristic of this time. For 'To neglect of learning genius owed its greater glory.' The age preferred to see its geniuses – from Stephen Duck to Chatterton and Burns – without learning.

Johnson, however, complained in his 154th *Rambler* that 'The mental disease of the present generation is a disposition to rely upon unassisted genius.' In his sober insistence in the 'Life of Cowley' that 'The true Genius is a mind of large general powers, accidentally determined to one particular direction',[7] Johnson can see the magic of Shakespeare as straightforwardly derived from close observation of the material of life. Johnson's reply to Fanny Burney's question concerning Shakespeare's invention of Caliban is positive and specific:[8]

> There is nothing so little comprehended among
> mankind as what is genius. They give to it all, when it

can be but a part. Genius is nothing more than knowing the use of tools; but there must be tools for it to use: a man who has spent all his life in this room will give a very poor account of what is contained in the next. (Miss Burney): Certainly, sir; yet there is such a thing as invention? Shakespeare could never have seen a Caliban. (J): No, but he had seen a man, and knew what a man is: He who would draw a monstrous cow, must first know what a cow commonly is; or how can he tell that to give her an ass's head or an elephant's tusk will make her monstrous? . . . Let two men, one with genius, the other with none, look at an overturned wagon – he who has no genius, will think of the wagon only as he sees it, overturned, and walk on; he who has genius, will paint it to himself before it was overturned, – standing still, and moving on, or heavy loaded, and empty; but both must see the wagon, to think of it at all.

It is clear that for Johnson the operations of the imagination in genius are commonplace and mechanically associative. They are based on memory and reflection rather than on that inner energy of emotion which can transcend reality to create new worlds of thought and feeling. It is a shrewd answer but a tame and pedestrian one. Johnson's predilection for the pathetic can fall, it will be remembered, into the sentimental: it is often associated with the everyday, the domestic. His dislike of the world of illusion emerges in his praise of the drama of Shakespeare as an antidote to it:[9]

> his drama is the mirror of life . . . he who has mazed his imagination, in following the phantoms which other writers raise up before him, may here be cured of his delirious ecstasies, by reading human sentiments in human language; by scenes from which a hermit may estimate the transactions of the world, and a confessor predict the progress of the passions.

Johnson's is a satisfying account for the common reader, and a memorable one; but these contemporaries were attempting to reach farther into less sure ground. William Duff in his *Essay on Original Genius* (1767) attempts to determine the role of fancy in the production of poetry, as distinct from that of genius: Wit and Humour 'are produced by the efforts of *rambling* and *sportive* Fancy' whereas genius 'proceeds from the copious effusions of a plastic Imagination': 'A vigorous, extensive and plastic Imagination is the principal qualification of the one [Genius], and a quick and lively Fancy the distinguishing characteristic of the other.'[10]

In Johnson's approach on the other hand there is no suggestion of the 'reverent and religious conception of the divine power of the artistic creator' acclaimed by Young, and by a whole generation of European writers, which returns[11]

> across the Channel, and is often found in the works of Coleridge, as when, for instance, he describes the imagination of the artist as an echo of what he calls the primary imagination, which is itself an analogue of creation, and its activity 'a repetition in the finite mind of the eternal act of creation in the infinite I AM'.

And it is when considering Shakespeare that Coleridge asserts: 'No work of true genius can want its particular form'. For the time being, however, though Johnson in the *Preface to Shakespeare* vindicates Shakespeare's genius by repudiating those criteria which condemn his mingling tragic with comic modes, it is on the grounds of truth to human experience, rather than to an awareness of the work of art as a microcosm of that experience.

V

The belief that the mark of original genius was an ability to create pure fiction was qualified in some quarters by the idea that success of this kind was due to favouring historical circumstances. Of course this had been implicit in the Augustan acceptance of the contemporary world as one cleared of superstition and prodigies: 'Nature well known, no prodigies remain.' And in such a world, it was recognised, certain kinds of writing were no longer possible and these kinds had traditionally been among the most attractive to the common reader. In the 419th *Spectator* Addison offered various observations on 'The Fairy Way of Writing' – legend, superstition and romance:

The Ancients have not much of this Poetry among them, for, indeed, almost the whole Substance of it owes its Original to the Darkness and Superstition of later Ages, when pious Frauds were made use of to amuse Mankind, and frighten them into a Sense of their Duty. Our Forefathers looked upon Nature with more Reverence and Horrour, before the World was enlightened by Learning and Philosophy, and loved to astonish themselves with the Apprehensions of Witchcraft, Prodigies, Charms and Enchantments. . . .

Among all the Poets of this kind our *English* are much the best . . . naturally Fanciful, and very often disposed by that Gloominess and Melancholy of Temper, which is as frequent in our Nation, to many wild Notions and Visions, to which others are not so liable.

The foundations are already laid for a national return to the inspiration of the Gothic as a reaction against the rational, lucid and social – but that will be looked at later in this chapter. What is of particular relevance here is the attempt to relate literature to the conditions of its time. And the preoccupation with the contemporary situation – which illustrates an awareness of peculiarly pressing contemporary difficulties – comes through the various interpretations of literary history, whether it is expressed in terms of a decline from the achievement of earlier writers, or of a simple evolutionary progress from barbarism to refinement. Young asks:

But why are originals so few? not because the writer's harvest is over, the great reapers of antiquity having left nothing to be gleaned after them; nor because the human mind's teeming time is past, or because it is incapable of putting forth unprecedented births; but because illustrious examples engross, prejudice, and intimidate. (pp. 275–6)

Goldsmith, dividing ancient learning into three periods, that of poets, of philosophers, and, in its decline, that of criticism, associates the last period with the state of taste in his own time:[12]

Original productions seldom appeared, and learning, as if grown superannuated, bestowed all its panegyric

upon the vigour of its youth, and turned encomiast
upon its former achievements. . . . Under the
auspicious influence of genius, arts and sciences grew
up together, and mutually illustrated each other. But
when once Pedants became lawgivers, the sciences
began to want grace, and the polite arts solidity; these
grew crabbed and sowre, those meretricious and
gawdy; the philosopher became disgustingly precise,
and the poet, ever straining after grace, caught only
finery.

An increase of criticism is . . . 'the natural consequence of learning's becoming universal'; and 'Criticism', he concludes, is the
'natural destroyer' of 'polite learning'.

So the conception of literary forms as ideals which dominated
criticism with considerations of genre, unity, conduct and style,
seemed by now to have replaced the supposed irregularities and
original brilliance of earlier writers in the non-classical tradition
with a mere polished perspicuity and refinement. With the
acclaim of the genius of Shakespeare, and to a lesser extent, of
Spenser, came an awareness of the absence from modern literature
of greatness of imagination. Dryden had noted it at an early stage:

Our age was cultivated thus at length
But what we gained in skill we lost in strength;
Our builders were with want of genius curst.
(Prologue to *The Double Dealer*, 1694, 11–13)

And it was natural, of course, that Pope's achievement should
be succeeded by a reaction, and a reaction which was not only
associated with the newer emphasis on the emotional response to
art and nature, but which was exacerbated by the dominant
interpretation of literary history as one of progression towards
refinement. It was an interpretation which gained strength from
the conscious pride in good sense and patriotic feeling which had
shaped the Augustan literary sensibility. But with the reaction
came a strengthening of the feeling, implicit in the energy with
which Ancients and Moderns controversy was debated, that the
age was not suitable for poetry, and this is associated with the
long-standing repudiation of fancy and superstition, and of the
uninhibited play of the imagination on the feelings. After praising

Milton's achievement, Collins concludes that it cannot be repeated:

> I view that Oak, the fancied Glades among,
>   By which as Milton lay, His Ev'ning Ear,
> From many a Cloud that drop'd Ethereal Dew,
>   Nigh spher'd in Heav'n its native strains could hear:
>   On which that ancient Trump he reach'd was hung;
>   Thither oft his Glory greeting,
>   From Waller's myrtle shades retreating,
> With many a Vow from Hope's aspiring Tongue,
> My trembling Feet his guiding Steps pursue;
>   In vain – Such Bliss to One alone,
>   Of all the Sons of Soul was known,
>   And Heav'n and Fancy, kindred Pow'rs,
>   Have now o'erturned th'inspiring Bow'rs,
> Or curtain'd close such Scene from ev'ry future View.
>
> ('Ode on the Poetical Character', 1746)

Richard Hurd, examining Spenser's debt to the romances of the age of chivalry, comments in a celebrated passage on the fortunes of poetry since the age of Elizabeth 'when reason was but dawning, as we may say, and just about to gain the ascendant over the portentous spectres of the imagination. Its growing splendour in the end, put them all to flight, and allowed them no quarter even among the poets:

> Henceforth the taste of wit and poetry took a new
> turn: and the *Muse*, who had wantoned it so long in
> the world of fiction, was now constrained against her
> will,
>
> To stoop with disenchanted wings to truth, . . .
>
> What we have gotten by this revolution, you will say, is
> a great deal of good sense. What we have lost is a world
> of fine fabling; the illusion of which is so grateful to the
> *charmed Spirit*, that, in spite of philosophy and fashion,
> *Fairy* SPENSER still ranks highest among the poets; I mean,
> with all those who are either come of that house, or have
> any kindness for it.

> Earth-born critics, my friend, may blaspheme:
> But all the GODS are ravish'd with delight
> Of his celestial song, and Music's wondrous might.
>
> (pp. 349–50)

Gray saw literature as 'drawing apace to its dissolution' (*Letters*, i, 265), and in 1750, as the verses in magazines and newspapers weakly echoed the strains of Pope, or Milton, as the case might be, a writer in the *Monthly Review* commented:

> in our later times, so large has been the inundation of
> rhiming trumpery from the press, that even the name
> of a poet, and of poetry, are become so cheap, so
> contemptible, and, in some instances, so abominable,
> that a real genius is often ashamed to be ranked among
> the sons of the muses, tho' in company even with
> Homer, Horace, and Milton. (iv, 29)

VI

The assumption that great poetry is capable of being produced only at certain times and in certain countries which are particularly favourable to the writer is shown in commentaries on Homer, and, of course, on the Scriptures. Thomas Blackwell's *Enquiry into the Life and Writings of Homer* (1735) accounts in this way for Homer's success in the epic: 'by the *united* Influence of the happiest CLIMATE, the most natural MANNERS, the boldest LANGUAGE, and most expressive RELIGION: when these were applied to such a Subject as the War between Greece and Troy, they produced the ILIAD and ODYSSEY.' It is no wonder, he thinks, that two such poems should appear only once in three or four thousand years, considering how many 'rare CHANCES' and 'uncommon INGREDIENTS' had combined to make them excel. He concludes that Homer wrote his epics simply by representing 'things both in his own and other Countries, *almost as he heard them talked of*'.[13] The poet's weaknesses were to be accounted for in the same way. 'HOMER was a compleat *natural Painter* of the Ways of Men', wrote John Brown in his *History of the Rise and Progress of Poesy* (1764), 'but an imperfect moral Painter from the *unpolished Genius* and *barbarous Legislation* of the Age in which he lived'.[14]

86

Robert Lowth's approach is similar. In the lectures on Hebrew poetry delivered at Oxford in 1741, but not translated and published until 1753, he associates the poetry of a period with the way of life of the people who wrote it. Similarly, Robert Wood was later to attempt to explain the superiority of classical writers of pastoral:[15]

> When the cares, as well as the pleasures of the country were compatible with the highest rank, and the prince and the peasant were literally united in the same person; elevation of sentiment and expression belonged to the royal shepherd, and were found in rural life. Hence it is that Oriental pastoral, though obscure and defective in the art of composition, affords the boldest flight of genius of this kind. . . . The modern Arab, in whom I have seen the characters of prince, shepherd, and poet, united, retains, in his compositions of this kind, the wildness, irregularity, and indelicacy of his forefathers, with a considerable share of the same original glowing imagination, which we could discover, even in their extempore productions, and under the disadvantage of crude and hasty translation.

Blair accounts for the success of Ossian, in his *Critical Dissertation* (1763), in terms of the society which produced him:[16]

> Irregular and unpolished we may expect the productions of uncultivated ages to be; but abounding at the same time with that enthusiasm, that vehemence and fire, which are the soul of poetry: for many circumstances of those times which we call barbarous, are favourable to the poetical spirit. The state in which human nature looks wild and free, though unfit for other improvements, certainly encourages the high exertions of fancy and passion.

VII

Closely related to this assumption that to create was to observe and depict from actual life, to paint the manners of a place and period, was the appreciation of literature of very different kinds, native and exotic. Ballad and song collections become more numerous, reaching a climax of critical acclaim in Percy's *Reliques* of 1765. Much earlier, in his preface to one of the first of many collections of early poetry, Allan Ramsay had written:[17]

> *Readers* of the best taste and most exquisite Discernment frequently complain of our *modern Writings*, as filled with affected Delicacies and studied Refinements, which they would gladly exchange for that natural strength of Thought and Simplicity of Style our Forefathers practised: To such, I hope, the following *Collection of Poems* will not be displeasing.
>
> When these good old *Bards* wrote, we had not yet made Use of imported trimmings upon our Cloaths, nor of foreign Embroidery in our writings. Their *Poetry* is the product of their own Country, not pilfered and spoiled in the transportation from abroad; their Images are native, and their *Landskips* domestick; copied from those Fields and Meadows we every Day behold.
>
> The *Morning* rises (in the Poet's Description) as she does in the *Scottish* Horizon. We are not carried to *Greece* or *Italy* for a Shade, a Stream or a Breeze. The *Groves* rise in our own Valleys; the *Rivers* flow from our own Mountains, and the *Winds* blow upon our own Hills.

National and historical interests combine to reassert the superiority of native literature. I referred earlier to Addison's association of romance, superstition and legend with an English tradition of writing. This had flourished in 'the dark ages', and was prized because of its charmed hold over the credulity of men. The great exemplar of this type of writing is Spenser, extolled by Milton in 'Il Penseroso' as among these 'great Bards' who

> In sage and solemn tunes have sung,
> Of Turneys and of Trophies hung;
> Of Forests and inchantments drear,
> Where more is meant than meets the ear.

(117–20)

We are, of course, approaching via Spenser and the manners and superstitions of the age of chivalry a term which is peculiarly central to the expression of the sensibility of these years – the 'Gothic'. It will be considered closely in the context of Thomas Warton's work, but it comes in here as the key term in Richard Hurd's *Letters*. Hurd identifies the medieval way of life, portrayed in the romances of chivalry, as 'Gothic', as opposed to the classical or heroic.

Basing his conclusions, as we might expect, on the premise that whatever affects the imagination and passions most strongly is the superior work of art, he argues the superiority of Gothic subject-matter to Grecian. Admitting that 'Much has been said and with great truth, of the felicity of HOMER's age, for poetical manners', he continues:

> But . . . as HOMER was a citizen of the world, when he had seen in *Greece*, on the one hand, the manners he had described, could he, on the other hand, have seen in the West the manners of feudal ages, I make no doubt but he would certainly have preferred the latter. . . . The current popular tales of Elves and Fairies were even fitter to take the credulous mind, and charm it into a willing admiration of the *specious miracles* which wayward fancy delights in, than those of the old traditionary rabble of Pagan divinities. And then, for the more solemn fancies of witchcraft and incantation, the *Gothic* are above measure striking and terrible.
> (*Letter* vi, pp. 280–1 and 283)

Quoting Addison's paper on 'The Fairy Way of Writing' he proceeds to commend the fancies of 'these bards' as 'More sublime, more terrible, more alarming' than those of the classic fablers: 'In a word, you will find that the *manners* they paint and the *superstitions* they adopt are the more poetical for being *Gothic*' (pp. 289–90).

VIII

Here the 'poetical' is identifiable with the forcible occupation of the reader's sensibility by the poet, and this is assumed to be achieved most readily by the use of 'Gothic' material. The implications of this for poetry are far-reaching, and Hurd instances great poets in support of his argument:

> The greatest geniuses of our own and foreign
> countries, such as ARIOSTO and TASSO in *Italy*, and
> SPENSER and MILTON in *England* were even charmed
> by the *Gothic* romances. Was this caprice and
> absurdity in them? or, may there not be something in
> the *Gothic* Romance peculiarly suited to the view of a
> genius, and to the ends of poetry? and may not the
> Philosophic moderns have gone too far in their
> perpetual ridicule and contempt of it? (*Letter* i, p. 239)

After one has made allowances for the universal tendency to swing from one extreme position to another in matters of taste, two points remain at issue. The first we have met repeatedly before, in one form or another: that in the conscious association of poetry with satire and manners, poets seemed to have diminished the natural faculty of poetry to impress itself on the mind of the reader by exalting or transporting him beyond the trivia of existence.

That this is a commonly felt human need is perhaps most clearly seen in the cult of the Gothic. In the eighth number of *The Bee* Goldsmith observed: 'We have a *wondering quality* within us. . . . It is, therefore, one of the most unthankful offices to go about to expose the mistaken notions of witchcraft and spirits; it is robbing mankind of a valuable imagination, and of the privilege of being deceived' (1759). And Walpole, that shrewd observer of man and society, makes a rather surprising admission in a letter dated 5 January 1766, which Edith Birkhead quotes in her account of *The Tale of Terror* (1921):

> Visions, you know, have always been my pasture; and
> so far from growing old enough to quarrel with their
> emptiness, I almost think there is no wisdom
> comparable to that of exchanging what is called the
> realities of life for dreams. Old castles, old pictures, old
> histories, and the babble of old people make me live
> back into centuries that cannot disappoint one. One holds

fast and surely what is past. The dead have exhausted
their power of deceiving! (p. 18)

Walpole had, of course, already produced by this time the first
Gothic novel in *The Castle of Otranto*. In his case, and in that of
Hurd and Thomas Warton, it is the picturesque and romantic
trimmings of the past (as present in medieval and Italian
romances) that are dearly prized. They enable the poet and his
reader to gain access to a different world, exotic and charged
with a sensuous pleasure in the shifts from one association in the
mind to another. So Thomas Warton opens his 'Pleasures of
Melancholy' in Miltonic vein:

> Beneath yon ruin'd Abbey's moss-grown piles
> Oft let me sit, at twilight hour of Eve,
> Where thro' some western window the pale moon
> Pours her long-levell'd rule of streaming light;
> While sullen, sacred silence reigns around,
> Save the lone screech-owl's note, who builds his bow'r
> Amid the mould'ring caverns dark and damp.
>
> (28–34)

The awareness of his surroundings, is, for the persona assumed by
the poet, a pictorial awareness, at an hour free from all distur-
bance, of the remains of a departed religion. So the 'lone' screech-
owl intensifies his solitude. Following Milton's steps, but adapting
the statement and the emotion to his own time and situation,
Warton gives emphatic expression to a sense not of loneliness
merely but of an isolation essential to the true poetic experience:

> Nor undelightful is the solemn noon
> Of night, when haply wakeful from my couch
> I start: lo, all is motionless around! . . .
> All Nature's hush'd in silence and in sleep.
> O then how fearful is it to reflect,
> That thro' the still globe's aweful solitude
> No Being wakes but me!
>
> (50–8)

> . . . let the sacred Genius of the night
> Such mystic visions send, as SPENCER saw,
> When thro' bewild'ring Fancy's magic maze,

To the fell house of Busyrane, he led
Th'unshaken Britomart; or MILTON knew,
When in abstracted thought he first conceiv'd
All heav'n in a tumult, and the Seraphim
Come tow'ring, arm'd in adamant and gold.

(62–9)

The intentional exploration of visual effects made sensuous by the use of evocative words and play of vowel texture is obvious in the last line.

IX

Attention is increasingly focused on the essential nature of poetry and on the kind of genius shown by the poets of the past. So in Gray's 'Bard' and 'The Progress of Poesy' and Collins's 'Ode on the Poetical Character' the development of poetry and the attributes of the poet are set before the reader. For subtlety in attempting to capture the stuff of poetry in terms of the past there is little to rival Gray's odes. In the intricate musicality which results from his handling of the Pindaric form the reader finds now this, now that response evoked: at one moment the utterance is dramatic, at the next there is the elegiac appeal of plangent repetition. Intricacy of rhyming enhances the dancing effectiveness which Mrs Garrick admired in the odes. Walpole wrote to Lord Lyttelton on 25 September 1757 that the public

> have cast their eyes over them, found them obscure,
> and looked no farther, yet perhaps no composition
> ever had more sublime beauties than are found in
> each. . . . The description of Shakespeare is worthy
> Shakespeare: the account of Milton's blindness, though
> perhaps not strictly defensible, is very majestic: The
> character of Dryden's poetry is as animated as what it
> paints. . . . As Greek as the expression *many-twinkling*
> is, it struck Mrs Garrick, and she says, on that whole
> picture, that Mr. Gray is the only poet who ever
> understood dancing.

The odes were bold attempts to write true poetry, intricate in form, imbued with sensuous descriptive effects and an overall pattern of significant feelings and reflections. In 'The Bard', sequences of imagery in a series of climaxes effected by the stanzaic patterning of the poem crystallise into personifications to give a climactic assertion of the power of poetry:

> The verse adorn again
> Fierce War, and faithful Love,
> And Truth severe, by fairy Fiction drest.
> In buskin'd measures move
> Pale Grief, and pleasing Pain,
> With Horrour, Tyrant of the throbbing breast.

The movement through varying patterning of statement and tone in the address to Edward is halted by the admonition to the king:

> A Voice, as of the Cherub-Choir,
> Gales from blooming Eden bear;
> And distant warblings lessen on my ear,
> That lost in long futurity expire.
> Fond, impious Man, think'st thou, yon sanguine cloud,
> Rais'd by thy breath, has quench'd the orb of day?
> To-morrow he repairs the golden flood,
> And warms the nations with redoubled ray.

The personification of the sun as it continues to warm the earth is associated with the power of poetry which transcends that of monarchs and time itself. The accelerating movement of the verse suggests the mounting exaltation of the speaker, and the reader is then dramatically and suddenly distanced from the whole situation in the return to the narrative mode of the concluding couplet describing the self-immolation of the Bard:

> 'Enough for me: With joy I see
> The different doom our Fates assign.
> Be thine Despair, and sceptr'd Care,
> To triumph, and to die, are mine.'
> He spoke, and headlong from the mountain's height
> Deep in the roaring tide he plung'd to endless night.

Gray's view of the 'Progress of Poesy' concludes with a moving exaltation of the true spirit of poetry: the rhyming of the lines dances on to display his technical mastery in verse. This throws

93

into relief the Bard's ambition to transform his idealising vision into a limited but definite poetic accomplishment which he describes in terms such as Wordsworth might almost have echoed in the 'Intimations of Immortality' ode, for Dryden:

> Bright-eyed Fancy hovering o'er
> Scatters from her pictur'd urn
> Thoughts, that breathe, and words, that burn.
> But ah! 'tis heard no more –
> Oh! Lyre divine, what daring Spirit
> Wakes thee now? tho' he inherit
> Nor the pride, nor ample pinion,
> That the Theban Eagle bear,
> Sailing with supreme dominion
> Thro' the azure deep of air:
> Yet oft before his infant eyes would run
> Such forms, as glitter in the Muse's ray
> With orient hues, unborrow'd of the Sun:
> Yet shall he mount . . .

The lift in the verse which coincides with 'Spirit' recalls Milton's enchanted description of the phoenix in 'Samson Agonistes' (1,699–1,707) in its creation of a climax sustained in the mind of the reader, with dramatic effectiveness of feeling in tune with tone.

So 'The Minstrel', 'The Bard', Ossian and the Rowley poems – begun, according to Chatterton, in 1769 – capture for the generation of Beattie, Gray, Macpherson and Chatterton a world in which recognisably poetic inspiration takes over from the demands of everyday reality. The opposition between the two worlds had been expressed by Thomson in his 'Castle of Indolence' (1748), as it was later by Tennyson in his 'Palace of Art'. The mellifluous creation of a dream-world is the distinctive feature of 'The Castle of Indolence', though it is the vehicle for a moral:

> A pleasing Land of Drowsy-hed it was:
> Of Dreams that wave before the half-shut Eye;
> And of gay Castles in the Clouds that pass,
> For ever flushing round a Summer-Sky:
> There eke the soft Delights, that witchingly
> Instil a wanton Sweetness through the Breast,

And the calm Pleasures always hover'd nigh;
But whate'er smack'd of Noyance, or unrest,
Was far far off expell'd from this delicious Nest.

(canto i, st. vi)

Spenser's *Faerie Queene* as well as Milton's minor poems were a new source of invention for those seeking poetic structures different from those of the Augustans. They were characteristically structures or fictions through which the evocation of different and highly personal feelings might affect the reader to an intimate emotional response, which might well be accompanied by an acquiescence in a general truth – as in 'The Bard'. To achieve this a diction had to be shaped and different forms experimented with. Metaphor, that hallmark of poetry, had been used by Pope at his best with an energy and wit which relied on verbal precision and rational analysis for its full effect. For a more personal, individual verse, expressing (at its most characteristic) feelings of a private kind and yet retaining social sentiments without resorting to the satiric mode, allegory, personification, and symbol seemed naturally to offer fresh scope for invention. So in 1746 Collins published his 'Odes on Various Allegoric and Descriptive Subjects', and in 1751 Johnson commended allegory: 'To imitate the fictions and sentiments of Spenser can incur no reproach, for allegory is perhaps one of the most pleasing Vehicles of instruction' (*Rambler*, no. 121). Writers who felt they belonged to an imaginatively impoverished tradition sought various means of renewing the true fount of poetry which they became increasingly aware they had inherited, not only from Spenser, Shakespeare and Milton, but from the bards and minstrels whose works had nourished and inspired the genius of their successors.

X

No one would quarrel with the general opinion that it is the novel which expresses the major creative impulse of the forty-odd years which separate the death of Pope from the publication of the *Lyrical Ballads*. Yet the obvious success of the novel, and the technical brilliance of Pope, have encouraged an oversimplifying approach to mid-eighteenth-century poetry.

95

In the long series of critical dismissals from which only a few poems emerge with credit one finds, of course, much that is just and discriminating. What is largely left out of account, though, is why these poets chose to write as they did. That their work is marked by certain idiosyncrasies – a reliance on pastoral modes and on a peculiarly artificial diction – and that it is often imitative of the minor verse of Milton, and to a lesser extent of Spenser, is insistently demonstrated. Eliot's is still a fairly representative indictment:[18]

> The eighteenth century in English verse is not, after
> Pope, Swift, Prior and Gay, an age of courtly verse. It
> seems more like an age of retired clergymen and
> schoolmasters. It is cursed with a Pastoral convention –
> Collins's Eclogues are bad enough, and those of
> Shenstone consummately dull – and a ruminative
> mind. And it is intolerably poetic. Instead of working
> out the proper form for its matter, when it has any,
> and informing verse with prose virtues, it merely
> applies the magniloquence of Milton or the neatness
> of Pope to matter which is wholly unprepared for it;
> so that what the writers have to say always appears
> surprised at the way in which they choose to say it.

There are certain odd assumptions here. One is prepared to join Eliot in his condemnation of the pastoral and to recall Dr Johnson's similar dismissal of the mode in 'Lycidas' as 'easy, vulgar, and therefore disgusting' (*Lives* ii, 163–4), until one wonders *why* this convention should be so common in this period. Why is to be poetic to be intolerable? And why should verse be informed with prose virtues? Both 'pastoral' and 'ruminative' after all, might equally well be applied to Wordsworth's 'Michael' – but in a context of approbation.

The key term, of course, is 'poetic'. Our own age has characteristically regarded the best poetry as conveying the depth and complexity of an adult mind in a real world, expressing its attitudes and emotions with a self-conscious irony. I. A. Richards indeed invokes the presence of irony as a touchstone for poetry and as the prime constituent of poetry of the highest order: 'Irony . . . consists in the bringing in of . . . opposite, the complementary impulses; that is why poetry which is exposed to it is not of the highest order, and why irony itself is so constantly a characteristic of poetry which is' (*Principles of Literary Criticism*, 1924, p. 250).

'Poetic' on the other hand, in a context where the reaction against the Georgians has for a long time marked the beginning of modern poetry, and Yeats's maturity is identified with his abandonment of the role of dreamer, has been accepted as denoting a verse which is deficient in maturity of feeling, inherently adolescent, escapist, and derivative from the world of literature rather than that of life. Identifying Eliot as the leader of a revolution in taste which changed the whole conception of what poetry should be like, George Macbeth sees the 'drive towards sincerity' as 'the dominant movement of the twentieth century'.[19]

The high valuation of sincerity in literature is to be found too in the eighteenth-century attempt to replace the criteria which had become too inflexibly based on the requirements of traditional kinds of writing by introducing new criteria associated with the actual responsiveness of the audience – an attempt which I examined in chapter 2, and of which the best exemplification is Johnson's *Preface to Shakespeare*.

The business of the critic is, traditionally, to discriminate for the readers of a particular generation, to make some assessment of the writing which is currently produced, and to relate the achievements of past literature to the insights of his own time, whether in terms of the author's genius, the social influences to which he is subjected, the demands of his audience, or the tradition to which he belongs or against which he may be reacting. The vocabulary of taste and feeling, however, which has been described in chapter 2, referred chiefly to responses to art, and (as I implied in commenting on Kames's attempts to systematise these) could be employed only in ways which might seem partial or arbitrary to the discrimination demanded by taste as well as by the developing sense of a national culture. Its advantage over that of the rules was its much greater flexibility. It could be applied to a wide variety of artistic forms to describe the nature of their impact on the audience. So it was equally appropriate to older literary forms, or to popular work. And it could be used to validate claims to wider critical attention of work which had been successful with its audience, but was of doubtful artistic status when judged by formal criteria – this is especially true of the ballad, the romance, the novel, of course, and tragi-comedy. Addison, in a well-known

Spectator (no. 70), had shown how it could be used to claim esteem for the ballad of Chevy Chase.

But a shift in the dominant critical vocabulary did not mean that there was no longer any necessity for the formulation of rules and methods of discrimination – though, as we have seen, this was not easy to effect in the context of the vogues for the sensational and horrific. So there were the attempts to relate certain types of subject-matter to certain emotional responses. And this, though welcomed by Johnson in the work of Kames and Burke, was not adequately adaptable to his own critical pronouncements.

The overall process of discrimination consisted for Johnson, as for his contemporaries, in applying the standards established by those works which had enjoyed 'continuance of esteem'. This principle Johnson enunciated in the tenth chapter of *Rasselas*, and, more carefully, in his *Preface to Shakespeare*. For Johnson criticism in practice, however, is a demonstration of the social and moral relevance of literature. In grasping the basic difficulty of all critical activity – how to formulate the relevance of art to life – Johnson aims in his *Preface* to vindicate Shakespeare from the prescriptions of petty authority by giving an account of his achievement, not in terms of ideal nature, of dramatic decorum, literary tradition and the rules, but in terms of real sublunary nature, and above all this means human nature. He falls back, that is, on that most flexible of criteria; one which can be used to bolster his prejudices as well as express his insights. His criterion of 'nature' is as wide as Dr Leavis's 'life'; and it has the potentialities which a strongly individual critical talent can employ to influence and educate the taste of his period.

XI

To employ 'nature' or 'life' as a criterion is to relate the concerns of literature to those of human existence in its full complexity of behaviour and feeling. But it has, it would appear, one disadvantage, and that disadvantage one which makes the criterion work against material where human life and emotions are less the object of concern than the creation of art which attempts to capture qualities of mood and feeling, so fictionalised and idealised in presentation that they are beyond any obvious translatability into normal experience. So the dismissive terms of this criticism – and I am not forgetting that it is criticism in which most profound and serious critical insights have been made – are 'escapist', 'fantasy', 'immature', 'visionary', 'fanciful', 'daydream', 'illusion' and so on. This is of further significance when we realise that to rely on 'nature' and 'life' as the focal points of critical appraisal is to rely on the substance of life itself, and the stuff of that abounds above all in that form which can most easily neglect the more intricate requirements of decorum with impunity, for social as well as artistic reasons – the novel. It is, of course, the form which has dominated literature from Johnson's day down to our own.

To attempt to modify a reliance on the flexible and complicated criteria of human emotions in a context which suggests reality (and characteristically, in the greatest novels, a predominantly social reality) is, I am aware, to fall into the danger of going to the other extreme and relying on form and technique as a basis for discrimination. In his Oxford lecture entitled 'Poetry for Poetry's Sake' (1901), Bradley enlarged on this difficulty in criticism: that in the linguistic habit of antithesising subject and form in a poem – which we see in terms of a microcosm – we fall inevitably into the language of antithesis. A poem's nature is, we see,[20]

> to be not a part, nor yet a copy, of the real world (as we commonly understand that phrase) but to be a world by itself, independent, complete, autonomous, and to possess it fully you must enter that world, conform to its laws, and ignore for the time the beliefs, aims, and particular conditions which belong to you in the other world of reality. . . . If substance and form mean anything in the poem, then each is involved in the other, and the question in which of them the value lies has no sense. . . . There is no such thing as mere form in poetry. All form is expression.

Hence the tendency to undervalue or abruptly dismiss certain kinds of literary statement is to exclude, or to be in danger of excluding, certain abstracted and idealised statements about experience which may seem to a critic writing at a particular time to be too rarified or fantastic. Both George Meredith and Virginia Woolf, as novelists, have suffered from this. It is something analogous to this kind of position, surely, which Dr Leavis is approaching when he comments on the influence of Keats on Victorian poetry:[21]

> The pre-Raphaelite cult of Beauty, which developed
> into the religion of Art (or the aesthetic religiosity), is
> the completest expression of that Victorian romanticism
> which in poetry draws so much on the Keats of *The
> Eve of St. Agnes*, *The Eve of St. Mark* and *La Belle Dame
> Sans Merci*. Victorian poetry in the central line that
> runs from the early Tennyson through Rossetti to
> Mr. Symons and his associates of the 'nineties turns
> its back on the actual world and preoccupies itself
> with fantasies of an alternative . . . the Victorian poetic
> day-dream does not suppose itself to have any serious
> relation to actuality or possibility.

In these terms the 'Ode on Melancholy' can be described as 'a prescription for making the most of your "sorrow's mysteries"'. Looking back in terms of his need of a tradition Leavis sees that aspect of Keats as originating an escapist cult, as Eliot deplored the poetic and pastoral preoccupations of pre-romantic poetry. It is – one would not deny – a mode of criticism which establishes traditions, sharpens discrimination, and raises specific theoretical issues. It is, less happily, the reason for the comments on 'Augustan' effects in the extraordinary number of notes which compose chapter 4 of *Revaluation*.

The opposition so frequently voiced between illusion and reality has, I would suggest, a built-in bias – semantically speaking – in favour of the latter. What is real, true, actual, human, natural, social and so on carries its own portmanteau of approbation. The merits of a work which does not meet these requirements tend to be neglected, and whole areas of poetic achievement have to be extricated from a submergence – often accepted as valid because pedagogically expedient – beneath the twentieth century's shaping of its literary heritage.

XII

So, to return to the eighteenth century, we find Dr Johnson dismissing the odes of Gray:

To select a singular event, and swell it to a giant's
bulk by fabulous appendages of spectres and
predictions, has little difficulty, for he that forsakes
the probable may always find the marvellous. And it
has little use: we are improved only as we find
something to be imitated or declined. I do not see that
The Bard promotes any truth, moral or political.
(*Lives*, iii, 438)

What is 'probable' is opposed to what is 'marvellous' in a self-
perpetuating association of probability with real everyday life,
and marvellous with fantasy, that is, escapism. Then there is
Johnson's comment on Collins:

He had employed his mind chiefly upon works of
fiction, and subjects of fancy; and, by indulging some
peculiar habits of thought, was eminently delighted
with those flights of imagination which pass the bounds
of nature, and to which the mind is reconciled only by
a passive acquiescence in popular traditions. He loved
fairies, genii, giants, and monsters; he delighted to
rove through the meanders of inchantment, to gaze on
the magnificence of golden palaces, to repose by the
waterfalls of Elysian gardens. . . . This idea which he
had formed of excellence, led him to oriental fictions
and allegorical imagery; and perhaps, while he was
intent upon description, he did not sufficiently cultivate
sentiment. . . . (*Lives*, iii, 337–8)

'This idea which he had formed of excellence'; 'fabulous appendages'; 'meanders of inchantment'. There seems to be some ideal
held in common by both Gray and Collins here according to
Johnson. It is interesting that Johnson loved reading romances;
'He used frequently to observe that there was more to be endured
than enjoyed in the general condition of human life' (*Life*, p. 442).
And when we look back at Addison, moving out from an interest
in evaluation for its own sake and the study of established classics
to a consideration of the engrossing pleasure to be gained from
literature, we return to the *Spectator*, no. 419, 'The Fairy Way of
Writing', writing which raises

a pleasing kind of Horrour in the Mind of the reader,
and amuses his Imagination with the Strangeness and
Novelty of the Persons who are represented in them.
They bring up into our Memory the Stories we have
heard in our Childhood, and favour those secret
Terrors and Apprehensions to which the Mind of Man
is naturally subject. . . . Men of cold Fancies and
Philosophical Dispositions, object to this kind of
Poetry, that it has not probability enough to affect the
Imagination . . . [but we] willingly give ourselves up
to so agreeable an imposture.

Addison is far readier to acknowledge the literary importance of
illusion than Johnson. The capacity for awakening excitement and
suspense, delight and surprise, are of central importance in the
experience of all art. The anonymous author of *Spenser Redivivus*
(1686), in an age geared to common sense and the exercise of
reason to dispel those superstitions which Sprat had so condemned,
had acclaimed Spenser's unparalleled use of enchantment and
vision in his *Faerie Queene*, observing:

Some there are that would so far unsoul Poesy, as to
allow nothing represented by it other than what
familiarly resembles the ordinary Results of our
Actions and Converse, and this they term likening of
Truth; not considering that there is a similitude
allowable for Contemplation and Opinion receiv'd by
Men. (Preface)

The 'Contemplation and Opinion receiv'd by men' of course, is
not merely the illusory world of fantasy and enchantment but
that also of ideal, vision and allegory, which is the artist's attempt
to clarify reality.

Johnson himself was frequently compelled when reading – as he
reveals in his notes on *Macbeth* and in his comments on Collins – to
acquiesce in popular traditions and outworn beliefs as necessary
fictions. He assumes in his *Preface* the influence of social beliefs and
superstitions on Shakespeare. And before embarking on the complex pattern of attitudes towards invention in the period which
succeeds the death of Pope and which produces the first great
novelists it is necessary to emphasise the peculiar dilemma which

confronted all writers, but poets in particular, at this time. For when the social and ethical impetus which inspired Augustan verse faltered, or the processes of history made it obviously less relevant, poets reacting against that type of verse were aware of the fact that they could no longer fall back on a commonly held system of belief, or even a common acceptance of the need for one. This is not to say that belief no longer mattered, but that what was held most in common was an ethical piety. For depth of spiritual insight as well as emotional concern writers were thrown back on their own feelings and sensations or on those inspired in them by past literature.

XIII

I mean, then – to draw the threads of the argument together – that what is particularly interesting about mid-eighteenth-century poetry is that it has to face a crisis, an apparent dearth of creativity, and that it does so in a way which has become more familiar to us in Victorian and Georgian poetry. It has to re-establish the role of poetry as of the world, yet transcending it; illuminating the spirit by reverting to other modes of apprehending life and its concerns; and extending the scope of poetry by making the reader's responsiveness its prime business – not his correction, nor his instruction, least of all his admiration compelled by technical brilliance. Moreover, it has to do this for what is by now a general reading public.

Roughly speaking, new modes of apprehending social relationships could be represented with greatest success in the novel. It was only here that the tensions between the demands of a traditional art form as it had evolved through the practice of a multitude of authors, and the various kinds of subject-matter – that tension which lies at the centre of artistic creativity – became irrelevant. And of these factors which determine the pattern of artistic creation – the particular tradition of the form or genre, the demands of the audience, the talent or genius of the artist, and the state of society – the two last favoured the emergence of a type of writing which would combine the appeal of the periodical essay with that of the romance. The periodicals themselves abounded with stories of contemporary society, and the reader's entertainment frequently exceeds his instruction as the follies and vices of the town are encountered by unsophisticated and inexperienced visitors.

Fielding's attempts in the preface to *Joseph Andrews* and the inaugural chapters to the books of *Tom Jones* to relate his novels to the classical epic are perhaps of less significance (his eye is on so many other things) than Sterne's awareness of his iconoclasm in *Tristram Shandy*. For Sterne a new kind of decorum arose out of his theme, the work organised itself in terms of new principles, but principles none the less. And this is also the case, as Johnson perceived, with Richardson in his exploration of the inner workings of a highly conscious and articulate individual caught in the pressures of a particular social situation – above all in *Clarissa*. Neither Richardson nor Sterne felt any responsibility towards a traditionally held concept of form. Smollett wrote as Defoe had done, omitting overt didacticism but steeping the reader in naval expeditions, colonial life or in the physical vicissitudes of contemporary existence.

So it was a form in which class interests and type histories of the day – in *Pamela*, *Clarissa*, *Roderick Random* and *Humphry Clinker* as well as in *Joseph Andrews* and *Tom Jones* – could take on a wider thematic significance as the study of mankind in society might be explored in terms of an analysis of the individual temperament, whether in Fielding's investigation of human nature, or Sterne's penetration of sensibility in *A Sentimental Journey*.

The novelist, then, taking human nature, or human beings in society as his subject, composed along a thread of action which might be dealt with as straight narrative, dramatic dialogue, personal or authorial reflection, or the juxtaposition of different attitudes to a particular situation in an epistolary convention to implicate the reader's responses more intimately. Or minor narratives in a different style might be introduced into the principal story – as in the work of Fielding and Smollett. Or the novelist might use the trappings of popular superstition and the horrors with which popular fiction had always abounded. The form seemed to have endless possibilities for reaching the reader.

In drama the excesses of the seventeenth century retreated before the demands for more varied and less morally reprehensible entertainment from more homogeneous audiences. When the Licensing Act of 1737 drew the teeth of dramatic satire, the variety of pantomime, opera, farce and burlesque flourished alongside the domestic, sentimental and sententious plays of the time. Foote, as stage-manager, actor and author, gained a wide following for his varied and novel entertainments – dancing, farce, burlesque – at the Haymarket in mid-century. Conventionality of theme in the drama, which above all other arts depended on the active and continuing support of a wide public, ensured that the stage should be 'a school of morality'.

XIV

Though many poets had continued to moralise their song in didactic and heroic couplets, there is as the century passes its turning-point an increasing recourse to blank verse, odes, ballads and sonnets. The subject-matter may be the domesticity of Thomas Edwards's sonnet 'On a Family Picture', which Dodsley included in the second volume of his *Collection* in 1748, real-life material (the 'Shipwreck' of Falconer, Langhorne's 'Chase') or familiar gossip, as in 'Anstey's Letter from Bath' (1766). Or it may be Mickle's gothic 'Ballad of Cumnor Hall'; but it is, at its most successful, the attempt to project individual feelings through various fictional or descriptive modes.

For Eliot the poets of this time shared the influence of Milton, of a pastoral poeticising tradition, and a dichotomy between thought – of a poor quality – and expression. For Arnold, however, Gray had been 'isolated in his century' because – in an age devoted to prose-writing – poetry necessarily 'obeyed the bend of mind requisite for the due fulfilment of this task of the century. It was intellectual, argumentative, ingenious; not seeing things in their truth and beauty, not interpretative.'[22] Back in the 1740s, however, for Mark Akenside, as he deliberated on the nature of inspiration in 'The Pleasures of Imagination', poets were 'chief' among men:[23]

> . . . eloquent men, who dwell on earth
> To clothe whate'er the soul admires or loves
> With language and with numbers.

All the elements and seasons of nature, he affirms,

> . . . declare
> For what th'eternal maker has ordain'd
> The pow'rs of man: we feel within ourselves
> His energy divine: he tells the heart,
> He meant, he made us to behold and love
> What he beholds and loves . . .

Energy and vitality of perception, receptivity, the awakening of the inner emotions of individual life, are the poet's privilege to experience and his task to transmit to others. But it is concerning his later lines on his youth in Northumberland:

> When all alone, for many a summer's day,
> I wander'd through your calm recesses, led
> In silence, by some powerful hand unseen . . .
> . . . studies which possess'd me in the dawn
> Of life, and fix'd the colour of my mind
> For every future year,

that Leavis, noting Nichol Smith's commendation of them, observes:[24]

> The point of Professor Nichol Smith's observation
> should be not that Akenside anticipates Wordsworth, but
> that Wordsworth, with an essential life of a very different
> order, has a certain eighteenth-century strength: it is not
> any 'romantic' spirit in Akenside that links him to
> Wordsworth, but the common-sense ethos and social
> habit implicit in that meditative verse – verse that . . .
> represents . . . a dull eighteenth-century by-line, one
> 'literary' in the bad sense.

The necessary acquiescence in the repudiation of a too-simple connection between the poets simply cannot be carried over to an acceptance of 'common-sense ethos and social habit'. This is patently irrelevant to Akenside's particular statements about his poetry and feelings. Whole tracts of the poem may be concerned with analysing the workings of the imagination, but here Akenside is fastening on a landscape of subjective significance and aiming to evoke a sympathetic emotional response from the reader:

> O ye Northumbrian shades, which overlook
> The rocky pavement and the mossy falls

> Of solitary Wensbeck's limpid stream;
> How gladly I recall your well-known seats
> Belov'd of old, and that delightful time
> When all alone. . .

Michael Bruce hails the cuckoo in a similar spirit:

> Sweet bird! thy bow'r is ever green,
> Thy sky is ever clear;
> Thou hast no sorrow in thy song,
> No winter in thy year!
>
> Alas, sweet bird! not so my fate,
> Dark scowling skies I see
> Fast gathering round, and fraught with woe
> And wintry years to me.
>
> (Ode: to the Cuckoo, 1770)

For Thomas Warton, writing 'On a Blank Leaf in Dugdale's *Monasticon*' (1777), the evidences of antiquity themselves stimulate his sensibility:

> Nor rough, nor barren, are the winding ways
> Of hoar Antiquity, but strown with flowers.

And other states of feeling are being articulated. The tones of Gray's 'Ode on a Distant Prospect of Eton College' (1742, published 1747) move from the personification of the emotions to the statement of common human vulnerability with which the last stanza opens:

> To each his suff'rings: all are men,
> Condemn'd alike to groan,
> The tender for another's pain;
> Th'unfeeling for his own.

The sense of a common fate has no longer a strong sense of metaphysical justification for that fate: it is something to be apprehended by each man on his own, and as such a cause for emotion of a subjective kind. So, in 1773, Cowper realises:

> The saint or moralist should tread
>   This moss-grown alley, musing, slow;
> They seek, like me, the secret shade,
>   But not, like me, to nourish woe.

Me fruitful scenes and prospects waste
　Alike admonish not to roam;
These tell me of enjoyments past,
　And those of sorrows yet to come.

('The Shrubbery', 1773, 17–24)

Reflections, sententiousness, all are personalised and become human and subjective, releasing an unprecedented and highly modulated range of feelings upon the responsive tastes and sensibilities of their readers, who, because the appeal is subjective and simple, can become directly involved.

　The expression of direct feeling was encouraged, of course, by the now flourishing tradition of hymn writing. Wesley's 'Wrestling Jacob' (1742) achieves a new simplicity and directness:

In vain Thou strugglest to get free,
　I never will unloose my hold:
Art Thou the Man that died for me?
　The secret of thy Love unfold;
Wrestling I will not let Thee go,
　Till I thy Name, thy Nature know.

(13–18)

It is Cowper's conclusion to 'The Castaway' –

'We perished, each alone'
　But I beneath a rougher sea
　And whelm'd in deeper gulphs than he –

that Virginia Woolf uses in *To the Lighthouse* to dramatise Mr Ramsay's suppressed feeling of remorse and despair.

XV

Where Augustan verse typically requires an assent to the argument of the poem, and the consequent subordination of the emotions, this later verse demands a response from the feelings. So in the two lines from Pope's Moral Essay, 'Of the Characters of Women':

Still round and round the ghosts of beauty glide
And haunt the places where their honour died,

(241–2)

we may be tricked into an emotional acquiescence by the first line and a half with its simple patterning and eerie suggestiveness but we are jerked sharply into an acceptance of the satirical proposition by the concluding half line. The attitudes of the reader are controlled by their appropriateness to the proposition which is being put forward by the poet.

One would normally associate Johnson with this kind of writing, so it is remarkably interesting that Housman should use the lines 'On the Death of Mr Robert Levet' –

> His virtues walked their narrow round,
> Nor made a pause, nor left a void;
> And sure the Eternal Master found
> The single talent well employed –

to illustrate his premise that 'to transfuse emotion – not to transmit thought but to set up in the reader's sense a vibration corresponding to what was felt by the writer – is the peculiar function of poetry.'[25] And with Housman's definition we are not far, either, from Eliot's own concern with the poet's structuring his emotion in poetry so that the reader's feelings are aroused.

It may seem perverse to argue the case for a common impetus among the widely varying merits and mediocrities of mid-eighteenth-century poetry. But I think such a case can be argued in terms of an awareness of 'That pleasing anxious being', that individual subjectivity in author and reader, in creation and response, which emerges as the achievement of the literature and philosophy of this time.

XVI

For Dr Leavis, the repudiation of everyday concerns by these poets is identified with a recourse to the 'poetical' – 'specialised (and conventional) sentiments and attitudes representing, as it were, a solemn holiday or Sabbath from the everyday serious'.[26] It is of course generally associated too with the mechanical recourse to a specialised poetic diction. Housman observed:[27]

> The way to write real poetry, they thought, must be
> to write something as little like prose as possible; they

devised for the purpose what was called a 'correct and splendid diction', which consisted in always using the wrong word instead of the right, and plastered it as ornament, with no thought of propriety, or whatever they desired to dignify.

And he chooses for condemnation the opening of Gray's 'Ode to Spring' as Wordsworth was for the same purpose to attack Gray's sonnet on the death of Richard West in the influential preface to the *Lyrical Ballads* of 1800. Gray's case for poetic diction, since his use of it is that which is chiefly called in question (though in this particular his achievement is frequently assimilated to that of any minor verse-writer who employs Latinate terms) is well worth looking at:[28]

> The language of the age is never the language of poetry; except among the French, whose verse, where the thought does not support it, differs in nothing from prose. Our poetry, on the contrary, has a language peculiar to itself, to which almost every one that has written has added something. In truth, Shakespeare's language is one of its principal beauties; and he has no less advantage over your Addisons and Rowes in this, than in those other great excellences you mention. Every word in him is a picture. Pray put me the following lines into the tongue of our modern dramatics –
>
> > But I, that am not shaped for sportive tricks,
> > Nor made to court an amorous looking-glass.
>
> and what follows? To me they appear untranslatable; and if this be the case, our language is greatly degenerated.

To recapture as far as possible the metaphorical life of poetry, to make poetry a speaking picture, Pope's syntax, geared to the verb as the focal point for the play of wit in the couplet, defeated the straightforward play of association on which the creation of mood and atmosphere depended. So, in addition to the use of exotic, remote or historical subject-matter, of the popular or supernatural in which Shakespeare had displayed his invention, and of the allegorical fiction in which Spenser and Milton had shone, there is developed a conscious exploitation of certain kinds of diction, and these of a predominantly descriptive character.

Leaving aside obvious archaisms and Miltonisms, which might be used with differing degrees of success, as they were for different ends – for burlesque, as in Philips's 'Splendid Shilling', or to create atmosphere, as in Thomas Warton's 'Pleasures of Melancholy' or playfulness as in Cowper's account of the game of chess or of the cultivation of cucumbers in 'The Task' – a special diction might be used to invigorate poetic perception in several different ways.

XVII

Gray employs different levels of diction to enhance the effective pathos of his theme. In the 'Sonnet on the Death of West' which Wordsworth condemned he begins by offering an orthodox idyllic morning which contrasts with the real feelings of the author who is indifferent to all temporal delights in the gnawing insistence of his sense of loss:

> In vain to me the smileing Mornings shine,
>> And redning Phoebus lifts his golden Fire:
> The Birds in vain their amorous Descant joyn;
>> Or cheerful Fields resume their green Attire:
> These Ears, alas! for other Notes repine,
>> A different Object do these Eyes require.
> My lonely Anguish melts no Heart, but mine;
>> And in my Breast the imperfect Joys expire.
> Yet Morning smiles the busy Race to chear,
>> And new-born Pleasure brings to happier Men:
> The Fields to all their wonted Tribute bear;
>> To warm their little Loves the Birds complain:
> I fruitless mourn to him, that cannot hear,
>> And weep the more because I weep in vain.

The delicate artificiality of the conventionally glad landscape contrasts poignantly with the direct statements of human sorrow. The device is used again, in a more complex way, in the 'Elegy

Wrote in a Country Churchyard' where the conventional literary landscape of the opening, and the conventional melancholy man of the conclusion

> Now drooping, woeful wan, like one forlorn,
> Or craz'd with care, or cross'd in hopeless love,
>
> (107–8)

are again poignantly juxtaposed with the personification of that death which threatens all human connections as well as human achievement whether of rich or poor:

> Can storied urn or animated bust
> Back to its mansion call the fleeting breath?
> Can Honour's voice provoke the silent dust,
> Or Flatt'ry sooth the dull cold ear of Death? . . .
>
> For who to dumb Forgetfulness a prey,
> This pleasing anxious being e'er resign'd,
> Left the warm precincts of the chearful day,
> Nor cast one longing ling'ring look behind?
>
> On some fond breast the parting soul relies,
> Some pious drops the closing eye requires;
> Ev'n from the tomb the voice of Nature cries,
> Ev'n in our Ashes live their wonted Fires.
>
> (41–4; 85–92)

The personification of death, endowed with vividly physical attributes – its dullness, coldness and dumbness, its powers of obliterating from human recollection which can only be partly and temporarily halted by the poet as by the epitaphs on the gravestones which have stimulated his reflections, and in terms of which he sees too his only immortality – is a characteristic aspect of the poetry of the time.

So too in Collins's 'Ode to Evening' the sensitivity of the poet's response to the beauty of nature is subsumed to a recognition of the relationship between the qualities of evening, freed from the turmoil of the day, and the tranquil reflection and contemplation which stimulate poetic sensibility. Johnson can use this kind of personification with dramatic weight, as Donald Davie has pointed out (*Purity of Diction in English Verse*, 1952):

> Condemn'd to hope's delusive mine,
>   As on we toil from day to day,
> By sudden blasts, or slow decline,
>   Our social comforts drop away.
>   ('On the Death of Mr. Robert Levet', 1–4)

For Johnson appreciates in poetry that elaborate personification and use of descriptive epithets which suggest a moral as well as an emotional atmosphere – as in his insistent appreciation of the famous passage from Congreve's *Mourning Bride*. The idyllic pastoral landscapes of Gray's poetry, then, are functional. So is that of Goldsmith's 'Deserted Village' which Crabbe was to repudiate in 'The Village' in the interests of 'truth'. There is a different kind of truth in Goldsmith, one which emotionally sustains the reader of poetry in bodying forth the experience of a commonly felt nostalgic recollection.

XVIII

The pastoral convention of which Eliot complained has been the refuge of poets time and time again from the sophisticated complexities of environments in which the power of illusion, and the visionary capacity of the poet, seemed to be denied. Milton's 'Lycidas', Arnold's 'Scholar Gipsy' and 'Thyrsis' alike evoke that purely fictional world where only the mischances of love or the inevitability of death disturb mankind as the seasons move in orderly progression and renewal. A recent account of the pastoral is of particular interest here:[29]

> The Pastoral represents a protest by urban man against
> certain distasteful aspects of his environment; it may
> be an excessive sophistication of intellectual activity, a
> preoccupation with industry and commerce or the
> hatreds and jealousies of political and military
> intrigue. Believing that the development of civilisation
> had corrupted human life, man longed to escape, now
> and again in the imagination, to an idealized world of
> simple shepherds, happy in the innocence and freedom
> of pastoral life and love.

So we have the idyllic charm of Goldsmith's 'Deserted Village'. The argument of Goldsmith's poem is against enclosures and the consequent depopulation of the village; but, as with Gray's 'Elegy', there is no need to deliberate the historical, economic or agricultural authenticity of the poem. We are given the experience of deprivation on different levels, personal and social. The lexical collocations of the first section, 'sweet', 'loveliest', 'smiling', 'lovely' – epithets traditionally associated in classical literature with the personification of the bounteous land – are related to the rural community in terms of engendering health and well-being, but at the same time with a nostalgia which accompanies something held in memory to be idealised there:

> Sweet Auburn! loveliest village of the plain,
> Where health and plenty cheer'd the labouring swain,
> Where smiling spring its earliest visit paid,
> And parting summer's lingering blooms delay'd:
> Dear lovely bowers of innocence and ease,
> Seats of my youth, when every sport could please,
> How often have I loiter'd o'er thy green,
> Where humble happiness endear'd each scene. . . .
>
> (1–8)

And now the eye of social man transforms the scene, imbuing it in retrospect with well-regulated industry, and an ideal community:

> How often have I paus'd on every charm,
> The shelter'd cot, the cultivated farm,
> The never-failing brook, the busy mill,
> The decent church that topp'd the neighbouring hill,
> The hawthorn bush, with seats beneath the shade,
> For talking age and whispering lovers made. . . .
>
> (9–14)

But the section concludes with a return to the personification of the village and the ideal loveliness of the opening lines is recalled only to force on the poet and the reader the sadness of the truth that they are now gone for ever:

> These were thy charms, sweet village; sports like these,
> With sweet succession, taught even toil to please;

These round thy bowers their cheerful influence shed,
These were thy charms – But all these charms are fled.
(31–4)

The reiterated use of the past tense here, given further emphasis in
the last line, is unexpectedly charged with melancholy by the
sudden shift to the present tense in the last half line. This effect is
reinforced by the replacement of 'thy' by the more immediate
'these' in the last line. The personification of the village with
which these charms are connected is unexpectedly succeeded by
the concluding exclamation in which the charms themselves move
into vivid personification in the course of their hasty and fearful
departure. The animation now given to 'charms' with the specific
force of 'fled', mimics the sense of deprivation so as to urge it on
the reader. In the second section the terms of the first are reiterated
and expanded, and the generality of the diction enables the poet
to claim a wider significance for his own personal feelings and
recollections:

Sweet smiling village, loveliest of the lawn,
Thy sports are fled, and all thy charms withdrawn;
Amidst thy bowers the tyrant's hand is seen,
And desolation saddens all thy green;
One only master grasps the whole domain,
And half a village stints thy smiling plain:
No more thy glassy brook reflects the day,
But chok'd with sedges, works its weedy way.
(35–42)

The choice of epithets is clearly directed by the desire to evoke the
awareness of the spoliation of the idyllic charm already so
insistently dwelt on. The smooth reflections of the brook giving
back with serene insistence the images of light and shade are now
destroyed as the true course of its bed is blocked, no longer kept
clear, just as in the world of men fertility and happiness have
departed with the breaking-down of the community, alike a
victim of economic change:

And, trembling, shrinking from the spoiler's hand,
Far, far away, thy children leave the land.
(49–50)

The Augustan awareness of the bond between the land and the community is present here again, but in terms of irremediable loss, which is the loss too of the poet as an individual, and as he concludes the poem, a loss likewise to poetry itself, which yet can evoke the reality of man's relation to the land in which he lives.

Personal feelings are combined with moral sentiments again in Gray's 'Ode on a distant Prospect of Eton College' as well as his 'Ode to Spring'. The private voice, the subjective presence of the poet is set alongside social truths with the effect of showing the dichotomy between the social ethos and the struggles of the subjective consciousness:

> Ah happy hills, ah pleasing shade,
> Ah fields belov'd in vain,
> Where once my careless childhood stray'd
> A stranger yet to pain!
> I feel the gales, that from ye blow,
> A momentary bliss bestow,
> As waving fresh their gladsome wing,
> My weary soul they seem to sooth,
> And, redolent of joy and youth,
> To breathe a second spring.
>
> (11–20)

But the moral to be drawn is rather wryly put:

> No more; where ignorance is bliss
> 'Tis folly to be wise.
>
> (99–100)

If we are to understand the nature of this kind of poetic statement it is not enough to analyse the syntax and diction in order to establish the odd felicity or extend our apprehension of a suggestiveness which had hitherto been passed over. There is another and more specific approach to the whole area of literary creativity at this time.

XIX

Empson describes pastoral composition as a 'process of putting the complex into the simple (in itself a great help to the concentration needed for poetry)'.[30] If the poet delivers us a 'golden' world as Sidney says, the pastoral comes nearer to it than any other literary form, and it is, as Johnson saw, a way of treating the material of poetry which has a special appeal to the general reader. Poets, at any rate, retreat there in persona, or in their own shape, as Milton claimed to have trod the dewy lawns with Edward King, as Goldsmith nostalgically recalls his teacher and the village clergyman in 'The Deserted Village', as Gray sets a melancholy man musing on a little community cut off from life's turmoils as well as life's opportunities in the 'Elegy'. The pastoral landscape rises, in 'Lycidas', in 'Thyrsis', in 'The Scholar Gipsy', to associate itself with the mourning for the passing of an ideal beauty, given physical presence in the death of the poet. As the pastoral inherited from the myth of the golden age the idea of a sympathetic bond between the natural world and its human inhabitants, one of the best-known poems in the English language evokes an awareness of personal deprivation, in terms of myth and isolation from society.

> The curfew tolls the knell of parting day,
> The lowing herd winds slowly o'er the lea;
> The ploughman homeward plods his weary way,
> And leaves the world to darkness, and to me.

The caesura in the last line cuts off the 'me' of the poem even from the ideal rustic landscape he is establishing. The mood of this central character is indeed projected in terms of the very literary gloom of this landscape with its rugged elms, moping owls and ivy-mantled tower. The isolation of the speaker in darkness which is emphasised in the first stanza is a darkness of the spirit as well as an absence of light, as the pervasive melancholy of the poem reveals. He is isolated from the rustic community by nightfall, by their presence being felt only in terms of their last resting place, and by his awareness of other classes of society and their attitudes towards the rustic poor. But Gray manages in the references to the hoary-headed swain's acquaintance with the melancholy chronicler of the rustic group – all essentially artificial and literary, melancholy man, swain and community alike – to establish the poet as aware of himself as a man among other men, yet cut off from the ordinary life of mankind, reflecting on the need for common human sympathy in the face of the inevitability of annihilation, seeing all his aspirations vain and his gifts wasted as those of these villagers have been, and finally laid to rest beneath an epitaph as crudely but piously composed as any of those in the churchyard.

The ruminative vein of which Eliot complained runs throughout, yet it is an integral part of the sensibility of a poet at this time that he should search among his own responses and compose from his own subjective feelings, to seek out within the poetic tradition whatever enabled him to escape from the everyday and mundane. This was one way, it seemed, to bring back true poetry into the English tradition and to defeat the pervasive irony and denial of straightforward emotion in verse of Pope and his school. And Johnson after all rejoiced to concur with the common reader, for 'by the common sense of readers uncorrupted with literary prejudices, after all the refinements of subtlety and the dogmatism of learning, must be finally decided all claim to poetical honours.'

> The *Church-yard* abounds with images which find a mirrour in every mind, and with sentiments to which every bosom returns an echo. The four stanzas beginning 'Yet even these bones', are to me original. I have never seen the notions in any other place; yet he that reads them here, persuades himself that he has always felt them. Had Gray written often thus, it had been vain to blame, and useless to praise him.
> (*Lives*, iii, 441–2)

XX

Perhaps it is as well to look at the strongest evidence for regarding these poets as having a special achievement which distinguished them from their antecedents or their successors. In his *Reflections on Werther*, Goethe remarks:[31]

> The Gessner etchings . . . heightened our longing for pastoral scenes, and a short poem that was ecstatically received in our small circle also affected us so that we seemed to have eyes for nothing else. 'The Deserted Village', by Goldsmith, was enjoyed by people on

every level of education. In it all those things were described, not as living or still effective but as a part of a past, lost existence, which we wanted to see with our own eyes, which we loved and valued and sought avidly in the present. . . . Here we found our honest Wakefield again in his well-known surroundings, no longer vividly portrayed, but a shadow recalled by the elegiac poet's soft lament. The very idea of such a description is felicitous as soon as one has decided to recall the innocent past in a mood of sweet sadness.

A little later he comments:

Strangely enough, our father and teacher, Shakespeare, who knew so well how to spread brightness, also helped to increase our gloom. Hamlet and his monologues remained ghosts that haunted us.

Goethe sees some continuity in terms of Werther's melancholy between the literary appeal of Shakespeare's Hamlet and that of the mid-eighteenth-century writers – he goes on from here to describe the impact of Ossianic melancholy. And he makes it clear, as Johnson did in the case of Gray, that the nature and strength of the appeal of this poetry was to general human feelings, not social but intensely subjective.

XXI

So in an attempt to combat what seemed to be the inevitable consequences of literary sophistication in loss of imaginative vitality, eighteenth-century poets turned instead to exploring the recesses of the human heart and rendering their own feelings and sense of isolation from the busy development of a growing industrial civilisation by returning to traditional fictions and older literary models. The dilemma recurs whenever one literary tradition has become ossified, or when it seems to have lost a quality which is permanently recognisable as poetical – a transmutation of real experience into a highly ordered structure of quintessential feelings. So their creative dilemma coincides with a more significant one – a quest for the poetical. And their own particular achievement expressed at its best in only a few poems, it is true, but all the same characteristic of their own time, lay in the expression and exploration of a range of feelings, largely aroused in terms of association and therefore intimately linked with the operations of memory and responsiveness to past literature. Aware of their feelings as held in common with those of other human beings, they could appeal to a wider audience: possessed as many of them were by sensibilities which isolated them from the complexities of social life, they established as the hallmark of their work, and of English literary influence on the continent, a melancholy nostalgia which came from a tension between their inner apprehension of a subjective isolation and an awareness of their own responses as individuals to the changing world around them.

Notes

1 'Preface to *De Arte Graphica*', *Of Dramatic Poetry*, i, 85.
2 *English Critical Essays (Sixteenth, Seventeenth and Eighteenth Centuries)*, ed. E. D. Jones (London, 1947), 273–4.
3 'Shakespeare: An Epistle to Mr. Garrick' (1760), *Oxford Book of Eighteenth Century Verse*, 411.
4 *The Rise of English Literary History* (Chapel Hill, 1941), 49–50.
5 See chapter 1, p. 24.
6 Letter x, *Works*, 8 vols (London, 1811), iv, 321, 323–4.
7 *Lives*, i, 2.
8 *The Diary and Letters of Madame D'Arblay*, ed. Charlotte Barrett, 6 vols (London, 1905), ii, 271–2.
9 *Johnson on Shakespeare*, ed. W. Raleigh (London, 1908), 14.
10 Pp. 52, 58.
11 See Wellek, *op. cit.*, 49–50.
12 'An Enquiry into the Present State of Polite Learning in Europe', *Collected Works of Oliver Goldsmith*, ed. Arthur Friedman, 5 vols (Oxford, 1966), i, 267, 268, 287.
13 *Enquiry into the Life and Writings of Homer* (London, 1735), 345–6.
14 John Brown, *The History of the Rise and Progress of Poetry, Through its Several Species* (Newcastle, 1764), 67.
15 *Essay on the Original Genius and Writings of Homer* (1769; London, 1824), 109–10.
16 Blair, *The Poems of Ossian*, ii, 154.
17 'The Ever Green' (1724), in Jones, *op. cit.*, 399.
18 'Poetry in the Eighteenth Century', *From Dryden to Johnson* (Pelican Guide to English Literature), iv, 274–5.
19 *Penguin Book of Victorian Verse* (London, 1969), 33.
20 *Oxford Lectures on Poetry* (1909), 5.

21 *Revaluation* (London, 1949), 255–6, 260.
22 'Thomas Gray', *Essays in Criticism*, 2nd series (Everyman; London, 1915), 92.
23 'The Pleasures of Imagination', iv (1772); iii (1774); iv (1772).
24 *Revaluation*, 109.
25 A. E. Housman, 'The Name and Nature of Poetry', *Selected Prose*, ed. John Carter (Cambridge, 1961), 172.
26 *Revaluation*, 116.
27 *Op. cit.*, 177–8.
28 *Correspondence*, i, 103.
29 Robert Coleman, 'Pastoral Poetry', *Greek and Latin Literature: A Comparative Study*, ed. John Higginbotham (London, 1969), 101.
30 *Some Versions of Pastoral* (Peregrine Books; London, 1966), 25.
31 *The Sorrows of Young Werther and Selected Writings* (Signet classics; New York, 1962), 135 and 144.

Four

Poetry versus Good Sense: Joseph Warton and the Reaction against Pope

I

In chapter 1 of *Biographia Literaria* Coleridge considers the relevance of poetry to his own development. He explicitly relates his awareness of true poetry to the work of William Lisle Bowles:[1]

> At a very premature age, even before my fifteenth year, I had bewildered myself in metaphysicks, and in theological controversy. Nothing else pleased me. . . . This was, beyond doubt, injurious both to my natural powers, and to the progress of my education. It would, perhaps, have been destructive had it been continued; but from this I was auspiciously withdrawn . . . chiefly by the genial influence of a style of poetry so tender and yet so manly, so natural and real, and yet so dignified and harmonious, as the sonnets, &c. of Mr. Bowles.

So, he continues:

> If in after time I have sought a refuge from bodily pain and mismanaged sensibility in abstruse researches, which exercised the strength and subtlety of the understanding without awakening the feeling of the heart, still there was a long and blessed interval, during which my natural faculties were allowed to expand, and my original tendencies to develope themselves; my fancy, and the love of nature, and the sense of beauty in forms and sounds.

The blossoming of the faculties as they are alerted to beauty and develop a capacity for response is seen by Coleridge as the direct result of reading Bowles's poetry. And this is that awareness of a separate and precious identity which strengthens and reanimates the entire being. The effect of this kind of poetry is contrasted with that of Pope in Coleridge's admission that although

> I was not blind to the merits of this (Pope's) school, yet as from inexperience of the world, and consequent want of sympathy with the general subjects of these poems, they gave me little pleasure, I doubtless undervalued the *kind*, and with the presumption of youth withheld from its masters the legitimate name of poets. I saw that the excellence of this kind consisted in just and acute observations on men and manners in an artificial state of society as its matter and substance . . . the matter and diction seemed to me characterized not so much by poetic thoughts, as by thoughts *translated* into the language of poetry.

From his reading, and an examination of its impact on his opinions and sensibility, Coleridge attempts to establish his own criteria of literary excellence:

> According to the faculty or source, from which the pleasure given by any poem or passage was derived, I estimated the merit of such poem or passage. As the result of all my reading and meditation, I abstracted two critical aphorisms, deeming them to comprise the conditions and criteria of poetic style; first, that not the poem which we have *read*, but that to which we *return*, with the greatest pleasure, possesses the genuine power and claims the name of *essential poetry*. Second, that whatever lines can be translated into other words of the same language, without diminution of their significance, either in sense, or association or in any worthy feeling, are so far vicious in their diction.

This criterion of delight in response, a response renewed emotionally and strengthened by memory and association, is connected by Coleridge with the poetry of Bowles. The test of paraphrase is a traditional one, used by Quintilian, Horace, and Cowley, as it had also been employed by Joseph Warton to demonstrate Pope's deficiencies as a poet.

Bowles himself had been inspired by Warton, his teacher at Winchester School. On the death of his old headmaster he wrote:[2]

> Thy cheering voice,
> O Warton! bade my silent heart rejoice
> And wake to love of nature; every breeze
> On Itchin's brink was melody; the trees
> Waved in fresh beauty.

It is Bowles again who upholds the standards of a true poetry as distinct from that of Pope in one of the few controversies of English literary history, the Bowles–Byron–Pope quarrel which was sparked off by Bowles's edition of Pope in 1806. Byron championed Pope in 'English Bards and Scotch Reviewers' (327–84) where Bowles is satirised as the champion of 'Sympathy . . . Thou first, great oracle of tender souls'. The battle between the champions of rival views of poetic excellence persisted for twenty years. And in his 'Final Appeal to the Literary Public' (1825) Bowles refers to the principles of criticism he has employed having been learnt along with his idea of poetry and which to him are 'as invariable as nature, as eternal as truth', in the same 'academia' of his youth. These were the principles which he had outlined in the tenth volume of his edition of Pope:

> it will be readily granted that all images drawn from what is beautiful or sublime in the works of nature are more beautiful and sublime than any images drawn from art; and that they are therefore, *per se*, more poetical. In like manner the passions of the human heart which belong to nature in general are, *per se*, more adapted to the higher species of poetry than those which are derived from incidental and transient manners. ('Concluding Observations on the Poetic Character of Pope')

It is not the connection between Bowles and Coleridge which is of importance here so much as the clear existence of a distinct kind of poetry and school of criticism which is related directly to the influence of the Wartons, and indirectly to the context of taste and feeling which is distinctively that of an age of sensibility, of taste and feeling seen in terms of individual temperaments and

without the overtly transcendental and didactic implications of
the work of the major Romantic poets.

II

Joseph and his younger brother Thomas Warton were poets before
they became critics or literary historians. Their father, a man of
notoriously Jacobite persuasions, himself a serious versifier and a
staunch admirer of the minor poems of Milton, was Professor of
Poetry at Oxford from 1718 to 1728. In 1748 Joseph issued an
edition of the elder Thomas's poems by subscription. Among them
appears 'An Epistle to Dr. Young' (to whom his son was to dedicate
the *Essay on the Writings and Genius of Pope*), stanzas on biblical
themes, various odes, and a poem entitled 'Farewell to Poetry'.
His mode of describing the province of poetry is of some interest:

> *Arcadian* Scenes adieu! in *Cyrrha's* Vale
> No more I wander, where the loose-rob'd Nymphs
> *Pan* and *Sylvanus* play'd, while on their Heads
> The laughing Hours rain'd Roses; while to guide
> Their nimble Feet great *Phoebus* came and touch'd
> His soul-bewitching Lyre; no more I sit
> On murmuring Aganippe's mossy Brink
> And wait inspiring Dreams; nor Garlands weave
> Of sweet Parnassian Flowers for *Clio's* head.

The 'inspiring Dreams', the delight in classical myth and
legend, are located by Joseph Warton in the beauties of nature
which he taught his scholars to see as the source of true poetry. In
'The Enthusiast, or the Lover of Nature' (1744) Warton, taking as
his model Lucretius, and borrowing his title from Shaftesbury's
Enthusiast, embellishes a familiar theme in order to repudiate that
preference for the landscaping and civilising of nature characteristic
of the descriptive poetry of Pope:

> . . . can *Stow*
> With all her *Attic* fanes, such Raptures raise,
> As the Thrush-haunted Copse, where lightly leaps
> The fearful Fawn the rustling leaves along,

> And the brisk Squirrel sports from Bough to Bough . . .
>   The Bards of Old
> Fair Nature's friends, sought such Retreats, to charm
> Sweet *Echo* with their Songs . . .

The desire of the poet is, of course, to escape from the busy world
to a pastoral and primitive simplicity:

> O who will bear me then to western climes . . .
> There, fed on dates or herbs, would I despise
> The far-fetch'd cates of luxury, and hoards
> Of narrow-hearted avarice; nor heed
> The distant din of the tumultuous world.

And the same primitivistic yearning acquires a Virgilian dying fall
in a more successful passage from 'The Dying Indian':

> . . . I shall soon arrive
> At the blest island, where no tygers spring
> At heedless hunters; where ananas bloom
> Thrice in each moon; where rivers smoothly glide,
> Nor thund'ring torrents whirl the light canoe
> Down to the sea; where my forefathers feast
> Daily on hearts of Spaniards . . .

It was probably this aspect of Warton's work that Dodsley saw as
more suited to the general taste for poetry when he published the
odes of Warton in preference to those of Collins in 1746.[3]
   To introduce his volume of odes Warton issued a literary mani-
festo. His editor, Chalmers, later observed that the preface avows
'those sentiments on the nature of genuine poetry which he
expanded more at large afterwards, and which were the foundation of what has since been termed "the school of the Wartons".'[4]
That Warton's contemporaries as well as his successors recognised
the existence of such a distinctive group of poets there is no doubt.
In the concluding stanza of his 'Ode to Genius' Robert Lloyd, for
example, pathetically enquires:

> Why sleep the sons of genius now?
> Why, Wartons, rests the lyre unstrung?

The preface to the *Odes on Various Subjects* of 1746 is a conscious repudiation of the school of Pope in the interests of traditional poetic inspiration. It demands chiefly that the imagination and the emotions be accorded once again their rightful place in poetry:

> The public has been so much accustomed of late to didactic poetry alone, and essays on moral subjects, that any work, where the imagination is much indulged, will perhaps not be relished or regarded. The author therefore of these pieces is in some pain, lest certain austere critics should think them too fanciful or descriptive. But as he is convinced that the fashion of moralizing in verse has been carried too far, and as he looks upon invention and imagination to be the chief faculties of a poet, so he will be happy if the following Odes may be looked upon as an attempt to bring back poetry into its right channel.

The indulgence in the imagination is an end in itself, particularly as the faculties of invention and fancy are the distinctive gift of the poet. Above all, contemporary poetry needs redirecting into its traditional course.

It was therefore natural that Warton should proceed to write his most ambitious critical work *An Essay on the Writings and Genius of Pope* in order to implement these principles; and above all to affirm that the proper stuff of poetry was not the world of everyday life, nor for him did it lie, as it did for his brother, in the realm of classical myth or legend, medieval romance, or the fancies and superstitions of earlier ages which older poets had employed. Nor was its world that of satiric or didactic statement. The world of true poetry is one of emotional responsiveness to a picturesque or literary as opposed to a social environment.

The dedication of the *Essay* is addressed to Edward Young who, three years later, produced his *Conjectures on Original Composition*. In this, it will be remembered, Young exhorts the poet to surrender to the promptings of his individual sensibility, to his own originality. In his dedication, Warton, announcing that 'The Sublime and the Pathetic are the two chief nerves of all genuine poesy' asks a question which has reverberated through criticism from Johnson to Leavis; 'What is there very Sublime or very Pathetic in POPE?' Listing four classes of poet, beginning with the truly sublime and pathetic—Spenser, Shakespeare and Milton, Warton proceeds to place other English poets in their different categories. Ethical and panegyrical poets fall into a second class; witty, tasteful and fanciful writers into a third, and the smooth mellifluous versifiers, a fourth. Since he has already described Pope as like Boileau, 'Incapable . . . du sublime qui élève l'âme, et du sentiment qui l'attendrit . . . laborieux, sévère, précis, pur, harmonieux' ('Incapable . . . of that sublimity which uplifts the soul and of that sentiment which softens it . . . hard-working, exact, precise, lucid and harmonious') – for Warton confesses himself 'Unwilling to speak out in plain English' – as having merely a clear head and an acute understanding which fit him for 'Morality and not Poetry', the reader is left to anticipate that Pope will eventually be ranked in the third or possibly even in the fourth class.

The ambiguities of statement and attitude in the dedication provide the key at once to the ways in which the *Essay* was received by Warton's contemporaries; to the influence it exerted on later writers; and, more important, to the attention it attracted as a document of crucial importance in the charting of attitudes to eighteenth-century taste. Its challenging tone is similar to that of Young's *Conjectures*; and its reception was in many ways similar, most reviewers seeing in it little that was unconventional, and yet subsequent writers on the period regarding it as revolutionary.[5]

III

With the *Essay on the Writings and Genius of Pope* we have for the first time in English criticism a full-length evaluation of a modern author by a man who is consciously reacting against the current poetic tradition. It is moreover a work which in intention employs the criteria of taste in so far as the sublime and the pathetic are declared to be the two emotions appropriate to great poetry. So the book might be expected to be a practical application of those principles of taste and expressions of sensibility which we have considered so far.

Already in poetry they are associated with the cultivation of a sensibility of heart which is not necessarily social and which is

primarily a felt extension of personality on the part of the individual. But, of course, if it is the fate of the minor poet that his work
be assimilated to a tradition or traditions which have been
delineated by the shifting modes of criticism, the fate of the minor
critic is even more obscure. It is only if he chances to make a
pronouncement which seems to a later generation of writers a
prediction of what has come to pass that his words assume a
significance which can sometimes be very different from that of
their original context. In so far as the business of the critic is to
act as a social intermediary or assessor between literature and its
audience, his attempts to lay claim to the chief role of criticism,
which is to establish principles of taste, are generally collapsed by
later writers into a series of crude classifications of influences,
schools and theories with which histories of criticism in particular
abound. His fate in literary history is little better, for here he is
still a prey to whichever period and from whichever point of
view the history happens to be written. To impose traditions on
criticism may be as necessary as to impose criteria on literature;
but it is a process which inevitably deprives an area of human
activity of much of its value and most of its interest.

Some scholars have, of course, tried to establish an ideal of
completely objective historicism in literary criticism. R. S. Crane
for instance has described his ideal history of criticism as[6]

> free to exhibit critics speaking for themselves with
> respect to problems not set for them, after the event,
> by the historian, but such as they themselves had
> formulated in the process of solving them; and its
> criteria of praise and blame would be based on no
> demand for uniformity to a particular idea of
> excellence in criticism but solely on an estimate of how
> much different critics were able to accomplish with the
> principles, materials, and devices at their disposal.

It is of course an impossibility to achieve this degree of object-
ivity: each age is attracted to that in the past which it seeks in its
own, but it is as necessary as ever to stress the complexity and
range of earlier critical approaches to literature, and to understand the special qualities of individuals who are generally agreed
to have made distinctive contributions to literary history or
criticism. The fate of the Wartons in particular, as is the fate of all

those writers who fall into the forty or fifty years conveniently but unfairly simplified in terms of the decay of neoclassicism and/or the development of pre-Romanticism, has been to be peculiarly vulnerable to this in terms of current fashions in literary history. So H. A. Beers in his *History of English Romanticism in the Eighteenth Century* (1899) describes Joseph Warton as venturing 'to uphold the then paradoxical thesis that Spenser was as great a man as Pope' and the *Essay* as 'revolutionary' (pp. 32–3, 213). E. J. Morley described the *Essay* as 'an original and daring piece of criticism, which marked the author out as an independent thinker, who refused to bow the knee to the "commonsense" verdicts of his day',[7] while more recently René Wellek in the first volume of his *History of Modern Criticism 1750–1950: The Later Eighteenth Century* writes:

> Practically all critical theory since Johnson has run in the opposite direction [to an appreciation of generalities] . . . The view was not unknown to the 18th century, and we shall describe the trend towards particularity in Joseph Warton, George Campbell, and others. (p. 86)

Joseph Warton's treatment of Pope, and Thomas Warton's of Spenser, as well as reflecting the preoccupations of criticism in this period, involve issues of permanent literary importance: the nature of poetry and the conditions under which the various poetic modes flourish. It is time to look at Joseph Warton's intention and preoccupations in his *Essay*. To do this it is as well first to establish the general pattern of his literary activities, and then to consider the ways in which he uses the criteria he has chosen – obviously, in this case, the sublime and the pathetic.

IV

Warton's first publication, a prose satire, *Ranelagh House* (1744) describes a guided tour round the world of the dead where Pope is found frequenting the society of the philosophers rather than that of the poets. After 'The Enthusiast' and *Odes on Various Subjects* came a work on which Warton clearly placed his hopes of patronage and preferment, his edition of Virgil (1753). This includes his

own verse translations of the Eclogues and Georgics and dis-
sertations on pastoral, didactic and epic poetry, with Christopher
Pitt's translation of the *Aeneid*, a dissertation by the influential
Bishop Warburton, and new observations by Joseph Spence,
Pope's confidant and previously Professor of Poetry at Oxford.

In the same year Johnson invited Warton to assume responsibility for the critical papers in the *Adventurer*: he and Warton
were both literary protégés of Robert Dodsley; and both were to
become members of the Literary Club, founded in 1764, of which
Burke, Reynolds and Garrick were members.

Warton's *Adventurer* essays fall into three main groups. Six are
fairly conventional occasional papers dealing with the poverty and
difficulties of poets, politeness, and contemporary morals and
manners. The second group consists of essays of more specifically
literary interest: an imitation of Longinus in the guise of 'a new
MS translated', and observations on Simonides and Menander; a
paper on the Ancients and Moderns controversy; a comparison
of the merits of the *Odyssey* with those of the *Iliad*; comments on
the absence of originality in contemporary literature (significantly
titled: 'Paucity of Original Writers. Passages which Pope has
borrowed pointed out'); a paper on blemishes in *Paradise Lost*;
and thirdly, five essays on Shakespeare's genius as revealed in a
consideration of *The Tempest* and *King Lear*.

Warton's chief claim to consideration by historians of literature
– *The Essay on the Writings and Genius of Pope* – was published
anonymously in 1756; the 700 copies of the first edition sold well
and the work was re-issued in 1762, and again in 1772 (while a
pirated edition appeared in Dublin in 1764), though its review of
Pope's works was not completed until 1784, when a second
volume, and a reprint and a new edition of the work appeared in
the same year. Warton's last completed work, an edition of Pope,
was undertaken at the request of a group of booksellers and
published in 1797. When he died in 1800 he was engaged on an
edition of Dryden, which was prepared for publication by his son.
Warton's contributions to this are negligible.

Most of Warton's life was spent at Winchester. He was at school
there with Collins before going to Oriel College, and returned as
usher in 1755. He became headmaster in 1766, resigning in 1793
to retire to Wickham. From Winchester a group of minor poets
emerged, maintaining a tradition which had originally included

Collins and Warton, and which produced Russell and Bowles. In his *Biographical Memoirs of the Reverend Joseph Warton, D.D.* Warton's biographer, Wooll, remarks that it was Warton's insistence on verse translation as a basic form of instruction at Winchester that encouraged the poetic talents of his pupils. Certainly among the Warton MSS. at Trinity College, Oxford, is a host of such exercises, sometimes bearing well-known names – that of Robert Lowth's son, for example.

The greater part of Warton's criticism is, however, concentrated on the poetry of Pope. Whatever idiosyncrasies, pedantries and irrelevances in general emerge from his work, there is everywhere a continuing opposition to the kind of poetry Pope wrote. There is, too, a commitment to the need for a strongly emotive content in poetry, whether evoked in terms of nature or in response to the highest achievements of the literature of the past.

V

As Warton's scholarship is of less interest here than his criticism there seems to be no need for a full consideration of his translations and his edition. But several of his early comments on Virgil are of particular interest, and show a consistency of viewpoint continuous with that of the preface to the *Odes*, and the *Essay on Pope*.

In the dedication of the *Virgil* to Sir George Lyttelton, at that time one of the Lords Commissioners of the Treasury, whose chaplain Warton became, there is a defence of the great founder of the pastoral genre, in terms specifically of his originality:

> There are few images and sentiments in the Eclogues
> of Virgil, but what are drawn from the Idylliums of
> Theocritus: in whom there is a rural, romantic
> wildness of thought, heighten'd by the Doric dialect;
> with such lively pictures of passions, and of simple
> unadorned nature, as are infinitely pleasing . . .
> Theocritus is indeed the great store-house of pastoral
> description; and every succeeding painter of rural
> beauty (except THOMSON in his Seasons) hath copied
> his images from him, without ever looking abroad
> upon the face of nature themselves. And thus a set of

hereditary objects has been continued from one poet to
another, which have been often made use of without
any propriety as to age or climate. (p. iii)

The absence of originality is an absence of original response,
which has resulted in second-hand observation and consequently a
lack of relevant feeling in relation to the objects described. It is
this feeling which Warton has especially singled out for praise –
'lively pictures of passions and of simple unadorned nature' – as
promising a 'rural, romantic wildness of thought,' which the mind
may explore. The imagery used must have the metaphorical
force of 'living words', he adds two pages later; for where in
Homer:

> If the arrows which are impatient to destroy, and
> the spears that *thirst* to drink blood, are so deservedly
> admired in the Iliad, Virgil doubtless merits equal
> praise, for giving life and feeling, love and hatred, hope
> and fear, wonder and ambition, to plants and to trees
> and to the very earth itself . . . all the creation is
> animated.

This does not, however, prevent Warton from apologising for using
such 'coarse words' as dung and ashes in his translation. Clearly
propriety and elegance are more to be deferred to here than
expressiveness.

The problems of innovation and invention become directly
related to the imaginative and emotional vitality of the writer
and, of course, to his use of allegory and personification and his
capacity to make these come alive to the reader. And despite his
long quotations from different critical authorities – Du Bos and
Castelvetro – and unacknowledged plagiarism from Addison,
Pope, Lowth and Johnson, Warton maintains his grasp of a
principal theme. That nature will always affect the imagination
more than art is an observation he has borrowed from Addison,
but for him the affecting is an authentic emotional experience and
can only be marred by any affectation of thought or expression
which distracts the reader from the experience of the overall
feeling. So he concludes his 'Dissertation on Pastoral' in the first
volume by referring to its Italian practitioners – Tasso, for
example – and condemning as defects of this kind their 'false

Thoughts, and Glittering Conceits', as quite contrary to Nature and Truth'. Fontenelle has failed in writing sophisticated pastorals featuring gallant shepherds and instead of ridiculing the simplicity of Theocritus and Virgil, he should have explored the reasons for their success.[8] On the other hand, Warton is by no means advocating – and this might too readily be assumed – a simple reliance on classical models. Of Boileau's work he remarks that it contains

> all that could be expected from a man of strong sense
> and keen observation (tho' perhaps of no warm
> poetical genius) who had spent his life in studying and
> defending the ancients, and had formed his taste upon
> the Greek and Roman models alone.

To imitate nature itself is essential to the pastoral mode: the introduction of sophistication will make the form appear ridiculous. But in didactic poetry there is little opportunity for this kind of original imitation; it is therefore a kind of writing which has to be specially assisted by the devices and techniques of poetry. It must rely on local effects to catch the emotions, and hence the attention, of the reader.

Castelvetro, the learned Italian commentator on Aristotle's *Poetics*, had declared, that if Virgil had written nothing but the Georgics, he ought not to have been enrolled among the number of the poets. Warton sees the question as a more complicated one. 'Surely', he comments,

> the poet is an imitator, when he paints any object of
> universal nature, animate or inanimate, whether he
> speaks in his own person or introduces speakers; tho'
> indeed imitations of the latter species have not the same
> dignity or vitality with those of human manners,
> passions, and characters. (i, 396)

In didactic poetry, though, there is a special problem, for:

> Profess'd teaching is highly disagreeable to the natural
> pride of man, as it implies a superiority of
> understanding over the person instructed. That
> precepts may gain an easy admission into the heart, it
> is necessary to deliver them in a concealed indirect
> manner, divested of all pretensions to a larger share of
> reason, and of all dogmatical stiffness. (*ibid.*)

So the creative gift of the poet is exercised only in raising and enlivening his subject. To write in didactic vein the poet:

> should turn *rules* in to *images*; he should describe
> things by their effects, and speak of them as already
> done, instead of regularly ordering the manner in
> which they should be done; and throw in
> circumstances and adjuncts, that may forcibly strike
> the imagination, and embellish and conceal the
> dryness of the subject. (i, 398)

So Philips in his *Cyder* has settled on a pathetic anecdote to enliven the course of his instruction. And digressions are best:

> A stroke of passion is worth a hundred of the most
> lively and glowing descriptions. Men love to be moved,
> much better than to be instructed. . . . The
> understanding feels no pleasure in being instructed
> twice in the same thing; but the heart is capable of
> feeling the same emotion twice, with great pleasure.
> (i, 400)

This last statement concerning the pleasure of recapturing emotion is closely comparable to Coleridge's remarks quoted at the beginning of this chapter, and that this should be so is sufficient warning against too dogmatic a grouping of authors in terms of schools and influences. For Warton has selected this aspect of Du Bos's *Réflexions* as relevant to what he wants to emphasise at this point, and no one, so far as I know, has placed Du Bos, Warton and Coleridge in the same tradition. Warton does not always do this; he often contents himself with providing a conducted tour of pastoral, didactic, or epic poetry with profuse quotations from commentators, but here he goes on to bring in different critical considerations bearing on the same point. Landscape painting requires human interest to arouse that feeling in the beholder which will make him respond; so the landscapes of Poussin and Rubens embrace human figures and actions, evincing a knowledge of the human heart. For, Warton concludes – and here he is specifically of his time in relating a critical platitude to didactic poetry and those elements of the pathetic which can make it of general human interest: 'without something of the pathetic, something that comes home to our business and bosoms, as Lord

Bacon expresseth it, no didactic poem can possibly be interesting.'

Warton's enthusiasm for Akenside's 'Pleasures of Imagination' enables him to conclude the 'Dissertation on Didactic Poetry' by quoting the extracts on greatness, wonderfulness and beauty, as showing the noble exemplification of the sources of the pleasures of poetry and the imagination. And it is only just to remark that these comments often show merely a capacity for rhapsodic encomia. Elsewhere, too, as is naturally the case when the major works of one of the greatest classical authors are under review, there is a good deal of reliance on traditional commentary and inherited criteria – nature, elegance, simplicity and even the rules. There is, after all, no case for approaching Virgil as anything but a great exemplar in all three genres and as such his traditional claim to the highest achievement is explored and justified.

The partisans of the Moderns, for example, had criticised the *Aeneid* for its defective moral; the weakness of Aeneas as epic hero; narrative errors, lengths of similes, and extensive plagiarism. Deriving his argument on epic from Bossu, Warton replies that though the end of tragedy is to arouse fear and pity, that of the epic is to stimulate admiration and love; and he follows Dryden and Rapin in maintaining that the character of Aeneas is perfect. He seems to infuse a more recent influence when he comments in pedestrian fashion that the actions of Aeneas are 'informed or regulated by religion and therefore he is far more amiable than Anchises or Ulysses'.

The fluid criterion of 'truth to nature' which might so easily be dismissed as mere critical commonplace, is related by Warton to the way in which a play maintains an imaginative unity, rather than a generalised aspect of human experience – as it does for Johnson – so though he does maintain the importance of the unities he also censures declamation as the bane of true tragedies, deploring the introduction of sententious reflections by modern authors (and one has only to read Addison's *Cato*, Edward Young's *Busiris* or Johnson's *Irene* to see the force of this). For Warton, nature is primarily external, next a matter of human feelings, lastly of that consistency of imagination which has been repeatedly manifested in great literature. In appreciating the importance of human feelings, and of the necessity for these to be expressed in general yet poignant terms which may be felt to be common to all, he comes close to Johnson's position, as we shall see when we look at his observations on Shakespeare. In his love of the particulars of external nature as an opportunity for originality of perception, and in his emphasis on the relevance of classical, Hebraic and modern literature as alike offering a common kind of imaginative and emotional experience, he is nearer to Gray and Collins, and indeed to Cowper, who, after all, consciously attempted to bring back into his own translation of the *Iliad* the noble simplicity of the original, and to rescue it from the 'petticoats' into which Pope was felt by Edward Young to have forced it.[9]

VI

Chief among Warton's preoccupations in his occasional papers – where after all he follows his inclinations more freely than in the rest of his work – is a high valuation of the richness of the ancient writers – classical and Hebraic – as against the moderns, except in wit and satire. Warton exalts the fertility of Shakespeare's genius, and all writers are evaluated in terms of their appeal to the emotions. So he follows both Lowth and Longinus in *Adventurer*, no. 51, in insisting on the inherent sublimity of the Bible:

> Had I been acquainted with this wonderful volume
> [the Bible] while I was writing my treatise on the
> Pathetic, I could have enriched my work with many
> strokes of eloquence, more irresistibly moving than any
> I have borrowed from our three great tragedians, or
> even from the tender Simonides himself.

And in order to affect, to achieve pathos and sublimity, the writer is advised to be particular and exact in his description or realisation of his idea, so that the reader may receive a speaking picture of what he is trying to convey. So we have the need for exactness in detailed description, and for detailed personification and allegory. In the same paper Warton writes:

> It is the peculiar privilege of poetry, not only to place
> material objects in the most amiable attitudes, and to
> clothe them in the most graceful dress, but also to give

life and motion to immaterial beings; and form, and
colour, and action, even to abstract ideas; to embody
the virtues, the Vices, and the Passions; and to bring
before our eyes, as on a stage, every faculty of the
human mind.

The last part of the extract is particularly worthy of note. The
faculties of the human mind themselves, in all their emotional
states and complexities, are to be presented in terms of action and
personified to attain a new kind of originality. For poetry is an art
whose essence is imitation; and if the emotions are not to be dealt
with in this way by the poet his opportunities for originality are
negligible. In the creation of type characters or type situations,

> The causes that excite and the operations that
> exemplify the greater passions, will always have an
> exact coincidence, though perhaps a little diversified
> by climate or custom; every exasperated hero must
> rage like Achilles, and every afflicted widow mourn
> like Andromache.

But in the varied emanations of the feelings in action in a particular situation lies the root of an individual author's capacity to
express his meaning. For 'Letters written from the heart and on
real occasions contain just pictures of life and manners, and are
the genuine emanations of nature.' In his discussion of *The
Tempest* (*Adventurer*, no. 97) there is a delicate sensitivity in his
commendation of the particularity and inventiveness of the
'highly poetical' evocation of silence:

> Pray you tread softly, that the blind mole may not
> Hear a foot-fall . . .

And in approaching *Lear* (no. 116) Warton characteristically
suggests a parallel between Shakespearian and Greek tragedy;
and he develops the moral which is to be drawn from the dramatic
situations:

> On his [Lear's] first appearance in this situation [on
> the heath] he draws an artful and pathetic comparison
> betwixt the severity of the tempest and of his daughters. . . .
> He concludes with a sentiment finely suited to his condition,

and worthy to be written in characters of gold in the closet of every monarch upon earth:

> O! I have ta'en
> Too little care of this. Take physic pomp!

At the same time he can be caught up by the force of the play: 'The heart of Lear having been agitated and torn by a conflict of such opposite tumultuous passions, it is not wonderful that "his wits should now begin to unsettle".' Lear's lines

> Pray do not mock me . . .
> . . . Do not laugh at me;
> For as I am a man, I think that lady
> To be my child Cordelia.

are extolled for their 'humility, calmness and sedateness' (no. 122).

VII

But the sensitivity to the emotional orchestration of a passage, or its concrete suggestiveness, coupled as it often naturally is with an eye for an overall moral effect, can lead the subjective judgment (as it is geared almost exclusively to feelings) astray into a crude sensationalising of certain kinds of material. This emerges in a way which may now be seen as typical of the times, in the notes on the first book of the *Aeneid* where Aeneas meets his mother Venus:

> This is a most entertaining and delightful scene.
> A great prince thrown by a tempest upon a strange
> coast, doubtful of its inhabitants . . . is wandering in a
> wood; meets a person whom he knows not, but who
> appears to be a beautiful virgin. He supposes her a
> nymph, or a goddess, in that lovely romantic dress. . . .
> She tells him a most surprising story relating to the
> place in which she finds him, gives him advice and
> comfort; afterwards appears to be indeed a goddess,
> and not only so, but his own mother, and then leaves
> him in suspense and anxiety. The solitude of the recess,
> the unexpectedness of the meeting, the surprising
> adventure, all conspire to fill the soul with ideas of

pleasing melancholy, and impatient expectation of the event. (420n)

A more obvious example occurs in his discussion of *The Tempest*:

> He has there given the reins to his boundless
> imagination, and has carried the romantic, the
> wonderful, and the wild, to the most pleasing
> extravagance. The scene is a desolate island; and the
> characters the most new and singular that can well be
> conceived, a prince who practises magic, an
> attendant spirit, a monster the son of a witch, and a
> young lady who had been brought to this solitude in
> her infancy, and had never beheld a man except her
> father. (*Adventurer*, no. 97)

Warton praises imaginative creativity most frequently when fictional or figurative creation on an obvious level is involved. So poetical, that is, allegorical and figurative passages are praised: 'The circumstances of Famine, Sword, and Fire, submissively waiting the orders of their master, when they should be let loose to action, is new and sublime' (*Aeneid* x, 399n, ix, 1,054n, and xii, 458n).

A similar sensationalising process is seen when the pathetic is not only applied, with a just discrimination, to Dido's silence in book 6 of the *Aeneid*, but becomes mere sentimentality in the encomium of the deer pursued by the huntsmen:

> These most beautiful and pathetic lines are so moving,
> as scarce to be read without tears. I would recommend
> them to some of our British heroines, who have had the
> honour of cutting a stag's throat, after a chase in
> Windsor Forest. (*Aeneid*, vii, 624n)

So, to emphasise Virgil's status as a pathetic poet, Warton remarks: 'It lay in his power alone, to have enriched the Roman poesy with what it so greatly wanted, and what is perhaps a more useful work than an epic poem itself, A PERFECT TRAGEDY', and he describes Virgil as 'steeping his song in tears' (Postscript, iv, 396). Associated with this must surely be Warton's predilection for Otway (as Johnson's for Congreve's *Mourning Bride*), so that he ranked that author, when placing British poets in order of merit in the dedication to his *Essay*, in the same class with Shakespeare and Milton.

VIII

The commendation of local beauties on grounds of sublimity, pathos, or vividness of realisation in detail, could not, however, be relied on to provide an adequate criterion for that final assessment of a work in relation to other works which the critic felt it his business to make. And so Warton can praise the content of Shakespeare's plays, and respond to their variety of effect, yet condemn Shakespeare as an artist because of his violation of formal requirements of the drama which survive for Warton as a set of objective standards. For example he comments on the neglect of the unities. He condemns the sub-plot in *Lear*, for instance (though Johnson was later to defend it), as distracting, and censures the improbability of the cliff episode and the cruelty which Goneril and Regan are allowed to show, as well as the breach of decorum in the blinding of Gloucester (*Adventurer*, no. 122).

Warton's choice of critical authority – notably in his use of French critics in his dissertations in his *Virgil* – often seems to run oddly counter to his personal enjoyment. His reading is extensive, and his interest in literary effects far-ranging as it emerges from the notes on Virgil and from the periodical essays alone. He employs criteria of subjective taste alongside older formal criteria identified with the hierarchy of the kinds, and so with the nature of established cultural standards. When both standards are employed as having an equal validity in an attack on a particular poet for the kind of poetry he writes, apparent confusion arises. None the less the articulation of the equal importance of both poses a permanent critical problem, the reconciling of subjective reaction with the general appraisal; but, more immediately, it emphasises the new authority of the criteria of taste.

IX

'The Sublime and the Pathetic are the two chief nerves of genuine poesy. What is there very Sublime or very Pathetic in POPE?' To George Sherburn the dedication[10]

> hardly does more than reaffirm the commonplace of
> neoclassical criticism, that ranks the epic, tragedy and
> great ode as the higher poetry, and the *genres* written
> by Pope as the lesser poetry. There is little that is
> revolutionary or 'romantic' in the position, nor was it
> total damnation in Warton's day or in his eyes to be
> called a 'poet of reason'. In his essays prefixed to Pitt's
> *Virgil* in 1753 Warton is tolerant of didacticism in
> poetry and not at all 'advanced'.

I have referred earlier to valuations of Warton as a revolutionary, a pre-Romantic. Here is Warton as an Augustan. The truth is, of course, as the consideration of the 'poetical' in chapter 3 was intended to show, that a regard for didacticism in poetry is not incompatible with seeing the true role of poetry in a different way as non-didactic, nor is it incompatible with that continuing preference for a sententious or improving content which accompanies the direct expression of feeling – as Warton's comment on the meeting between Venus and Aeneas shows. The two are not necessarily identical but they are by no means opposed.

From the outset it is clear that Warton's attack is directed against Pope as epitomising a certain type of poetry:

> No love of singularity, no affectation of paradoxical
> opinions, gave rise to the following work. I revere the
> memory of POPE, I respect and honour his abilities;
> but I do not think him at the head of his profession.
> In other words, in that species of poetry wherein POPE
> excelled, he is superior to all mankind: and I only say
> that this species of poetry is not the most excellent one
> of the art.

So far this would be mere commonplace, agreeing with several assessments of satire, and indeed of Pope's achievement in relation to other poets in, for example, Ayre's *Memoirs of the Life and Writings of Alexander Pope* (1745) and Dodsley's 'Ballance of Poets' (*Museum*, 1746). In the 'Ballance of Poets' great poets are ranked not only on the 'particular parts' of their poetry, but on their work as a whole and its relative importance to that of other writers.

Pope is well placed in the different categories under which poetic merits are arranged: as 'Critical Ordonnance'; 'Pathetic Ordonnance'; 'Dramatic Expression'; 'Taste'; 'Colouring'; 'Versification' and 'Moral'; but his final rating is far inferior to Shakespeare's. Homer and Shakespeare rank highest; next, Milton and Virgil; Spenser comes fourth and Pope fifth. The writer explains:

> This general [final] estimate is also necessary . . . as
> some of the Articles [criteria] are applied equally to
> every Species of Poetry; so that a Satirist will be rated
> as high, in that Article, as an Epic Poet; provided
> his Ordonnance be as perfect for Satire as that of
> the other is for Heroic Poetry. Upon this Account,
> Justice to the Manes of the diviner Poets requires
> that we should recognise their Pre-eminence upon the
> Whole, after having thus set their Inferiours
> upon a level with them in particular Parts.

The question of criteria and evaluation is, then, a difficult one. In the Dedication Warton attempts to develop his own. He proceeds:

> We do not, it should seem, sufficiently attend to the
> difference there is, betwixt a MAN OF WIT, A MAN OF
> SENSE, and a TRUE POET. Donne and Swift were
> undoubtedly men of wit, and men of sense: but what
> traces have they left of PURE POETRY? . . . Which of
> these characters is the most valuable and useful is
> entirely out of the question: all I plead for, is, to have
> their several provinces kept distinct from each other;
> and to impress on the reader, that a clear head, and
> acute understanding are not sufficient, alone, to make a
> POET; that the most solid observations on human life,
> expressed with the utmost elegance and brevity, are
> MORALITY and not POETRY; . . . and that it is a
> creative and glowing IMAGINATION, 'acer spiritus ac
> vis', and that alone that can stamp a writer with this
> exalted and very uncommon character, which so few
> possess, and of which so few can properly judge.

And he proceeds to employ the method prescribed by Horace,

and, as we have seen, referred to by Coleridge, of rewriting the passage of poetry in question as prose.

Invention and originality in the poet, pathos and sublimity in the poem, with a vividness and particularity of illustration that enable the emotions to be more easily aroused, in association with a reflection which is at the same time moral and aesthetic – these are the guiding lines one would anticipate Warton employing when he examines Pope's works in his attempt to determine how far the greatness of recent poetry compared with that of the past. Such interests, when employed as constituent parts of Warton's critical method, lead – as this minor poet, after all, is both scholar and pedagogue – to disconcerting digressions on matters associated with the form, or even more remotely with the content of whatever poem is being discussed.

X

The first volume of the *Essay* deals with the early poetry of Pope, and therefore with his descriptive and emotional pieces: the Pastorals, 'The Messiah', 'Windsor Forest', the 'Elegy to the Memory of an Unfortunate Lady', and the Epistles of 'Sappho to Phaon' and 'Eloisa to Abelard', with which the volume concludes, as well as with the 'Essay on Criticism'. The hundred pages which are disproportionately devoted to this poem provide a great many opportunities for digression on the history of learning which was one of Warton's literary preoccupations. 'The Rape of the Lock' is examined as demonstrating Pope's originality in his chosen genre, and as exhibiting the excellent range of satiric effects which might be achieved by a highly gifted modern author.

Warton's critical approach in the opening section 'Of the PASTORALS, and the MESSIAH, an Eclogue', is interesting in two ways. He begins by employing the criterion of originality, complaining that: 'It is something strange, that in the pastorals of a young poet there should not be found a single rural image that is new: now this I am afraid is the case in the PASTORALS before us' (p. 2), and he contrasts the pastorals of Theocritus as 'richly and circumstantially delineated.' It follows that again originality lies in particularised description.

The poet described what he saw and felt; and had no
need to have recourse to those artificial assemblages of
pleasing objects which are not to be found in nature.
. . . The beauties of that luxurious landscape, so richly
and circumstantially delineated in the close of the
seventh idyllium, where all things smelt of summer and
smelt of autumn . . . were present and real. (pp. 3–4)

This is of course connected with the second criterion – the pathetic
– where Warton compares Pope's fourth eclogue to 'Lycidas'.
Declaring this one of Milton's 'most exquisite pieces' Warton
comments: 'The mention of places remarkably romantic, the
supposed habitation of Druids, bards, and wizards, is far more
pleasing to the imagination, than the obvious introduction (as in
Pope) of Cam and Isis' (p. 7). Scenic descriptions are both the
potential source of originality and of feeling, for in the 'Dissertation
upon Pastoral Poetry' to which I have already referred Warton
had identified the love of natural scenery as a very important
passion in its own right and one common to all mankind:

The Love of the Country is so strong a Passion, that it
can hardly be ever obliterated or overcome: tho'
Business and Amusements, or criminal Pursuits, or
Conveniences, or Courts, carry Men into Cities, yet
they still continue fond of Fields and Forests, of
Meadows and Rivulets . . .

And he continues:

the finest Pieces of Architecture would lose their
Beauty, if rural Objects were not interposed among
them . . . this is owing to the superior Powers which
the Works of Nature hold above those of Art, to affect
and entertain the Imagination. (i, 36)

So it is natural that he should look for both originality and
consequently authenticity of personal response in Pope's nature
poetry, notwithstanding the objection to this approach which was
emphatically expressed by Johnson later in his 'Life of Pope': 'To
charge these Pastorals with want of invention, is to require what
was never intended.'

Invention in terms of scenic description (the subject of section

2 is 'Windsor Forest') is spontaneously engendered by those reflections which proceed naturally from the train of associations set up in the mind by the object or description offered by the poet. So Denham is commended, as 'Cooper's Hill' shows the individual responding to the stimulus of the scene so that the reflections in the poem occur

> much in the same manner as the real sight of such
> scenes and prospects is apt to give the mind a
> composed turn, and incline it to thoughts and
> contemplations that have a relation to the object.
> This is the great charm of the incomparable ELEGY
> written in a Country Church-yard. Having mentioned
> the rustic monuments and simple epitaphs of the
> swains, the amiable poet falls into a very natural
> reflection:
>
>> For who, to dumb forgetfulness a prey,
>> This pleasing anxious being e'er resign'd,
>> Left the warm precincts of the chearful day,
>> Nor cast one longing lingering look behind?
>
> (pp. 30–1)

So Warton justly, if superficially, commends the way in which Pope introduces a pathetic reflection into 'Windsor Forest':

> When Pope therefore has described a pheasant shot,
> he breaks out into a very masterly exclamation,
>
>> Ah! what avail his glossy varying dyes,
>> His purple crest, and scarlet-circled eyes,
>> The vivid green his shining plumes unfold,
>> His painted wings, and breast that flames with gold!
>
> Where this exquisite picture heightens the distress,
> and powerfully excites the commiseration, of the
> reader. (p. 33)

XI

What emerges as we read on from section to section is Warton's return over and over again to the natural disposition, genius or bent of mind of the poet as a major consideration in criticising the literary work. The nature of the poetic talent of Pope is compared with that of other writers, his performances set against other works in the same kind. The long 104-page section on the 'Essay on Criticism' is accounted for by this. For Pope's genius is suited to didactic and moral poetry, and the poem is therefore 'a masterpiece in its kind' (p. 100). A clear head and strong sense were the characteristic qualities of Pope and the circumstances of Pope's life had favoured the cultivation of these qualities. So, if Pope had attempted the epic,

> so DIDACTIC a genius would have been deficient in that SUBLIME and PATHETIC, which are the main nerves of the epopea . . . he would have given us many elegant descriptions, and many GENERAL characters, well drawn; but would have failed to set before our eyes the REALITY of these objects, and the ACTIONS of these characters . . . POPE's close and constant reasoning had impaired and crushed the faculty of imagination . . . the political reflections . . . would have been more numerous than the affecting strokes of nature. (p. 280)

And while one cannot accept the antithesising of the faculties with which the observation begins, the general conclusion is not so different from Coleridge's comments on this kind of poetry quoted at the beginning of this chapter for one to dismiss the passage entirely. Apart from this, and the regard for originality, simplicity, sublimity and pathos, Warton's observations are true to pattern – digressive, pedantic, garrulous, occasionally gossipy, and too often, where relevant, merely commonplace. But the range of reading and reference is still extraordinary and helps to account for a broad sympathy and flexibility of appreciation which can enter into the pathos of the story of Ugolino in Dante's *Inferno* (pp. 254–5), Addison's *Cato* as a 'fine dialogue on Liberty' (p. 261), and *Lear* and *Macbeth* as striking instances of 'what interesting tragedies may be written, without having recourse to a love-story' (p. 265). This last is in contrast to Rowe, whose 'genius was rather delicate and tender, than strong and pathetic; his compositions sooth us with a tranquil and tender sort of complacency, rather than cleave the heart with pangs of commiseration' (pp. 272–3).

On a more general level Warton is inclined to attribute the dominance of satire to the growth of the rational spirit of enquiry. Announcing that 'In no polished nation, after criticism has been much studied, and the rules of writing established, has any very extraordinary work ever appeared' (p. 203), he offers a tentative explanation:

> Whether or no, the natural powers be not confined and debilitated by that timidity and caution which is occasioned by a regard to the dictates of art: or whether, that philosophical, that geometrical, and systematical spirit so much in vogue, which has spread itself from the sciences even into polite literature, by consulting only REASON, has not diminished and destroyed SENTIMENT; and made our poets write from and to the HEAD rather than the HEART: or whether, lastly, when just models, from which the rules have necessarily been drawn, having once appeared, succeeding writers, by ambitiously endeavouring to surpass those just models, and to be original and new, do not become distorted and unnatural, in their thoughts and diction. (pp. 203–4)

Though this last reflection has a continuing relevance, Warton does not find opportunity to explore it further as he does the opposition between the head and the heart, for immediately he turns to consider 'The Rape of the Lock' as a proof of his thesis, and as an 'heroic-comic poem', 'the most excellent kind of satire' (p. 205). It is an essentially modern and British achievement. For the French:

> in point of DELICACY, ELEGANCE, and fine-turned RAILLERY, on which they have so much valued themselves, they have produced nothing equal to the RAPE OF THE LOCK. It is in this composition Pope principally appears a POET; in which he has displayed more imagination than in all his other works taken together. (p. 248)

The pathos of the 'Elegy to the Memory of an Unfortunate Lady' and still more of 'Eloisa to Abelard' is brought to the reader's attention in all its variety and depth as Warton moves slowly through the poems. In the case of the latter he quotes copiously from the lovers' letters to illustrate developments in the poem. And so he reaches his conclusion:

> THIS EPISTLE, is, on the whole, one of the most highly finished, and certainly the most interesting, of the pieces of our author; and, together with the ELEGY to the Memory of an Unfortunate Lady, is the only instance of the Pathetic POPE has given us. I think one may venture to remark that the reputation of POPE, as a poet, among posterity, will be principally owing to his WINDSOR-FOREST, his RAPE OF THE LOCK, and his ELOISA to ABELARD; whilst the facts and characters alluded to and exposed, in his later writings, will be forgotten and unknown, and their poignancy and propriety little relished. For WIT and SATIRE are transitory and perishable, but NATURE and PASSION are eternal. (pp. 333-4)

It is an orthodox conclusion which might have been reached by many writers of the time; but the question Warton had begun by asking remained unanswered. He continued to raise it in one form or another throughout his life; but at this point the nature of Warton's attitude to Pope, and his use of various criteria must give place to the next major issue to be considered – the ways in which contemporary taste changed. This may be usefully examined in relation to the impact of Warton's work.

XII

Verdicts on the first volume, for as such it was received, were on the whole favourable, though for rather different reasons. The *Monthly Review* criticised the dedication, with its ranking of poets,[11] and Warton accordingly altered this in the second edition to meet the criticism – for he had originally placed Lee and Otway in the first class.

Johnson's review appeared in the *Literary Magazine*, and while complimenting Warton on the range of knowledge exhibited there, he also finds it an 'entertaining miscellany', a compound of 'critical remarks and literary history'.[12] Later, of course, he supposed that Warton's delay in issuing a second volume was due to his pique in not persuading the world to his, he implies, rather perverse opinion concerning the poet:

BOSWELL   'Why, Sir, should that prevent him from continuing his work? he is an ingenious Counsel, who has made the most of his cause – he is not obliged to gain it.'

JOHNSON   'But, Sir, there is a difference when the cause is of a man's own making.' (*Life*, p. 475)

But the statements must have seemed acceptable enough to the general public. Dodsley, devoted to Pope's memory as that of a friend and patron, demurred at Warton's dogmatic tone in the dedication, and would not publish the work himself. But he took some trouble to get it published and he urged Warton to complete the second volume. Warburton, while antagonised to some extent by Warton's criticism of his edition of Pope, would have attacked with his customary brutality if he had had any glimpse of the connection which was later to be suggested between the *Essay* and Pope's subsequent loss of reputation. Warton's own patron, Lord Lyttelton, himself defended Pope's didactic poetry in his *Dialogues of the Dead* (1760). That Warton was conscious, however, of the nature of his attack on Pope is another question; for the time being it was at any rate clear that any originality of statement concerning the nature of true poetry on which he seemed to pique himself in the first volume had for the time being escaped notice. It was not until later that the implications of the tone of the dedication were fully realised. By that time Young had attacked Pope's versification and lack of originality; Webbe, Pope's style; and Duff, his genius.

But lives of the poet continued to appear: Dilworth's in 1759, Roberts's in 1761; and the long-awaited Warburton biography, written by Ruffhead, appeared in a volume of the 1769 reprint of Warburton's edition. Ruffhead attacks Warton: 'It would seem as if he thought that the true poet, was to write nothing but what bore the stamp of poetic fury and inspiration'. Adding what seems to be a reasonable objection:[13]

If the critic means, that we do not find in Pope a
poem, in which the *sublime* and the *pathetic* constitute
the character of the whole: this is only saying, in
other words, what every one knows, that Mr. Pope
never composed a tragedy, or an epic poem. But, if he
means to deny, that there are a thousand passages in
Pope's poems, in which the *sublime* and the *pathetic* are
displayed in their utmost force and perfection; this is a
mistake, that all who have eyes, or hearts, or heads,
must be convinced of.

Nine years later, in 1778, appeared a champion of Pope's poetic
reputation, Percival Stockdale, who, in *An Inquiry into the Nature
and Genuine Laws of Poetry including a particular defence of the Writings
and Genius of Mr. Pope*, reveals a public awareness of the existence
of the Wartons as leaders of a literary faction, at the same time
exhibiting on his own account an undoubtedly conservative, not
to say reactionary, attitude. The present state of taste is, in his
opinion, sadly degenerate – the popularity of Ossian and the
Wartons is symptomatic of this decline:[14]

Their *Gothick* souls are only stimulated with the
transcendently sublime; or, in other words, with the
unnatural, the gigantick, and the incoherent. . . . If
you can only astonish Them, They will immediately
pronounce you sublime. In sentiment, give them all the
extravagance, and madness of ill-imagined passion.
In painting, let all your figures be grotesque; let all
your colouring be Chinese. Give Them a huddle, a
crash of objects; the grandeur of Sir William Chambers;
– the very Advertisements of a Langford; – the very
Poetry of the Wartons.

Clearly the Wartons were seen as representative of certain
aspects of contemporary taste, and equally clearly their public
image was a gross caricature of their criticism and scholarship in
classical as well as modern literature.

XIII

But none of the reactions sees the questioning of Pope's appeal to
the reader as having substantial importance. Nor does Warton at

any stage establish this approach clearly or consistently. So the most powerful answer to his findings on other criteria – the poet's originality, use of imagination, depth of feeling – is given by Johnson in the *Lives* of 1782. Wherever Warton's criticism of Pope is sufficiently specific he counters it. Johnson agrees that Pope's fundamental intellectual characteristic was good sense, but he vigorously defends the poet in a well-known passage:

> But good sense alone is a sedate and quiescent quality, which manages its possessions well, but does not increase them; it collects few materials for its own operations, and preserves safety, but never gains supremacy. Pope had likewise genius; a mind active, ambitious, and adventurous, always investigating, always aspiring; in its widest searches still longing to go forward, in its highest flights still wishing to be higher; always imagining something greater than it knows, always endeavouring more than it can do.
> (iii, 217)

Rather weakly Johnson adds that Pope 'gathered his notions fresh from reality, not from copies of authors, but from the originals of Nature'. None the less Johnson finally subordinates Pope to Dryden on the criterion of original genius; and, to judge from his use of a stock metaphorical comparison, it is because of a genius which in Dryden goes beyond trammels of sophistication and refinement of ideas; it has more emotional and emotive energy:

> Dryden's page is a natural field, rising into inequalities, and diversified by the varied exuberance of abundant vegetation; Pope's is a velvet lawn, shaven by the scythe, and leveled by the roller.
>   Of genius, that power which constitutes a poet; that quality without which judgment is cold and knowledge is inert; that energy which collects, combines, amplifies and animates; the superiority must, with some hesitation, be allowed to Dryden. It is not to be inferred that of this poetical vigour Pope had only a little, because Dryden had more; for every other writer since Milton must give way to Pope; and even of

Dryden it must be said, that if he has brighter
paragraphs, he has not better poems. Dryden's
performances are always hasty. . . . The dilatory
caution of Pope enabled him to condense his sentiments,
to multiply his images, and to accumulate all that
study might produce or chance might supply. If the
flights of Dryden therefore are higher, Pope continues
longer on the wing. If of Dryden's fire the blaze is
brighter, of Pope's the heat is more regular and
constant. Dryden often surpasses expectation, and
Pope never falls below it. Dryden is read with
frequent astonishment, and Pope with perpetual
delight. (p. 216)

Johnson then, chiefly questions the assumptions Warton makes
about true poetry and the criteria he adopts to determine Pope's
status as a poet. In his comments he offers a tacit challenge to
Warton's copious but unfulfilled promises of a particular application of his critical precepts: 'The Works of Pope are now to be
distinctly examined, not so much with attention to slight faults
or petty beauties, as to the general character and effect of each
performance' (pp. 222–4). 'Windsor Forest' and the ethic epistles
show the imagination 'which strongly impresses on the writer's
mind, and enables him to convey to the reader the various forms of
nature, incidents of life, and energies of passion', and that
judgment 'which selects from life or nature what the present
purpose requires, and, by separating the essence of things from its
concomitants, often makes the representation more powerful than
the reality' (p. 247). But the breakdown of poetic qualities is less
convincing when we come to Pope's diction. He 'had the colours
of language always before him, so that he had in proportions very
nicely adjusted to each other, all the qualities that constitute
genius' (p. 247). And in this connection Johnson's comments on
the translation of the *Iliad* reveal a refusal to examine the issues
raised by Warton and other critics of Pope:

His version may have been said to tune the English
tongue; for since its appearance no writer, however
deficient in other powers, has wanted melody. Such a
series of lines so elaborately corrected, and so sweetly
modulated, took possession of the publick ear; the

> vulgar was enamoured of the poem, and the learned
> wondered at the translation . . . the purpose of a
> writer is to be read, and the criticism which would
> destroy the power of pleasing must be blown aside.
> Pope wrote for his own age and his own nation: he
> knew that it was necessary to colour the images and
> point the sentiments of his author; he therefore
> made him graceful, but lost him some of his sublimity.
> (p. 238)

Johnson seems to be turning a blind eye on his own assumption
that 'nothing can please many, and please long, but just representations of general nature.' By defending Pope's attempt to
meet the taste of his time be betrays some uneasiness in admitting
the loss of sublimity in the translation, but rhetorically turns and
rends the questioner to repress the argument:

> After all this, it is surely superfluous to answer the
> question that has been asked, whether Pope was a poet,
> otherwise than by asking in return, if Pope be not a
> poet, where is poetry to be found? To circumscribe
> poetry by a definition will only show the narrowness
> of the definer, though a definition which shall exclude
> Pope will not easily be made. Let us look round upon
> the present time, and back upon the past; let us
> enquire to whom the voice of mankind has decreed
> the wreath of poetry; let their productions be
> examined, and their claims stated, and the pretensions
> of Pope will no more be disputed.

Then he adds:

> if the writer of the *Iliad* were to class his successors, he
> would assign a very high place to his translator,
> without requiring any other evidence of Genius.
> (pp. 251–2)

As a reply to Warton this reads like sound sense. Yet as Johnson
returns to the question of Pope's status as a poet again and again
there remains a suspicion that some problem lies half glimpsed and
still unanswered.

XIV

The second volume of the *Essay* appeared in 1782. That it was still awaited with curiosity is clear from the *Critical Review*'s comment that 'this work has been awaited, and even called for, by the public'.

In his advertisement Warton refers to the fact that the first two hundred and one pages – including the comments on the 'Imitations of Chaucer', on the 'Essay on Man' and the greater part of the 'Moral Essays' – had been printed over twenty years before. That the number of copies sold was considerable, and probably met a demand far greater than that for the original *Essay*, twenty-six years earlier, may be deduced from the different versions of volume 2 which preceded the issue of the fully revised second edition, all within the year. At first the publisher seems merely to have used up the pages printed in the early 'sixties to which Warton referred in the advertisement. To these Warton's subsequent comments were added to make up a bulky second volume. Next a reprinting of the work was made with the running headings 'Essay on the Writings and Genius of Pope', though the 1762 title *Essay on the Genius and Writings of Pope* was used. Finally the material was split into two volumes of equal size for the complete reprinting of the fourth edition.[15]

But the second volume was everywhere regarded as a disappointment. The examination of Pope's works is patched and rambling, with sections written at varying intervals of time and spatchcocked together, resulting in a more obviously digressive pattern of irrelevant or barely relevant material than in the first volume. A contemporary reviewer found the style and method alike 'too familiar and gossiping. . . . And the rambling desultory manner in which he digresses into subjects of general criticism, should have pointed out to him the necessity of an index'.[16]

The limp and pedestrian comments on Pope's style; the increasing frequency of pedantic digressions; the blatantly cursory account of 'The Dunciad' betray an overall absence of concern with the kinds of poetry – chiefly didactic and satiric – which remained to be considered. Warton seems to be more concerned with replying to Johnson, when he upholds the orthodoxy of the 'Essay on Man' and defends it against Johnson's imputations on Pope's ability to reason in verse; and the poet's abstemiousness, for example, is stressed to offset Johnson's criticism of his greed. Warton concentrates on the more obvious theme of his whole work, concentrating on the individual author and abandoning the general problem. Pope's predominant talent was not his imagination: he was pre-eminent as a moralist and satirist,

> The perusal of him affects not our minds with such
> strong emotions as we feel from *Homer* and *Milton*; so
> that no man of a true poetical spirit, *is master of himself*
> while he *reads* them. Hence, he is a writer fit for
> universal persual; adapted to all ages and stations;
> for the old and for the young; the man of business
> and the scholar. He who would think *Palamon and
> Arcite*, the *Tempest* or *Comus*, childish and romantic
> might relish POPE.

There is still the insistence on a 'true poetical spirit' as the superior faculty of response to poetry. The nature of Pope's appeal is a limited though a general one, and cannot awaken or nourish the imagination, only please the understanding. 'Surely', Warton continues,

> it is no narrow and niggardly encomium to say he is
> the great Poet of Reason, the *First* of *Ethical* authors in
> verse. And this species of writing is, after all, the
> surest road to an extensive reputation. It lies more
> level to the general capacities of men, than the higher
> flights of more genuine poetry. We all remember when
> even a Churchill was more in vogue than a Gray.
> (pp. 478-9)

The sentiments of Pope and Addison might remain in vogue as embodying admirable precepts of social and general value, but for Warton it is Gray who enshrines for his own time the true spirit of poetry. Stumbling over criteria of feeling and form, almost tedious in his insistence on often mechanically applied terms of appreciation – sublimity, pathos, liveliness, correctness and elegance – Warton brings his work to a conclusion by opposing Johnson in placing Pope above Dryden, but asserting the supremacy of Gray. For Warton true poetry had not died with Pope, it was capable of being renewed and brought back into its right channel. The artist's potentiality for creation had not been exhausted by earlier achievements, and whenever enthusiasm and feeling could be aroused in the reader, there the true province of poetry had been illuminated once again. So, returning to his question of 1756, he ends the second volume:

> *Where* then, according to the question proposed at the
> *beginning of this Essay*, shall we with justice be
> authorized to place our admired Pope? Not, assuredly,
> in the same rank with *Spenser*, *Shakespeare*, and *Milton*;
> however justly we may applaud the *Eloisa* and *Rape*
> of the *Lock*; but, considering the correctness, elegance,
> and utility of his works, the weight of sentiment, and
> the knowledge of man they contain, we may venture
> to assign him a place *next* to *Milton*, and *just* above
> *Dryden*. Yet, to bring our minds steadily to make this
> decision, we must forget, for a moment, the divine
> *Music Ode* of *Dryden*; and may perhaps then be
> compelled to confess, that though Dryden be the
> greater genius, yet *Pope* is the better artist.
>
> The preference here given to POPE, above other
> modern English poets, it must be remembered, is
> founded on the excellencies of his works *in general*, and
> *taken all together*; for there are parts and passages in
> other modern authors, in *Young* and in *Thomson*, for
> instance, equal to any of POPE; and he has written
> nothing in a strain so truly sublime, as the *Bard* of
> *Gray*. (pp. 480–1)

Fanny Burney recalled, on meeting Joseph Warton, that Dr Johnson had called him a 'rapturist', and herself observed: 'His ecstacies are excited so readily, from the excessive warmth of his disposition, and its proneness to admire and wonder.'[17] Warton remained, for all his pedagogy and plagiarising – which reached their climax in his edition of Pope – capable of genuine enthusiasm for literature, and of a concern with experiencing it as something different from everyday life and manners.

His responsiveness to particular literary effects is manifest in the *Essay* as it was in the periodical papers. In Pope's 'Epistle to the Earl of Oxford', he finds 'a weight of sentiment and majesty of diction which our author has nowhere surpassed'; in lines 267–80 of the first epistle of the 'Essay on Man', the 'exalted description of the omnipresence of the Deity' almost tempts him to retract his 'assertion that there is nothing transcendently sublime in POPE' (p. 137). He gives a surprisingly detailed appreciation of certain effects in the character of Sporus in the 'Epistle to Arbuthnot' (pp. 320–5); and of the line 'Where sprawl the Saints of VERRIO and LAGUERRE' ('Epistle to the Earl of Burlington') Warton emphasises the felicity of the verb: 'One single verb has marked with felicity and force the distorted attitudes, the indecent subjects, the want of nature and grace, so visible in the pieces of these two artists' (pp. 255–6). The spectator's reaction to the ceiling of the chapel at Chatsworth, and to those of other eighteenth-century mansions will often echo this of Warton. And if he had the lamentable lack of taste to suggest an amended puctuation for the opening of Gray's 'Elegy': 'The curfew tolls! The knell of parting day!' in the notes to his edition of Pope (v, 207), his love of sensational elements in literature did not blind him to the splendour of the lines:

> Thence a new world to Nature's laws unknown,
> Breaks out refulgent, with a heav'n its own:
> Another Cynthia a new journey runs,
> And other planets circle other suns.
> The forests dance, the rivers upward rise,
> Whales sport in woods, and dolphins in the skies.

Though his admiration is constrained again to cliché which is here almost misleading – unless we remember the elasticity with which picturesqueness could be applied: 'The . . . lines contain some of the most forcible and lively descriptions any where to be found: and are a perfect pattern of a clear picturesque style' ('The Dunciad', Book iv. 1. 282n. *Works*, v).

XV

Warton's lack of flexibility in critical appreciation is characteristic. He cannot anywhere compete with Johnson in vigour and lucidity of articulation. But what makes his work interesting is that incessant pondering of the essential separation between poetic

experience and social truths. The individual can benefit emotionally from great poetry in a way in which he cannot benefit from
Pope's poetry.

Among the Warton MSS. in Trinity College library are what
seem to be several attempts made by Warton to answer the
question he poses at the beginning of his *Essay*: 'The Sublime and
the Pathetic are the two chief nerves of genuine poesy. What is
there very Sublime or very Pathetic in POPE?' Here there is a
simplified and rather different version of the conclusion:

> Where then may we place our admired bard? Not
> with Spencer &c. – but next after Dryden in the 2ᵈ
> class – He suppress'd enthusiasm – he kept company
> with politicians statesmen &c. – he adhered to polished
> Life –
> Ld. Bolingbroke led him to read the *french*
> Moralists – He became the first of *moral* poets – He
> kept to present *Life* – the *topics* of the Day – perhaps in
> the sight of this, when he saw this was the (His) true
> method to become famous, not by pursuing a *higher*
> Species of Poetry – observe that Churchill is more
> talked of than Gray – Gray our best *poet* – I think Ld.
> Bolingbroke a great hand in making Pope a moral
> poet – Ld. Bolingbroke himself had no Taste of true
> poetry & Pope fell into his tastes of all sorts.
> What he *could* or might have done is most uncertain
> – What he *did* must be argued from. Certain it is that
> except Abelard and the Rape there is not much other
> poetry – He imitated those parts of Horace which
> Horace himself says are not poetic – & wrote some
> original Epistles in *imitation* of these unpoetic pieces –
> No absurdity – no incorrectness in his Works – fit for
> Universal perusal – for the old and the young –smooth
> – even – sober – & pleasing – What sort of sensation
> do his Works give in comparison of Milton? What
> Segrais said long ago – Le Siècle est devenu prosaique
> – Formed on Boileau his darling Poet.

But Warton adds a comment, showing himself uneasily aware
of the potential absurdity of refusing to any particular kind the

status of poetry: 'I am sensible that this may be confining poetry *too* much to *one* species perhaps'. None the less, elsewhere we find a fragment referring to Pope as a 'prose poet', on reading whose work 'we feel a gentle complacency; and that sort of tranquil assent to the truth of his doctrines, that we experience from the theorems of Geometry'. . . . 'The reading Pope will never make a young man a *poet*: it may I shall be bold enough to say make him a better [?] man of taste & knowledge of the world' (Trinity College MSS.).

XVI

Warton's conclusion seemed an anticlimax to most commentators. Nathan Drake asked: 'Who, indeed before the commencement of Mr. Warton's criticism thought of estimating the poetical genius of Pope higher than that of Shakespeare and Milton?'[18] And Chalmers points out that Warton 'at length persuaded the world that he did not differ from the common opinion so much as was supposed', and that the dedication to the *Essay* had expressed 'no new doctrine', but had been taken from Phillips's *Theatrum Poetarum* (1675), where a distinction is made in the preface between poets of wit and poets of passion. Chalmers reveals how far taste in poetry had shifted by this time (1810), observing that whatever objections were raised to the *Essay*, 'while that blind admiration of Pope which accompanied his long dictatorship continued in full force':

> It is now generally adopted as the test of poetical merit
> by the best critics, although the partialities which
> some entertain for individual poets may yet give rise to
> difference of opinion respecting the provinces of
> argument and feeling. (p. 152)

The *Essay* was, however, followed by the edition of Pope in 1797. Like its predecessors the work was modelled on Warburton's plan, with the inclusion of items which had previously been omitted, chiefly on account of their grossness, and of a large number of letters. And just as the *Essay* revealed an authorial method best suited to the compilation of an edition, the edition materially consisted of a reproduction, with slight readjustments, of the material of the *Essay*.

It is interesting, however, that his attitude towards Johnson, who had died in 1784, becomes openly antagonistic, and he opposes his own valuation of poetry to that of his critic. At one point he bundles together a heterogeneous list of topics on which he stresses his disagreement with Johnson, concluding with the 'Odes of Gray'. In volume 1 he attacks Johnson's criticism of these as showing 'more strong sense than a just relish for true poetry' and wishes that Johnson's 'strange and unwarrantable' dismissal of them 'could be sunk into oblivion'.

Later he remarks:

> Johnson's mind was formed for the Didactic, the Moral
> and the Satiric; he had no true relish for the higher
> and more genuine species of poetry. Strong couplets,
> modern manners, present life, moral sententious
> writings alone pleased him. Hence his tasteless and
> groundless objections to the Lycidas of Milton and to
> the Bard of Gray. Hence his own Irene is so frigid and
> uninteresting a tragedy; while his imitations of Juvenal
> are so forcible and pointed. His Lives of the Poets are
> unhappily tinctured with this narrow, prejudiced, and
> confined notion of poetry, which has occasioned many
> false or spurious remarks, and many ill-grounded
> opinions, in a work that might have been, and was
> intended to have been, a manual of good taste and
> judgment.

Whilst deferring to Johnson's criticisms on particular aspects of Pope's work, he maintains an opposition between the poetry of Milton and Gray and that of Johnson, Swift, and, indirectly, Pope: 'I know not of any work of the Dean's that can be strictly called *poetical*. Our *Bards* of this species are numerous.'

Warton's own attitude towards the edition is made sufficiently clear in a letter he wrote to a friend in December 1795:[19]

> Rejoice with me . . . that I have finish'd my labours on
> Pope for the press, and we have begun to print. But
> this is the sort of work in which there can be little
> curious matter on so known and so beaten a subject –

and no very correct writer can be a good subject for criticism – to be always commending is tedious and almost as bad as to be always censuring.

The more rigorous editorial practices introduced by Malone and Stevens were not adopted by Warton. Nor did he attempt to cast any light on the doubts which Johnson had expressed concerning Pope's manipulation of his correspondence and his conduct in relation to Addison, the Duchess of Marlborough and the Duke of Chandos. Though he introduces a large number of letters which Warburton had not included they are badly arranged. The nine-volume edition which had aroused the interest of the public on account of Warton's long preoccupation with its subject was a disappointment, as Mathias made clear, when he cruelly described Warton disappointing 'the publick hope', to drivel[20]

> o'er the page of POPE –
> Whilst o'er the ground that WARBURTON once trod,
> The Winton pedant shakes his little rod.

XVII

The extent to which Warton influenced the nineteenth-century reaction against Pope is difficult to determine. The attacks of Macaulay, De Quincey and others are associated with Cowper's complaint that Pope had made poetry 'a mere mechanic art', and with Johnson's deprecation of the weaknesses and pettiness of Pope's private character. Of all the nineteenth-century writers after Bowles, John Dennis most closely approaches Warton's attitude to the poetry of Pope. Acquiescing in Pope's status as a writer of classic importance, he nevertheless concludes:[21]

> He has written none of the verses which children love,
> nor any lines which grown-up people care to croon
> over in moments of weakness or sorrow. In his works the
> wit o'ertops the poetry, the intellect gets the better of
> the heart, and thus he wins admiration from his readers
> rather than affection.

Warton's various inconsistencies are less relevant than the

undoubted authenticity of his preoccupation with a problem which has so far seemed insoluble, even if not capable of being adequately formulated. The gap between the world of private feeling and cultural approval, of the enjoyment which is spontaneous, uninhibited and refreshing and that which is the product of a sensibility cultivated to the point where our emotions are often to a major extent surrendered to current modes in cultural standards is one which Warton would not, of course, have recognised.

The separation between the cultural tradition and the personal enjoyment of the individual, however, the extent of his real involvement with art, remains a problem of major importance. The poetry of Dryden and Pope tends on the whole to be less popular with undergraduate students than that of any other major poets writing in modern English. Admiration of skill, analysis of technical brilliance, do not compensate for a quality which appeals to the individual in terms of the orchestration of emotions and feelings in the highly wrought structures which Donne, Keats, Wordsworth, Shelley, Eliot and Yeats have to offer. It might be argued that the fully mature taste for poetry does not differentiate between the poetry of thought and that of feeling: it might be argued that the poetry of thought – as C. Day Lewis argued in the preface to his translation of the *Georgics* – only shows how it feels to think: that the test of paraphraseability of contents is ludicrously inadequate. And these arguments might be accepted; yet there still attaches to the experience of art the quest for the expression of a fuller emotional awareness than the Augustans thought fitting to express in their poetry. To write for the general and social response was to neglect the individual feelings of humanity. Johnson's comment that the absence of human experience from *Paradise Lost* militates against a spontaneous sympathetic response to the action can be associated with Richards's comment on Matthew Arnold:[22]

> the arts are inevitably and quite apart from any
> intentions of the artist an appraisal of existence.
> Matthew Arnold when he said that poetry is a
> criticism of life was saying something so obvious that
> it is constantly overlooked. The artist is concerned with
> the record and perpetuation of the experiences which

seem to him most worth having . . . he is also the man who is most likely to have experiences of value to record. . . . His experiences, those at least which give value to his work, represent conciliations of impulses which in most minds are still confused, intertrammelled and conflicting. His work is the ordering of what in most minds is disordered. That his failures to bring order out of chaos are often more conspicuous than those of other men is due in part at least to his greater audacity; it is a penalty of ambition and a consequence of his greater plasticity. Instead of recognising that value lies in the 'minute particulars' of response and attitude, we have tried to find it in conformity to abstract prescriptions and general rules of conduct.

To Warton and his contemporaries large areas of what was considered appropriate poetic experience had disappeared under the pressure of the 'abstract prescriptions and general rules of conduct' of social, didactic and ethical verse. Pope remained a major English poet but it was necessary that after him different kinds of expression should, if possible, be reclaimed for poetry. That Warton expressed this so dogmatically ensured its memorability; that he identified it with a repudiation of the achievment of the most recent major poet may (as Johnson suggested) have been perverse, but it gives him an obvious historical significance.

To the Wartons and those of their contemporaries who regarded authentic poetry only as that which is a source of pleasure and delight fostering the illumination of human experience and the enlarging of human sensibility, it was essential to separate poetry from the socially didactic and ethical and to identify a correct taste with a susceptibility to the sublime and the pathetic. And for them poetry was no longer to be divorced from illusion and fantasy, but the ways in which illusions had been given literary form in the past were to be examined that they might be used to foster the poetical spirit of their own generation. It is to this investigation of the nature of true poetry, rather than to the more audacious but ultimately baffling aim of demonstrating its nature in terms of its absence from the work of a major poet – which was what after all, Joseph Warton seemed to be attempting in the

Essay – that Thomas Warton devoted his skill as poet and anti-quarian.

Notes

1 *Biographia Litereria*, ed. J. Shawcross, 2 vols (Oxford, 1939), i, 9–10, 11, 14.
2 'A Monody on the Death of Dr. Warton', *Poetical Works*, ed. C. C. Clarke (Edinburgh, 1868).
3 See Ralph Straus, *Robert Dodsley, Poet, Publisher and Playwright* (London, 1910), 87, 153.
4 Alexander Chalmers (ed.), *The Works of the English Poets from Chaucer to Cowper*, 21 vols (London, 1810), xviii, 146.
5 See Paul F. Leedy, 'Genres Criticism and the Significance of Warton's *Essay on Pope*', *Journal of English and Germanic Philology*, xlv (1946), 140–6; Joan Pittock, 'Joseph Warton and his Second Volume of the Essay on Pope', *Review of English Studies*, xviii (1967), 264–73.
6 'On Writing the History of English Criticism, 1650–1800', *University of Toronto Quarterly*, xxii (1952), 376–91.
7 'Joseph Warton's Criticism of Pope', *Modern Language Notes*, xxxvi (1921), 276.
8 See J. M. Congleton, *Theories of Pastoral Poetry in England, 1684–1798* (Gainsville, 1952).
9 Warton, *op. cit.*, 291. Cf. Cowper: 'the sublime of Homer in the hands of Pope becomes bloated and tumid, and his description tawdry'; *Letters*, ed. J. G. Frazer, 2 vols (London, 1912), i, 400.
10 *The Early Career of Alexander Pope* (Oxford, 1934), 10.
11 See E. N. Hooker, 'The Reviewers and the New Criticism 1754–70', *Philological Quarterly*, xiii (1934) 189–202. *Monthly Review*, xiv (1756), 528–54, and xv (1756), 52–78.
12 Reprinted in *Works*, ed. Arthur Murphy, 12 vols (London, 1806), ii, 413–23.
13 Owen Ruffhead, *The Life of Alexander Pope, Esq., Compiled from Original Manuscripts with a Critical Essay on his Writings and Genius* (London, 1769), 433, 422.
14 Percival Stockdale, *An Inquiry into the nature and Genuine Laws of Poetry, including a particular Defence of the Writings and Genius of Mr. Pope* (London, 1778), 128–30.
15 W. D. MacClintock, *Joseph Warton's Essay on Pope. A History of the Five Editions* (London 1933); G. B. Schick, 'Delay in Publication of the Second Volume of Warton's "Essay on Pope"', *N. & Q.* no. 200, 67–9; Pittock, *op. cit.*
16 *The Monthly Review*, lxvi (1782), 271.
17 *The Diary and Letters of Madame D'Arblay*, ii, 180, 'He is what Dr. Johnson calls a rapturist', and (iii, 4).

18 *Essays, Biographical, Critical and Historical*, 2 vols (London, 1810), ii, 133.
19 Wooll, *Biographical Memoirs of the Revd. Joseph Warton, D.D.* (London, 1806), 405–6.
20 *The Pursuit of Literature* (8th ed. revised; London, 1798), Dialogue IV (1797), ll. 479–82.
21 *Studies in English Literature* (London, 1876), 60.
22 *Principles of Literary Criticism* (London, 1948), 60–1.

Five

The Taste for the Gothic: Thomas Warton and the History of English Poetry

I

When Johnson's *Dictionary* appeared in 1755 it contained no reference to the word 'Gothic'. Yet Horace Walpole had succumbed to the spell of Gothic architecture in building his castle at Strawberry Hill in 1750, and the vogue for Gothic as well as Chinese in design is attested by Robert Lloyd in his description of 'The Cit's County Box' (1757):

> The traveller with amazement sees
> A temple, Gothic or Chinese,
> With many a bell or tawdry rag on
> And crested with a sprawling dragon,
> A ditch of water four foot wide . . .
> With angles, curves, and zig-zag lines . . .

The taste for the nebulously exotic, wild or fanciful could be localised to best effect for several reasons in those periods of history which might be thought to have produced Gothic buildings. When Walpole published his *Castle of Otranto* in 1764 he subtitled it 'A Gothic Tale'. And as the Gothic novel developed in the work of Clara Reeve, Charlotte Smith, Ann Radcliffe and 'Monk' Lewis it held spellbound a reading public wider and more heterogeneous than ever before. So in *Northanger Abbey* (written in 1798) even the judicious Henry Tilney confesses himself incapable of leaving *The Mysteries of Udolpho* half-finished, while the story affords his girlish heroine not only 'the luxury of a raised, restless, and frightened imagination' but an inability to control her state of mind when she at last encounters an authentic abbey.

II

Clearly Gothic architecture was of less significance, culturally speaking, than the emotions it aroused by its associations, its suggestions of the manners and trappings of what was supposed to have been the medieval way of life. But the cultivation of a taste for the Gothic in the novel was to a considerable extent a continuation, at a culturally more sophisticated level, of the tales of heroic deeds, bloody murders and supernatural horrors which had been the fiction of the unrefined reading public as far back as the sixteenth century.

In the later seventeenth century 'Gothic' had become equivalent to rude, barbarous and uncouth: its primary connection after all was with the race of vandals which had overrun and demolished the civilisation of ancient Rome. For this reason it was inherently opposed to classicism, while the 'Gothic' in relation to the architecture and literature of the medieval period was likewise associated with whatever was extravagant, fanciful, wild and uncontrolled by the overall sense of design and function which was so pre-eminently the virtue of the buildings and literary forms of classical antiquity.

The difficulties of providing a definition for so potentially ambivalent a word are best illustrated by Addison. In the *Spectator*, no. 415, he compares the two types of architecture in terms of their effect on the mind:

> Let any one reflect on the Disposition of Mind he finds
> in himself, at his first Entrance into the *Pantheon* at
> *Rome*, and how his Imagination is filled with something
> Great and Amazing; and, at the same time, consider
> how little, in proportion, he is affected with the inside
> of a *Gothick* Cathedral, tho' it be five times larger than
> the other; which can arise from nothing else but the
> Greatness of the Manner in the one, and the Meanness
> in the other.

But, somewhat paradoxically, in defending his admiration for the ballad of Chevy Chase, he removes the ballad from its historical context and employs it as a neoclassical touchstone of true taste:

> I know nothing which more shews essential and
> inherent Perfection of Simplicity of Thought, above
> that which I call the Gothick Manner in Writing, than
> this, that the first pleases all Kinds of Palates, and the

latter only such as have formed to themselves a wrong
artificial Taste upon little fanciful Authors and
Writers of Epigram. *Homer, Virgil, or Milton*, so far as
the language of their poems is understood, will please
a Reader of plain common Sense, who would neither
relish nor comprehend an Epigram of *Martial*, or a
Poem of *Cowley*: So, on the contrary, an ordinary
Song or Ballad that is the Delight of the common
People, cannot fail to please all such Readers as are
not unqualified for the Entertainment by their
Affectation or Ignorance; and the Reason is plain,
because the same Paintings of Nature which
recommend it to the most ordinary Reader, will appear
Beautiful to the most refined. (no. 70)

Cowley and Martial are, then, Gothic in their artificiality and
fancifulness. But this was inevitably an ephemeral distinction,
only sustained by the familiar Gothic–Grecian antithesis. More
generally acceptable is the verdict on contemporary taste which I
cited in chapter 1:

I look upon those writers as Goths in Poetry, who,
like those in Architecture, not being able to come up
to the Beautiful Simplicity of the old *Greeks* and
Romans, have endeavoured to supply its Place with all
the Extravagancies of an irregular Fancy. . . . The
Taste of most of our *English* Poets, as well as Readers,
is extremely *Gothick*.

To set the classical against the English tradition in this way is to
associate the violations committed by Spenser and Shakespeare,
for example, against the classical modes of composition in epic
and tragedy, with the wild and fanciful exuberance of Gothic
architecture. And so indeed John Hughes attempted to defend
Spenser's *Faerie Queene* three years later, by suggesting that in
structure it resembled a Gothic rather than a Grecian edifice.
Pope employed the same analogy in expressing his appreciation
of Shakespeare in 1725: Gothic architecture is 'more strong and
solemn' than neat modern buildings; 'Nor does the whole fail to
strike us with greater reverence, though many of the parts are
childish, ill placed and unequal to its grandeur.'

III

In his account of *The Gothic Revival* Sir Kenneth Clark quoted the analogy employed by Hughes and Pope to show that although[1]

> These two passages have been much quoted by
> historians of literature to prove that Gothic architecture
> influenced literary taste. . . . I think the reverse is true.
> We accept as almost axiomatic the generalisation
> that in England a love and understanding of literature
> greatly exceeds, and indeed swamps, appreciation of
> the visual arts; and a new current of taste is likely to
> be first felt in a literary channel. Shakespeare and
> Spenser would be appreciated before a Gothic
> cathedral; and in fact it was the analogous forms of
> these great writers which shed lustre on the despised
> architectural style. Above all it was Shakespeare, so
> unmistakably great in defiance of all the rules of
> Aristotle, who broke the back of classical prejudice. If
> Aristotle's rules could be defied with success, why not
> those of Vitruvius too? Gothic architecture crept in
> through a literary analogy.

But the experience derived from the poetry of Spenser or the plays of Shakespeare could not be justified seriously enough to counter criticisms of defects in structure and tone merely in terms of an architectural analogy. Sir Kenneth Clark himself concluded that the writers of the Gothic novel:

> have their place in the Gothic Revival because they
> show the frame of mind in which the multitude of
> novel-readers looked at medieval buildings. But if we
> search the second half of the eighteenth century for
> literary influences on the Gothic Revival we need not
> spend time on the *Castle of Otranto*'s offspring, but on
> those books which show a real interest in the middle
> age, a veneration for its arts and manners, and a
> serious study of its monuments.

We are in the province not only of imaginative response to literature but of antiquarianism and scholarship:

When antiquarianism reappears as a vital interest it
is in the persons of Gray and Warton. Now Gray and
Warton were poets. Their enthusiasm for Gothic
springs from a literary impulse which first made itself
felt as antiquarianism was beginning to decline. This
literary impulse, if anything, can be called the true
starting-point of the Gothic revival.

IV

If indeed there was a decline in antiquarianism – though the
Society of Antiquarians was incorporated in 1751 – it was chiefly
in terms of its social acceptability. The study of the abstruse and
recondite to no socially useful end had been pilloried by Pope
when he placed Thomas Hearne in the third book of his 'Dunciad'
(1728):

> 'But who is he, in closet close y-pent,
> Of sober face, with learned dust besprent?'
> 'Right well mine eyes arede the myster wight,
> On parchment scraps y-fed, and Wormius hight.
> To future ages may thy dulness last,
> As thou preserv'st the dulness of the past!
> 'There, dim in clouds, the poring Scholiasts mark,
> Wits, who like Owls, see only in the dark,
> A Lumberhouse of Books in ev'ry head,
> For ever reading, never to be read! (185–94)

The cultural gap between the antiquarian and the man of taste
narrowed as the study of registers and chronicles became essential
to the work of the scholar and critic. The work of editors like
Warton, Percy and Ritson was only made possible by the per-
severance of those whom Pope had so lightly dismissed. Hearne's
editions of the chronicles of Robert of Gloucester (1724) and Peter
Langtoft (1725), Ames's *Typographical Antiquities* (1749), with its
description of the contents of Malory's *Morte Darthur*, Walpole's
Catalogue of Royal and Noble Authors (1758) augmented the earlier
work of Bale, Camden, Leland, À Wood, and their successors,
Oldys, Wanley and Hickes. New areas of literary enquiry were
opened up by the cataloguing of manuscript collections. Oxford

University published a catalogue of manuscripts in 1697; Wanley's catalogue of the Harleian collection, published by order of the trustees of the British Museum in 1759, contained substantial extracts from some of the entries; and in 1767 the Oxford University published a catalogue of the manuscripts held by the Oxford and Cambridge colleges. Abroad St Palaye published his *Mémoires de l'Ancienne Chévalerie* in 1759.

The publication of early literature, whether in the reprinting of *England's Helicon*, or *Tottel's Miscellany*, Dodsley's *Select Collection of Old Plays* (1744), or in contemporary collections like those of Ramsay, met a demand not from scholars so much as from the general public. So Shenstone wrote to Percy in 1760 urging him to publish the manuscript ballad, song and romance material which he had discovered, but not without making certain alterations and improvements which would adapt the original material to the taste of the general reader, for[2]

> All People of Taste throu'out the Kingdom will rejoice
> to see a judicious, a correct and elegant collection of
> such Pieces. For after all, 'tis such Pieces that contain
> ye true Chemical Spirit or Essence of Poetry, a little
> of which properly mingled is sufficient to
> strengthen and keep alive very considerable Quantities
> of the kind. 'Tis ye voice of Sentiment rather y^n the
> the Language of Reflection, and adapted peculiarly to
> strike ye Passions, which is the only Merit of Poetry
> that has obtained my regard of late.

Shenstone was proved right. And after all it was Macpherson who by decking out legendary scraps with biblical cadences and contemporary sentiments achieved so great a success with *Ossian*. The cultivation of the public taste had never blended more happily with the growth of a sense of historical perspectives and an illuminating and revivifying range of imaginative expression in earlier literature. When Warton discovered James I's *Kingis Quair* Percy wrote to him at Oxford:[3]

> Were I at the fountain head of literature, as you are, I
> should be tempted to transcribe some of the curiosities
> that lie mouldering in your libraries for publication – I
> am persuaded this of James would be acceptable to the

public, both to the Antiquarians and men of taste: –
this and two or three other such pieces would make an
additional volume to the *Ever green* or Collection of ancient
Scots poems of which a second Edition has lately been
called for.

There was a general uneasiness felt among scholars lest they
should appear to their potential public as too pedantic, though
their keen interest in exact scholarly enquiry is illustrated in the
mid-century correspondence between Percy and his collaborators
– Warton, Evans, Farmer, Malone, Shenstone and Johnson. So
Warton explains to his readers the need for the investigation into
the use of romance, allegory and legend by Spenser in writing
the *Faerie Queene*:

> In reading the works of an author who lived in a
> remote age, it is necessary, that we should look back
> upon the customs and manners which prevailed in his
> age; that we should place ourselves in his situation,
> and circumstances; that so we may be the better
> enabled to judge and discern how his turn of thinking,
> and manner of composing were biass'd, influenc'd, and,
> as it were, tinctur'd, by very familiar and reigning
> appearances, which are utterly different from those
> with which we are at present surrounded. For want of
> this caution, too many readers view the knights and
> damsels, the turnaments and enchantments of Spenser
> with modern eyes, never considering that the
> encounters of Chivalry subsisted in an author's age, as
> as has been before hinted; that romances were then
> most eagerly and universally read; and that thus,
> Spenser from the fashion of his age, was naturally
> dispos'd to undertake a recital of Chivalrous
> achievements, and to become, in short, a ROMANTIC
> POET. (p. 217)

Spenser was, then, a poet conditioned by his environment as
much as Blackwell and Wood had shown Homer to have been,
and in the same way as Lowth had demonstrated the relationship
between the style and subject-matter of the Scriptures and the
customs and environment of the Hebrews.

As he shows in his use of terms in the 1765 *Preface* Johnson was quick to see the potentialities of this approach as a way out of the stalemate at which criticism seem to have arrived in working according to the requirements of ideal forms. He wrote to congratulate Warton on his achievement in a well-known letter:

> You have shewn to all, who shall hereafter attempt the study of our ancient authours, the way to success; by directing them to the perusal of the books which these authors had read. Of this method, Hughes and men much greater than Hughes, seem never to have thought. The reason why the authours, which are yet read, of the sixteenth century, are so little understood, is, that they are read alone; and no help is borrowed from those who lived with them, or before them.
> (*Life*, p. 190)

A second enlarged edition of the *Observations* came out in two volumes in 1762, in the same year as Hurd's *Letters on Chivalry and Romance*. Warton had, then, eight years earlier, already suggested what Hurd specifically undertook, a defence of the manners of chivalry as the most promising subject-matter for poetry; though he does not imply as Hurd does that the classical authors might have benefited from an acquaintance with chivalry and romance: the myths and legends of antiquity had, after all, afforded a similar repository of superstition and fancy. In the *Observations* of 1754 he wrote:

> Though the FAERIE QUEENE does not exhibit that economy of plan, and exact arrangement of parts which Epic severity requires, yet we scarcely regret the loss of these, while their place is so amply supplied, by something which more powerfully attracts us, as it engages the affection of the heart, rather than the applause of the head; and if there be any poem whose graces please, because they are situated beyond the reach of art, and where the faculties of creative imagination delight us, because they are unassisted and unrestrained by those of deliberate judgment, it is in this of which we are now speaking. To sum up all in a few words; tho' in the FAERIE QUEENE we are not

satisfied as critics, yet we are transported as readers.
(pp. 12–13)

The distinction Warton makes here between the reader and the
critic is one which he shows applies equally to the poet and the
critic. He concludes his postscript to the work with a quotation
from Spenser in which the critic identifies himself with the
statements of the poet:

> The waies thro' which my weary steps I guide,
> In this DELIGHTFUL LAND OF FAERY,
> Are so exceeding spacious and wide,
> And sprinkled with such sweet varietie
> Of all that pleasant is to ear or eye
> That I nigh ravisht with rare thought's delight,
> My tedious travel do forgett thereby,
> And when I gin to feel decay of might,
> It strength to me supplies, and cheares my dulled spright.

The same reaction to Spenser was expressed by Goldsmith in
the *Critical Review* for February 1759:

> There is a pleasing tranquillity of mind which ever
> attends the reading of this ancient poet. We leave the
> ways of the present world, and all the ages of
> primeval innocence and happiness rise to our
> view. . . . The imagination of his reader leaves reason
> behind, pursues the tale without considering the
> allegory, and upon the whole, is charmed without
> instruction.

Gray told Nicholls that 'he never sat down to compose poetry
without reading Spenser for a considerable time previously',[4] and
it was Gray whose odes, published at Strawberry Hill by Walpole
in 1757, were a deliberate attempt to recreate the tone and
subject–matter of Gothic poetry.

The enriching of the poet's imagination as well as the illumination and pleasure of the general reader were effected by Spenser,
and these two ends were those which Shenstone had referred to as
the impression created by the early poetry which he was encouraging Percy to publish in the letter I quoted earlier. With
Thomas Warton's work we move into more clearly defined areas

of Gothic inspiration where the colleges of Oxford, and cathedrals, abbeys and castles alike summon up the visions, which were for him the province of true poetry, while through an omnivorous appetite for antiquities and a real sensitivity to the romantic elements in the poetry of Spenser and Milton he evolves for the first time an interpretation of the development of a history of English poetry.

V

In 1748 William Mason published 'Isis', an elegy attacking the political principles and the dissipation of Oxford. The following year Thomas Warton, then aged twenty-one, replied in 'The Triumph of Isis', acclaiming Oxford as a bastion of enlightenment and a haunt of the Muses:

> Green as of old each olived portal smiles,
> And still the Graces build my Grecian piles:
> My Gothic spires in ancient glory rise,
> And dare with wonted pride to rush into the skies.
>
> (77–80)

It is the Gothic aspect of Oxford rather than the Grecian which is seen as the stimulus to reflection which awakens the poetic sensibility:

> Ye fretted pinnacles, ye fanes sublime,
> Ye towers that wear the mossy vest of time;
> Ye massy piles of old munificence,
> At once the pride of learning and defence;
> Ye cloisters pale, that, lengthening to the sight,
> To contemplation, step by step, invite;
> Ye high-arch'd walks, where oft the whispers clear
> Of harps unseen have swept the poet's ear;
> Ye temples dim, where pious duty pays
> Her holy hymns of ever-echoing praise;
> Lo! your loved Isis, from the bordering vale,
> With all a mother's fondness bids you hail!
>
> (149–60)

The poet's dedication to his vision connects Spenser's *Faerie Queene* with Milton's minor poems – there is the poet's awareness of his vocation in 'Lycidas' and the indulgence in contemplation as a means of gaining access to a variety of worlds in 'Il Penseroso'. Of Milton's description of the 'embowed roof' in this last poem Warton writes in the second edition of the *Observations*:

> Impressions made in earliest youth, are ever
> afterwards most strongly felt; and I am inclin'd to
> think, that Milton was first affected with, and often
> indulged the pensive pleasure, which the awful
> solemnity of a Gothic church conveys to the mind, and
> which is here so feelingly described, while he was a
> schoolboy at St. Paul's. The church was then in its
> original Gothic state, and one of the noblest patterns
> of that kind of architecture. (ii, 135)

Such solemn glooms were congenial to the youthful Warton's soul (his first poem of note, written when he was only seventeen, is 'The Pleasures of Melancholy') as they were, he thought, to the poets he loved best.

But Warton shows, too, an awareness of the danger inherent in prolonged introspection on the part of the poet. In 'The Suicide', for example, which Goethe mentions as influencing the sensibility of young Werther, the Muse is responsible for filling the poet's 'soft ingenious mind/With many a feeling too refined' so that

> More wounds than Nature gave he knew,
> While Misery's form his fancy drew
> In dark ideal hues, and sorrows not its own.
>
> (46–7, 52–4)

Later Warton made what has been regarded as a repudiation of his allegiance to the Gothic in his 'Verses on Sir Joshua Reynolds's Painted Window at New College, Oxford' (1778). He describes himself as having been:

> A faithless truant to the classic page, –
> Long have I lov'd to catch the simple chime
> Of minstrel harps, and spell the fabling rime.
>
> (8–10)

He dwells on the attractions of the Gothic at length, whilst assigning a controlling role to those of the Grecian:

> . . . chief, enraptured have I loved to roam,
> A lingering votary, the vaulted dome,
> Where the tall shafts, that mount in massy pride,
> Their mingling branches shoot from side to side;
> Where elfin sculptors with fantastic clue,
> O'er the long roof their wild embroidery drew;
> Where Superstition, with capricious hand,
> In many a maze the wreathed window plann'd,
> With hues romantic tinged the gorgeous pane.
>
> (17–25)

But as he looks at Reynolds's window he acknowledges the power of formal design and lucidity of colour:

> Sudden, the sombrous imagery is fled,
> Which late my visionary rapture fed;
> Thy powerful hand has broke the Gothic chain,
> And brought my bosom back to truth again;
> To truth by no peculiar taste confined,
> Whose universal pattern strikes mankind;
> To truth, whose bold and unresisted aim
> Checks frail caprice, and Fashion's fickle claim;
> To truth, whose charms deception's magic quell,
> And bind coy Fancy in a stronger spell.
>
> (61–70)

In Reynolds's window the Graces are wedded to 'the Gothic pile'. The Grecian is necessary to ensure permanence of appeal in checking the subjective waywardness of individual fancy. One might perhaps see this as reflecting the two aspects of taste at this time: the public and social taste which is a matter for critical discrimination and assessment according to recognisable and generally acknowledged principles, that taste which operates to establish standards and to 'improve opinion into knowledge'; and secondly, in the taste for the Gothic, that encouragement of an actively responsive sensibility, necessary to arouse in the reader, essential to stimulate the creative energy of the poet.

But to Warton the Grecian also was a source of poetical delight. He devoted his lectures in his two terms as Professor of Poetry at

Oxford (1756–66) to Greek poetry. In his inaugural lecture he shows a sensitive awareness of what is traditionally a vitally important but at this time neglected function of poetry.

In itself, he says, the reading of poetry nourishes the faculties of man and enlarges his potentialities for assimilating different kinds of wisdom:[5]

> the man who has spent his leisure for a time on these
> more polite and refined letters will thereafter follow
> up the more exacting and abstruse literature with
> greater acumen and with a mind more nimble and
> more ready to tackle any study you wish; he has also
> prepared for himself this pleasure in which he can
> withdraw into a tranquil haven from the tension of
> thought, and in which, exhausted and over-whelmed
> by over-work he can take refuge and find rest.

This, he concludes, is because:

> We humans are so shaped in our inner selves, there
> exists in us such a kind of delicate and fastidious
> feeling, that we are by no means content with things
> as they in fact are, suffering as we do from a certain
> dryness (to confess the truth) and poverty. . . . In all
> things . . . we strive for an outward beauty and
> charm. And human nature seems to seek out this end,
> that somewhere there may be accorded a place to that
> which we call refined and tasteful.

So he enlarges on the beauties of natural scenery as the divine provision made for this end, and, as he makes clear in his edition of Theocritus (comparing the pastorals of Theocritus with those of Virgil) it is the particular selection of detail which alerts the reader to an imaginative participation in the experience evoked by such a scene. This use of detail accounts to Warton for the superiority of Theocritus. 'Virgil becomes thin and meagre where Theocritus, treating the same matter, becomes fuller, copious and richer, because Theocritus describes things fully whereas Virgil only hints at them.' The pastorals of Theocritus as compared with those of Virgil exemplify beauty as opposed to mere symmetry and refinement. 'They (the pastorals of Theocritus) were beautiful

precisely because they preserved the unevenness of actual life.'
(preface). Of the description of the cup in the first idyll Warton
comments: 'the work [on the cup] consists of pastoral images,
beautiful and brilliant. In selecting these the taste of the poet is
seen no less than his invention. . . . I easily prefer the fulness of
Theocritus to the dryness and sparseness of Virgil' (i, 5n. line 27).

And in much of his own poetry he evokes the beauty of the
natural scene with what is essentially an attempt at a similar
delicacy and exactness. Although he begins his 'Ode on the First
of April' with the conventional classical personae:

> With dalliance rude young Zephyr woos
> Coy May,

he explores their significance on a different note: Spring creeps
timidly upon the land:

> Scant along the ridgy land
> The beans their new-born ranks expand:
> The fresh-turn'd soil with tender blades
> Thinly the sprouting barley shades:
> Fringing the forest's devious edge,
> Half robed appears the hawthorn hedge;
> Or to the distant eye displays
> Weakly green its budding sprays.

(27-34)

VI

The interests which have been traced so far account for the
pattern of Warton's work. He spent his life in Oxford, where he
became Fellow of Trinity in 1750, Professor of Poetry in 1756 and
Camden Professor of Ancient History in 1785; he occupied his
leisure with his brother in Winchester College or travelling round
the country examining buildings and landmarks of architectural,
historical or legendary interest. His observations on these fill
several notebooks and are still unpublished, though some of this
work was used (in illustrating places mentioned by poets) in *The
History of English Poetry* and in his edition of Milton's *Poems on
Several Occasions*.

His work falls under three main heads. First, there is the working out of an English poetic tradition which he explored in the *Observations on the Faerie Queene* (1754); the *History* (1774, 1778 and 1781); his *Enquiry into the Authenticity of the Poems attributed to Thomas Rowley* (1782), and lastly his edition of Milton's minor poems (1785). The second group consists of work in classical literature: his edition of the *Inscriptionum Romanarum Metricarum Delectus* (1758) accompanied the delivery of his still unpublished lectures on the Greek writers to which I have already referred; the *Anthologia Graeca* appeared in 1766; and in 1770, with a prefatory essay which was an enlarged version of his lecture on pastoral poetry, his edition of Theocritus. Into the third group falls his antiquarian or topographical work: his *Description of Winchester* (1750), his *Specimen of a History of Oxfordshire* (1782), and the essay on Gothic architecture which originally appeared as part of the two-volume second edition of *Observations* (1762). The bulk of the material of the *Life and Literary Remains of Ralph Bathurst* (in two volumes, 1761), and of the *Life of Sir Thomas Pope* (1772), fall into this category, as they are closely connected with the history of the university and were produced by Warton as Fellow of Trinity under the spur of desire for preferment. There are, apart from these, odd contributions to the *Idler* – merely of entertainment value – and his popular and still amusing burlesque of the anti-quarian pedantry of the language of guidebooks, *A Companion to the Guide and a Guide to the Companion* (1760). He became Camden Professor of Ancient History in 1785 and Poet Laureate in the same year. As laureate Warton is chiefly remarkable for con-triving, as Peter Pindar noted, to slide off the Royal Occasion into Gothic inspiration with a happy and congenital irrelevance.

In *The New Rolliad* (no. 1, 1785) Warton is described as approaching the King with a 'certain hasty spasmodic mumbling, together with two or three prompt quotations from Virgil', and as associating the efficacy of his talent as laureate with 'mist, darkness, and obscurity' in connection with 'the sublime and mysterious topics' he touches on in his odes (pp. 284, 206–7). Throughout his career there is a continual intermingling of his different interests so that the sensitivity of the poet often guides the researches of the antiquarian and the concern for the standards of taste and exactness of scholarship augments the delight in the exuberance of fancy.

VII

Having given a retrospective account of English poetry before Spenser in *Observations* Warton adds: 'from the age of Spenser, we shall find, that it (poetry) principally consisted in visions and allegories. Fancy was a greater friend to the dark ages, as they are called, than is commonly supposed' (ii, 101–2). He appends a note: 'This subject may, probably, be one day considered more at large in a regular history.'

His work on the Greek poets, and his researches into manuscript material, collating texts or consulting editions on Percy's behalf as well as his own – in a letter to Shenstone of 1762 Percy refers to Warton's sparing no pains in pursuing this kind of research – encouraged this ambition. In a letter to Percy in 1765 Warton expresses his intention of writing the history, and asserts that his materials for it are 'almost ready'.

In 1766 Warton informs Percy that he has had to lay the work aside to prepare the edition of Theocritus which had been commenced in 1758, but in July 1768 he declares the publication of the edition imminent and promises himself 'another Excursion into Fairy Land'. In the following year he declares: 'I am sitting down in good Earnest to write the History of English Poetry. It will be a large work; but as variety of materials have been long collected, it will be soon completed.'[6]

The preface to the *History* itself suggests that Warton's intention is eminently orthodox:

> In an age advanced to the highest degrees of
> refinement, that species of curiosity commences, which
> is busied in contemplating the progress of social life,
> in displaying the gradations of science, and in tracing
> the transitions from barbarism to civility.

Warton proceeds to insist on the sense of achievement which this must necessarily encourage, but apart from this social purpose there is another:

> In the mean time, the manners, monuments, customs,
> practices, and opinions of antiquity, by forming so
> strong a contrast with those of our own times, and by
> exhibiting human nature and human inventions in

new lights, in unexpected appearances, and in various forms, are objects which forcibly strike a feeling imagination.

This development in the argument is immediately checked, however: 'Nor does this spectacle afford nothing more than a fruitless gratification to the fancy.' The element of delight in the fancy and exuberance of earlier poetry is to be kept under the control of the social purpose of the history – to educate the public taste.

But the end of the third volume, published in 1781, saw Warton embarking on a 'general View and Character of the Poetry of Queen Elisabeth's age' and the few sheets of the fourth volume printed in his lifetime contained only an account of the satires of Marston and Hall. Other manuscript material was found to contain an account of the Elizabethan sonnet, but it seems a reasonable conclusion that Warton had little inclination to bring the historical account of English poetry beyond the Elizabethan period. His biographer, Richard Mant, considers the nature of the task remaining to be completed:

> The next part of his employment was to have been a particular examination of this, our Augustan age of Poetry; and having, like Aeneas, surmounted the difficulties, and escaped from the obscurity, of Tartarus, he was now about to enter on the Elysian fields . . . But notwithstanding the enjoyment of these scenes must have been so congenial to his mind; though in his first edition of Milton's juvenile poems in 1785 he announces that speedily will be published the fourth and last volume of the History of English Poetry; and though four years had elapsed since the publication of the third volume, and five years afterwards elapsed between this notice and his death, the work (from what cause it does not appear) was never completed: whether it was that the long duration of the same employment had in the end occasioned disgust; or whether his subsequent attention was nearly engrossed by Milton, and thus diverted from the masters to their greater disciple . . . Certain . . . it is, that the work was never brought to a conclusion, though the completion of it would have entitled him to the receipt

of a considerable sum: and there is reason to believe,
that not much was written beyond what is in the
possession of the public. (pp. l–li)

It was, in fact (as the reviewer of Mant's biography in the
Edinburgh Review to some extent realised), Warton's last work, the
edition of Milton's minor poems, which provided some kind of
conclusion – and indeed the only one which was logical – to the
massive undertaking of the *History*. Referring to the edition of
Milton's poems, the reviewer concludes: 'These commentaries
and his observations on Spenser, may now be regarded as in some
degree supplemental to his great unfinished work on English
poetry' (ii, 258).

The drift of Warton's comments on these poems reveals a
preoccupation with Milton as a neglected old English poet, the
inheritor of the fictions and fable of his predecessors, of the story of
'Cambuscan bold, Of Camball and of Algarsife', of 'masque and
antique pageantry'. It was this which attracted Warton in the
poetry of Milton, and it was almost certainly through these early
poems that part at least of the magic and enchantment which were
for Warton associated with the literature of the age of chivalry
and superstition made its appeal. Warton's emphasis on the way
in which Gothic and classical myth and legend go side by side
in Milton's poetry is a continuation of and a fitting chronological
conclusion to the interpretation of the nature of poetry which
emerges from the three completed volumes of the *History*.

VIII

This is to some degree confirmed by the way in which Warton
insisted on seeing the history of poetry evolve, a way which, as he
knew, ran counter to the interpretations of Pope and Gray.

Outlines for the *History* exist in four different forms: the first is a
brief sketch among Warton's manuscript annotations to his copy
of the *Faerie Queene*; the second is the general survey of the development of poetry to the eighteenth century given in the *Observations*;
the third was printed from the Trinity College MSS. by Clarissa
Rinaker; and the fourth occurs in Warton's reply to a letter from
Hurd which had contained Gray's plan for a history.

The first is a note in Warton's hand on the blank leaf facing the title page of 'Prothalamion':

> The Rise and Progress of Allegoric Poetry in England
> 'till it's Consummation in Spenser, & it's Decline
> after him. We have the visionary Poet, or
> personification before P. Plowman, who drew it from
> the Troubadours. After him came Chaucer, Gower,
> Lidgate, (Harding) Barclay, Hawes, Skelton bad.
> Sackville, Spenser and effects ended with Fletcher.

The account in the *Observations* begins:

> If we take a retrospect of english poetry from the age
> of Spenser, we shall find that it principally consisted
> in the allegoric species; but that this species never
> received its absolute consummation till it appeared
> with new lustre in the Faerie Queene . . . (ii, 101)

Chaucer's invention and humour, Lydgate's improvements in versification are considered; then Warton comes to Stephen Hawes – 'a name generally unknown, and not mentioned by any compiler of the lives of english poets':

> This author was at this period the restorer of invention,
> which seems to have suffered a gradual degeneracy
> from the days of Chaucer. He not only revived, but
> improved, the antient allegoric vein, which Hardyng
> had almost entirely banished. Instead of that dryness of
> description, so remarkably disgusting in many of his
> predecessors, we are by this poet often entertained
> with the luxuriant effusions of Spenser. (ii, 104)

The rise of classical studies in the reign of Henry VIII is related to a group of scholars 'and the Greek language, in which are reposited the treasures of true learning now began to be taught and admir'd'; with Skelton poetry made no advances in versification, nor was his allegorical poetry remarkable. Reference is made to the allegorising successes of Lindsay and Dunbar, and to those of Sackville as the precursor of Spenser. But:

> After the Fairy Queen, allegory began to decline,
> and by degrees gave way to a species of poetry whose

images were of the metaphysical and abstracted kind.
This fashion evidently took it's rise from the
predominant studies of the times.

Allegory, notwithstanding, unexpectedly rekindled
some faint sparks of its native splendor, in the
PURPLE ISLAND of Fletcher, with whom it almost as
soon disappeared: when a poetry succeeded, in which
imagination gave way to correctness, sublimity of
description to delicacy of sentiment, and majestic
imagery to conceit and epigram.

And he diagnoses the situation as it has affected the poetry of his
contemporaries:

Poets began now to be more attentive to words than to
things and objects. The nicer beauties of happy
expression were preferred to the daring strokes of
great conception. Satire, that bane of the sublime,
was imported from France. . . . The muses were
debauched at court, and polite life, and familiar
manners, became their only themes . . . The simple
dignity of Milton was either entirely neglected, or
mistaken for bombast and insipidity by the refined
readers of a dissolute age, whose taste and morals were
equally vitiated. (ii, 110–12)

It is in the second edition, in which Warton had clearly become
more confident of his own taste, that he explicitly associates the
rise of satire with this decline. After 'daring strokes of great
conception', Warton adds 'Satire, that bane of the sublime, was
imported from France'. He omits from the opening pages of the
second edition a reference to the 'bad taste' which prevailed
when Spenser began to write the *Faerie Queene*, and he softens his
earlier condemnation of Spenser's choosing to model his work on
that of Ariosto rather than Tasso – Ariosto's superior in 'conduct
and decorum'. Between 1754 and 1762 the attitude towards things
Gothic, strange or fanciful had clearly moved from a condemnation of its uncouth barbarism to what was at least an interested
curiosity.

The structuring of each account in terms of allegorical poetry is
the most obvious feature too of the third sketch – a plan which

was probably drafted some time in the 'fifties, as it repeats the reference to bad taste prevailing before Spenser which was rephrased to indicate a more neutral approach in the 1762 edition. Clarissa Rinaker comments that this draft is probably for the first volume as it was originally planned. The first item – the plan is again chronological in outline – refers to the Druids and Bards; the second to 'Pierce Plowman' as 'the first Allegorical Poem in our Tongue'; in the third Warton describes how 'The Allegoric inventive Vein seem'd in a little time to be lost'; fourth comes the revival of learning and the rise of polished verse with Wyatt and Surrey; lastly, 'A fine harvest of Poësy now shew'd itself in Q. Elizabeth's reign'.

IX

In 1770 Gray wrote, at Hurd's request, to Warton, who was by this time far advanced in his preparation of the first volume, offering his own sketch of a history and enquiring whether it corresponded with anything in Warton's own approach:[7]

> few of your friends have been better pleased than I,
> to find this subject, surely neither unentertaining nor
> unuseful, had fallen into hands so likely to do it
> justice; few have felt a higher esteem for your talents,
> your taste, and industry.

Gray's scheme is based on Pope's, which had appeared in Ruffhead's *Life* in 1769. It introduces the subject with a survey of Gothic and Saxon poetry. Gray bases his account on the assumption that there were different schools of poets, first, that of Provence to which Chaucer and his successors belonged; the second, the Italian school, which in turn influenced the lyric poetry of Surrey and his contemporaries. Next, in a fourth section, he deals with

> Spenser, his character: subject of his poem, allegoric
> and romantic, or Provençal invention; but his manner
> of tracing it borrowed from the second Italian School.
> – Drayton, Fairfax, Phineas Fletcher, Golding, Phaer,
> &c. This school ends in Milton. – A third Italian

school, full of conceit, begun in Queen Elizabeth's
reign, continued under James and Charles the First,
by Donne, Crashaw, Cleveland, carried to its height by
Cowley, and ending perhaps in Sprat.

Part V

School of France, introduced after the Restoration –
Waller, Dryden, Addison, Prior, and Pope – which
has continued to our own times.

Walpole felt after reading Warton's *History* that Gray's plan
had not been superseded and would have been far superior; and
although Warton is writing after completing only the first volume
it is obvious that this more systematic approach in terms of
schools, influences and kinds of writing might have produced a
more satisfactory treatment of the ways in which writing poetry in
English had developed. Warton replied in a letter which raises
points of considerable interest, while revealing his complete lack
of grasp of the overall structuring his material would require:[8]

Although I have not followed the plan, yet it is of
great service to me, and throws light on many of my
periods by giving connected views and details. I begin
with such an introduction or general dissertation
as you had intended, viz. on the Northern Poetry,
with its introduction into England by the Danes and
Saxons, and its duration. I then begin my history of
the Conquest, which I write chronologically in sections,
and continue as matter successively offers itself, in a
series of regular annals, down to and beyond the
Restoration. I think with you that dramatic poetry is
detached from the idea of my work, that it requires a
separate consideration and will swell the size of my
book beyond all bounds. One of my sections, a very
large one, is entirely on Chaucer, and will almost
make my first volume, for I design two volumes in
quarto. This first volume will soon be in the press. I
should have said before that though I proceed
chronologically, yet I often stand still to give some
general view, as perhaps of a particular species of

poetry, etc., and even anticipate sometimes for this purpose. These views often form one section, yet are interwoven with the tenor of the work, without interrupting my historical series. In this respect some of my sections have the effect of your parts or divisions.

The first three outlines of his survey show that what the letter to Gray implies has indeed happened. Warton is not so much concerned with historical developments in poetry, but with charting the fortunes of a type of poetry – that allegorical and inventive vein – which had for him the greatest appeal. His grounds for not employing the schemes of Pope or Gray he later enlarged on:

> To confess the real truth, upon examination and experiment, I soon discovered their mode of treating my subject, plausible as it is and brilliant in theory, to be attended with difficulties and inconveniences. . . . Like other ingenious systems, it sacrifices much useful intelligence to the observance of arrangement; and in the place of that satisfaction, which arises from a clearness and a fulness of information, seemed only to substitute the merit of disposition, and the praise of contrivance. The constraint imposed by a mechanical attention to this distribution, appeared to me to destroy that free exertion of research, with which such a history ought to be executed, and not easily reconcileable with that complication, variety, and extent of materials, which it ought to comprehend.
> (*Mant*, i, lxii–iii)

Warton's chief concern is not with standards or theories, but with research into, and making his readers acquainted with, the chief elements in that vein of poetic inspiration which had helped to produce England's greatest national poets. And this in consequence would improve the taste of his time.

X

Warton's plan for the *Observations* is based on an acceptance of current tools of analysis – the ways in which the author to be considered has imitated the work of his predecessors; the relationship between his style and his subject; and the chief characteristics of his poetry – in this case the allegorical. Spenser's indebtedness to the classical and Italian poets had received consideration from Warton's predecessors, Hughes and Upton. But, as Johnson noted in the letter I quoted earlier, Warton realised that a mass of popular romance and ballad material had been accessible to the poet. Employing therefore, an already accepted method of investigation Warton opened fresh perspectives of knowledge and established a new kind of relevance for popular literature and for the researches of the antiquarians.

For after establishing Spenser's indebtedness to the manners of chivalry and the literature of romance in section 10, 'Of Spenser's Allegorical Character', Warton goes on to mention the effects of public entertainments of his time on the invention of the allegory:

> Nor is it sufficiently consider'd, that a prevalent
> practice of Spenser's age contributed in a very
> considerable degree to make him an ALLEGORICAL POET.
> It should be remember'd that, in the age of which we
> are speaking, allegory was the subject and foundation of
> public shews and spectacles, which were then exhibited
> with a magnificence superior to that of former times; that
> the vices and virtues personify'd and represented by
> living actors, distinguish'd with their representative
> emblematical types, were generally introduc'd to
> constitute PAGEANTRIES, which were then the principal
> entertainments, and shewn not only in private, and
> upon the stage, but very frequently in the open streets,
> for solemnising any public occasion. (pp. 217–18)

Warton refers to Holinshed's description of the 'SHEW OF MAN-HOOD AND DESERT' at Norwich, and of a 'TURNEY' at Westminster. He draws the conclusion that 'Spenser's manner of allegorizing seems to have rather resulted from some of the spectacles just-mention'd, than from what he had red in Ariosto'. The researches of the antiquarian are demonstrated as necessary to a true understanding of the fabric of what was becoming more clearly recognisable as a complex and broad national literary heritage.

Warton points out that Spenser uses the allegory as a moral

vehicle in the manner of Ariosto in book 1, but that his characteristic method is different from Ariosto's:

> In fact, Ariosto's species of Allegory does not so much
> consist in impersonating the virtues, vices, and
> affections of the mind, as in the adumbration of moral
> doctrine, under the actions of men and women. On
> this plan Spenser's allegories are sometimes formed: as
> in the first book, where the Red-crosse Knight or a
> TRUE CHRISTIAN . . . defeats the wiles of Archimago,
> or the DEVIL, &c. (pp. 219–20)

And he adds a footnote:

> It is observed by Plutarch, that 'Allegory is that, in
> which one thing is *related* and another *understood*'.
> Thus Ariosto RELATES the adventures of Orlando,
> Rogero, Bradamante, &c. by which is UNDERSTOOD the
> conquest of the passions, the importance of virtue, and
> other moral doctrines; on which account we may call
> the ORLANDO a MORAL poem; but can we call the
> FAIRY QUEEN upon the whole a MORAL poem? is it not
> equally an HISTORICAL or POLITICAL poem? For though
> it may be, according to it's author's words, an
> ALLEGORY or DARK CONCEIT, yet that which is
> couched or understood under this allegory is the
> history, and intrigues, of queen Elizabeth's courtiers;
> which however are introduced with a Moral design.
> (p. 219n.)

For Warton the allegory of Spenser is peculiarly rich and
abundant: it is not merely a narration which can be given
interpretative gloss – as Plutarch had defined allegory and as
Ariosto had practised it. Nourished on the pageantry and romance
literature of his time, Spenser's imagination, peculiarly susceptible,
like that of all great artists, to the dominant modes of statement
of his age, became steeped in symbolic forms of expression so that
his poetry was not a direct representation but an imaginative
transformation of the experience available to him. In this Warton's
approach to Spenser resembles his observations on the excellence
of Theocritus as compared to Virgil in the pastoral. The details

of either allegory or pastoral are so presented that an ideal world is rendered real to the imagination of the reader. The tension between form and subject is resolved without, as in Ariosto or Virgil, the importance of the formal concerns dominating the experience offered by the poem. This is achieved by combining the natural representation of particularised and concrete detail to suggest the texture of real life to the reader with the formal structuring of that experience to produce a significant whole. And as the very use of allegorical form guarantees the intention on the poet's part of conveying to the reader some general, abstract truth, so the form or forms in which the allegory is cast may employ all the fantastic and beguiling creativity of the poet without the validity of a central theme being undermined, any more than the ebullient fantastic forms of Gothic architecture detracted from the awareness of the intention with which the building had been erected. The mind is led to ponder on the general theme by being alerted to responsiveness by local and specific details which the poet depicts.

It will be remembered that Warton sees a decline in poetry as 'Poets began . . . to be more attentive to words than to things and objects'. Following on the references to the indebtedness of Spenser to the spectacles and entertainments he saw for his allegory, Warton makes an important statement about the relationship between poetry and reality, beginning, it is true, conventionally enough:

> he [Spenser] has shewn himself a much more ingenious allegorist, where his IMAGINATION BODIES forth unsubstantial things, TURNS THEM TO SHAPE, and marks out the nature, powers, and effects of that which is ideal and abstracted, by visible and external symbols; as in his delineation of FEAR, ENVY, FANCY, DESPAIR, and the like. Ariosto gives us but few of these symbolical beings, in comparison of Spenser; and those which he has given us, are by no means drawn with that fullness and distinctness with which they are painted by the latter. And that Spenser painted these figures so fully and distinctly, may we not reasonably attribute it, to his being so frequently habituated to the sight of these symbolical beings, distinguished with

their proper emblems, and actually endued with
speech, motion, and life? (p. 220)

The principle is the same as that employed when he referred to
the impact of Gothic architecture on the youthful imagination of
Milton. It follows that Spenser's failures and inconsistencies – to
which an entire section of the *Observations* is devoted – are not
Warton's central concern. His chief interest is in showing how the
poet's mind was so furnished that it could excel in true poetry.
And it was the conditions in the age of Elizabeth which had
produced the fine harvest of poetry to which he refers in his
outline sketch for *History*.

XI

In his account of *Early English Stages, 1300–1576* (1959), Glynne
Wickham considers the modes of statement inherent in experience
offered by the pageant theatres which were erected in the streets
of a city to welcome a royal visitor:

> The nature of their content was sermon, spectacular
> and dramatic, the significance of which was
> specifically directed at the visitor but which the
> occasion caused author, actors and audience to share
> alike. In consequence of all these facts, thematic
> content took precedence over everything else in the
> construction of both text and spectacle. Where topical
> subject matter was inevitably of so personal a kind,
> courtesy, if nothing else, forbade bald statement.
> Instead, it suggested allegorical treatment. This could
> be scriptural, historical, mythological or whatever best
> fitted the occasion and justifies the remarks which
> Warton made in his *History of English Poetry* and which
> I quote in full since they appear to have sustained
> such unwarrantable neglect from subsequent historians
> of our drama:
> 'It seems probable that the PAGEANTS, which being
> shown on civil occasions, derived great part of their
> decoration and actors from historical fact, and

consequently made profane characters the subject of
public exhibition, dictated ideas of a regular drama
much sooner that the MYSTERIES; which being confined
to scripture stories, or rather the legendary miracles of
sainted martyrs, and the no less ideal personifications
of the christian virtues, were not calculated to make so
quick and easy a transition to the representations
of real life and rational action.' (pp. 62–3)

The variety of allegorical modes available, to which Professor
Wickham refers, was related to Spenser's allegorising by Warton
in the passage which I have already quoted from the *Observations*.
The closer the parallel to actual existence for the reader, the more
flexible the modes of treatment of that reality available to the
writer. It was historical fact that mattered:

Witches were thought really to exist in the age of
Queen Elizabeth, and our author had, probably, been
struck with seeing such a cottage as this, in which a
witch was supposed to live. Those who have perus'd
Mr. Blackwall's Enquiry into the Life and Writings
of Homer, will be best qualified to judge how much
better enabled that poet is to describe, who copies
from living objects, than he who describes, in a later
age, from tradition. (p. 267)

Warton's motivation in assembling the 'mass of raw materials
which Scott saw as preliminary to writing a history' rather than
as itself constituting the *History of English Poetry*, is, then, to
accumulate evidences of a tradition of true poetry and the
conditions of the ages from which it emerged. So in the second
edition of the *Observations* he concludes an account of the decora-
tions of various buildings with the sudden remark:

Taste and imagination make more antiquarians, than
the world is willing to allow. One looks back with
romantic pleasure on the arts and fashions of an age,
which

> Employ'd the power of fairy hands.   (ii, 234)

– a quotation from Gray which emphasises the bond of antiquarian enthusiasm which they shared.

XII

It is characteristic of Warton that from an apparently common-place standpoint he arrives at a surprising delicacy and subtlety of insight. The material available to the poet is of course modified by his characteristic responses to his environment. So in the section rather unpromisingly headed 'Of Spenser's Imitations of Himself', we have first the commonsense assertion that while the tracing of borrowings from other authors which Warton had dealt with so far is

> a business which proceeds upon an uncertain
> foundation, affording the amusement of conjecture
> rather than the satisfaction of truth; it may perhaps
> be a more serviceable undertaking, to produce an
> author's IMITATIONS OF HIMSELF: and this will be more
> particularly useful in the three following respects, viz.
> It will discover the FAVORITE IMAGES of an author; it
> will teach us how VARIOUSLY he expresses the same
> thought; and it will often EXPLAIN DIFFICULT passages,
> and words. (p. 181)

From a discussion of various passages he concludes that Spenser 'particularly excels in painting affright, confusion, and astonishment'. But Warton does not rest content with this generalisation. The poetry of Spenser conveys to him a certain quality of mind of the author, providing indeed a clue to that bent of disposition which causes the poet to dwell on certain kinds of experience and intensities of feeling. Of the account of Despair in book 1 Warton remarks:

> It is a trite observation, that we paint that best, which
> we have felt most. Spenser's whole life seems to have
> consisted of disappointments and distress; so that he
> probably was not unacquainted with the bitter agonies
> of a despairing mind, which the warmth of his
> imagination, and, what was its consequence, his
> sensibility of temper contributed to render doubly
> severe. Unmerited and unpitied indigence ever
> struggles hardest with true genius; and a good taste, for
> the same reasons that it enhances the pleasures of life,

sustains with uncommon tortures the miseries of that
state, in which (says an incomparable moralist) 'every
virtue is obscured, and in which no conduct can avoid
reproach; a state in which cheerfulness is
insensibility, and dejection sullenness, of which the
hardships are without honour, and the labours
without reward'. (pp. 193–4)

But while each bent of the creative mind is different, and poets
may suffer in a variety of ways, the prospects offered by antiquarianism are limitless and, given Warton's assumptions,
invariably rewarding. For him the unfolding of a *History of Poetry*
will inevitably be an investigation into the records of the past
combined with responsiveness to that poetry which delights
him most and this will be intermingled with antiquarian digression and extensive transcription.

XIII

In the preface to his *History* Warton shows above all a sense of his
obligation to his public:

We look back on the savage conditions of our ancestors
with the triumph of superiority; we are pleased to
mark the steps by which we have been raised from
rudeness to elegance: and our reflections on this
subject are accompanied with a conscious pride,
arising in great measure from a tacit comparison
between the feeble efforts of remote ages, and our
present improvements in knowledge.

But, none the less, to appreciate present achievements it is
necessary to gain insight into the manners of the past:

to develop the dawnings of genius, and to pursue the
progress of our national poetry, from a rude origin and
obscure beginnings, to its perfection in a polished age,
must prove an interesting and instructive investigation.
But a history of poetry, for another reason, yet on the
same principles, must be more especially productive of
entertainment and utility. I mean, as it is an art, whose

object is human society: as it has the peculiar merit,
in its operations on that object, of faithfully recording
the features of the times, and of preserving the most
picturesque and expressive representations of manners.
(pp. ii–iii)

So although the overt aim of the work is to improve his readers'
knowledge of the past, and extend their awareness of present
achievements and past ways of life, of different modes of thinking
and feeling, Warton soon discloses in discussing his plan where the
main emphasis of his work is to lie. He refers to his decision not to
employ the schemes of Gray or Pope on the grounds that:

The constraint imposed by a mechanical attention to
this distribution (of materials in Schools) appeared to
me to destroy that free exertion of research with
which such a history ought to be executed, and not
easily reconcilable with that complication, variety, and
extent of materials, which it ought to comprehend.
    The method I have pursued, on one account at
least, seems preferable to all others. My performance,
in its present form, exhibits without transposition the
gradual improvements of our poetry, at the same time
as it uniformly presents the progression of our language.
(p. v)

Unlike Gray he feels that the drama cannot properly be excluded:
though it can only of necessity be given a subordinate place in his
account, yet 'I flatter myself . . . that from evidences hitherto
unexplored, I have recovered hints which may facilitate the
labours of those, who shall hereafter be inclined to investigate the
antient state of dramatic exhibition in this country, with due
comprehension and accuracy' (p. vii). He defends himself in
advance against accusations of prolixity in quotation: 'it should
be remembered, that most of these are extracted from antient
manuscript poems never before printed, and hitherto but little
known. Nor was it easy to illustrate the darker and more distant
period of our poetry without producing ample specimens.'

In the mean time, I hope to merit the thanks of the
antiquarian, for enriching the stock of our early
literature by these new accessions: and I trust I shall

> gratify the reader of taste, in having so frequently
> rescued from oblivion the rude inventions and
> irregular beauties of the heroic tale, or the romantic
> legend. (p. viii)

The purpose of the *History* as he sees it at the beginning is to unearth discoveries, not to pursue an overall interpretation. It is not surprising that over a quarter of the first volume (the pages are not numbered) should consist of the two digressions which Warton asserts will consider 'some material points of a general and preliminary nature', and will at the same time 'endeavour to establish certain fundamental principles to which frequent appeals might occasionally be made, and to clear the way for various observations arising in the course of my future enquiries'. The two digressions are 'On the Origin of Romantic Fiction in Europe' and 'On the Introduction of Learning into England'. These two topics serve to indicate, as Warton claims, his main lines of investigation.

XIV

Whereas Percy had opened the *Reliques* with an account of the importance of the minstrels, Warton is concerned with the ways in which the fantasies of the romantic imagination reached Europe. The interpretation offered by Warburton, which had relied on the impact of the Saracens on the Spanish culture, was undermined by Percy's investigations into the dating of Spanish romance material. Warton quickly arrives at the fund of legend held in common by Celtic speakers: the stories of Wales and Brittany strongly resemble one another. Consequently on the fourth page of his Dissertation he observes that Milton 'mentions indiscriminately' the knights of Wales and Armorica as the customary retinue of king Arthur:

> – What resounds
> In fable or romance, of Uther's son
> Begirt with BRITISH and ARMORIC knights'.

He refers to *Ossian* as evidence of the intermingling of different influences:

It is indeed very remarkable, that in these poems the
terrible graces, which so naturally characterise, and
so generally constitute, the early poetry of barbarous
people, should so frequently give way to a gentler set
of manners, to the social sensibilities of polished life,
and a more civilised and elegant species of imagination.
Nor is this circumstance, which disarranges all our
established ideas concerning the savage stages of society,
easily to be accounted for, unless we suppose, that the
Celtic tribes, who were so strongly addicted to poetical
composition, and who made it so much their duty from the
earliest times, might by degrees have attained a higher
vein of poetical refinement, than could at first sight or
on common principles be expected among nations,
whom we are accustomed to call barbarous; that some
few instances of an elevated strain of friendship, of
love, and other sentimental feelings, existing in such
nations, might lay the foundations for introducing a
set of manners among the bards, more refined and
exalted than the real manners of the country; and that
panegyrics on those virtues, transmitted with
improvements from bard to bard, must at length have
formed characters of ideal excellence, which might
propagate among the people real manners bordering
on the poetical.

He cites Blair's defence of *Ossian*, and refers (in a note) with some
respect to Macpherson's. But Warton is mainly concerned with
establishing relationships between early literatures in which a
love of the marvellous and supernatural is manifested. So he
proceeds:

These poems, however, notwithstanding the difference
between the Gothic and the Celtic rituals, contain
many visible vestiges of Scandinavian superstition. The
allusions in the songs of Ossian to spirits, who preside
over the different parts and direct the various
operations of nature . . . entirely correspond with the
Runic system, and breathe the spirit of its poetry.

In support of this he cites instances from Olaus Wormius and

Olaus Magnus, as well as from Bartholin's *De Contemptu Mortis apud Daniis*, and the 'Hervarer Saga'. Tacitus joins Diodorus Siculus and Joannes Aventinus, Posidonius and Aelian in notes to support Warton's assertions concerning the subject matter of Scandinavian poetry. The giants, dragons and fairies on the other hand are attributed to Arabian influence, and their absence from the poems of Ossian is for Warton 'a striking proof of their antiquity'. The work of Evans is cited in confirmation of the absence of fantastic marvels of this kind from the productions of the ancient Welsh bards. And so he comes to his conclusion:

> Amid the gloom of superstition, in an age of the
> grossest ignorance and credulity, a taste for the
> wonders of Oriental fiction was introduced by the
> Arabians into Europe, many countries of which were
> already seasoned to a reception of its extravagancies,
> by means of the poetry of the Gothic scalds, who
> perhaps originally derived their ideas from the same
> fruitful region of invention. These fictions, coinciding
> with the reigning manners, and perpetually kept up
> and improved in the tales of troubadours and ministrels,
> seem to have centred about the eleventh century in the
> ideal histories of Turpin and Geoffrey of Monmouth,
> which record the supposititious achievements of
> Charlemagne and King Arthur, where they formed the
> ground-work of that species of fabulous narrative
> called romance. And from these beginnings, or causes,
> afterwards enlarged and enriched by kindred fancies
> fetched from the crusades, that singular and capricious
> mode of imagination arose, which at length composed
> the marvellous machineries of the more sublime
> Italian poets, and of their disciple Spenser.

The climax of fine fablings is exemplified in Spenser, so that control of the imagination by the judgment which is necessitated for the advance of society and the improvement of civilised life is achieved through the acquisition of wisdom. Hence the second dissertation deals, sequentially, with the introduction of learning into England.

Warton traces here the impact of the barbarian invasions on the Roman civilisation, the incursion of the Gothic disorder into

Roman 'peace and civility'. But not only did the Goths have the opportunity to acquire some degree of wisdom from their conquests: Warton observes that

> Their enemies have been their historians, who naturally painted these violent disturbers of the general repose in the warmest colours. It is not easy to conceive, that the success of their amazing enterprizes was merely the effect of numbers and tumultuary depredation. . . . Superior strength and courage must have contributed in a considerable degree to their rapid and extensive conquests; but at the same time, such mighty achievements could not have been planned and executed without some extraordinary vigour of mind, uniform principles of conduct, and no common talents of political sagacity.

Meantime Latin poetry had lapsed into barbarism – 'From the growing increase of christianity, it was deprived of its old fabulous embellishments, and chiefly employed in composing ecclesiastical hymns.' In monasteries, however, the spark of knowledge was kept alive, and with increasing stability libraries began to grow and learning again to flourish. Warton's attitude towards his material is shown when he considers the work of Bede: 'It is diverting', he writes, referring to the *Mélanges d'Histoire et de Littérature* (Paris, 1725) of 'Monsieur de Vigneul Marville',

> to see the French critics censuring Bede for credulity: they might as well have accused him of superstition. . . . He has recorded but few civil transactions: but besides that his history professedly considers ecclesiastical affairs, we should remember, that the building of a church, the preferment of an abbot, the canonisation of a martyr, and the importation into England of the shinbone of an apostle, were necessarily matters of much more importance in Bede's conceptions than histories or revolutions. He is fond of minute descriptions; but particularities are the fault and often the merit of early historians.

And earlier:

His knowledge, if we consider his age, was extensive
and profound: and it is amazing, in so rude a period,
and during a life of no considerable length, he should
have made so successful a progress, and such rapid
improvements, in scientific and philological studies,
and have composed so many elaborate treatises on
different subjects.

The deployment of an historical imagination is characteristic of
Warton's best work. Again, in the conclusion to the Dissertation,
he insists on the ways in which civilising influences may not
necessarily foster the growth of a civilising literature. In the
medieval period he sees in the growth of civil and canonical laws
an encouragement to pedantry and casuistry in the universities,
where jurisprudence 'was treated with the same spirit of idle
speculation which had been carried into philosophy and theology,
it was overwhelmed with endless commentaries which disclaimed
all elegance of language, and served only to exercise genius, as it
afforded materials for framing the flimsy labyrinths of casuistry.'
But, in any case, in spite of an increase of learning:

> The habits of superstition and ignorance were as yet
> too powerful for a reformation of this kind to be affected
> by a few polite scholars. It was necessary that many
> circumstances and events, yet in the womb of time,
> should take place, before the minds of men could be so
> far enlightened as to receive these improvements.

And he returns to his main theme before beginning the *History*
proper:

> But perhaps inventive poetry lost nothing by this
> relapse. Had classical taste and judgment been now
> established, imagination would have suffered, and too
> early a check would have been given to the beautiful
> extravagancies of romantic fabling. In a word, truth
> and reason would have chased before their time those
> spectres of illusive fancy, so pleasing to the imagination,
> which delight to hover in the gloom of ignorance and
> superstition, and which form so considerable a part of
> the poetry of the succeeding centuries.

XV

The experience of reading the *History* has been variously described as 'wading rather than reading' and as being guided by the 'torch of genius through ruins in which he [Warton] loves to wander'. The grounds for such apparently conflicting verdicts should by now have become clear. For Gibbon the *History* combined 'the taste of a poet with the minute diligence of an antiquarian':[9] and whereas the concern of the poet is with that poetry of the past which advanced the art of verse and at the same time awakened the imaginative response of the modern reader, the business of the antiquarian is with the reproduction of obscure material which illuminated the life of the past in which those poets wrote. It is the critic or man of taste who attempts to unite both interests, and this role of Warton's as professor and Poet Laureate is too often forgotten. Warton places his concern with poetry and manners, however, before any questioning of critical assumptions. It is on this account that his work suffers from a lack of discrimination between poets of very different levels of achievement but at the same time and for the same reason benefits from what is essentially a free exertion of research. In the infancy of historical accounts of poetry it was of greater importance to extend the imaginative awareness of the reader than to utter precepts and demarcate schools and influences and traditions.

Warton employs the greater part of his first volume in quoting from various romances of chivalry, and in giving accounts of contemporary pageants and miracle plays. He proceeds to *Piers Plowman* and Langland's use of personification and allegory, then to Chaucer, whose work marks at once the advent of pathos into literature and of some elegance and refinement into the vernacular. The lengthy appreciation devoted to Chaucer and the comparison of his work with that of his originals serves to emphasise the national genius of the poet and offers the best criticism of his work since Dryden.

But the expectations which were aroused by the first volume were not answered by the second. Although he begins with a valuable account of Gower, Occleve and Lydgate, emphasising considerations of style, dwelling appreciatively on passages of natural description and noting any indebtedness to romance material, Warton goes on to a protracted and detailed account of fifteenth-century translations from the classics into French and English, from Harding and the Lives of the Saints to Hawes, Skelton, the Scottish poets and the moralities and mysteries, with a digression on the acting of plays in schools and universities. It is disappointing that the Renaissance is described almost entirely in terms of the revival of learning, the increase in translations, the endowment of schools and colleges (material which Warton had employed in his lives of Pope and Bathurst), so that any element of exposition is buried beneath a mass of recorded detail. Vast tracts of this volume disappointed Warton's contemporaries by their dullness:

> The learned and ingenious Writer [comments the
> *Monthly* reviewer] has prosecuted his respectable
> labours with great assiduity, but, possibly, with too
> much prolixity. On that account only it is to be feared
> that his valuable book may become the solitary
> inhabitant of *consulted* libraries. . . . there is to certain
> minds a charm in the investigation of antiquity, which
> is not easily dissolved: and it is no wonder if, in tracing
> the progress of ancient genius, a writer whose pursuits
> have been congenial with his subject, should loiter in the
> fairy region through which he passes. (lix, 132)

XVI

The principal interest of this volume, however, was the lengthy dissertation on the Rowley poems. For although Warton goes so far as to say that if they were indeed authentic they might be considered to have redeemed the poetic reputation of the fifteenth century, he states at the beginning of his account that 'there are some circumstances which incline us to suspect these pieces to be a modern forgery' (p. 139). The sensitivity to different poetic modes of statement which was present in the comments on *Ossian* quoted earlier, is now brought to bear on the different aspects of Chatterton's forgeries. The Epistle prefixed to *The Tragedy of Aella* commends 'SOME GREAT STORY OF HUMAN MANNERS', as most suitable for theatrical presentation. But, says Warton:

this idea is the result of that taste and discrimination, which could only belong to a more advanced period of society.

But, above all, the cast of thought, the complexion of the sentiments, and the structure of the composition evidently prove these pieces not antient. (pp. 155–6)

And if the obsolete language be offered as proof:

As to his knowledge of the old English literature, which is rarely the study of a young poet, a sufficient quantity of obsolete words and phrases were readily attainable from the glossary to Chaucer, and to Percy's Ballads. It is confessed, that this youth wrote the *Execution of Sir Charles Bawdwin*: and he who could forge that poem, might easily forge all the rest. (p. 157)

Warton does not allow his sensibility to the poetry to distract him from the application of standards of scholarship. He concludes:

It is with regret that I find myself obliged to pronounce Rowlie's poems to be spurious. Antient remains of English poetry, unexpectedly discovered, and fortunately rescued from a long oblivion, are contemplated with a degree of fond enthusiasm: exclusive of any real or intrinsic excellence, they afford those pleasures, arising from the idea of antiquity which deeply interest the imagination. With these pleasures we are unwilling to part. But there is a more solid satisfaction, resulting from the detection of artifice and imposture. (p. 164)

Warton's *Enquiry into the Authenticity of the Rowley Poems* was published in 1782, and here his rigorous analysis of their forgeries was part of a defence of his standards of scholarship against the attacks of Joseph Ritson and others. He affirms roundly that if the Rowley poems are not established finally as forgeries 'the entire system that has hitherto been framed concerning the progression of poetical composition, and every theory that has been established on the gradual improvements of taste, style, and language, will be shaken and disarranged' (p. 8).

Earlier in the *Enquiry* Warton discusses the charges levelled against his scholarship by his critics, and compares them to 'the unexpected retort of Curll the bookseller, who being stigmatised by Pope for having been ignominiously tossed in a blanket, seriously declared he was not tossed in a blanket but in a rug' (p. 5). In his edition of Pope's *Works* Bowles remarks of Thomas Warton: 'So sweet was his temper, and so remote from pageantry and all affectation was his conduct, that when even Ritson's scurrilous abuse came out, in which he asserted that his [Warton's] back was "*broad enough*, and his heart *hard enough*" to bear any thing Ritson could lay on it, he only said, with his usual smile, "*A black letter'd* dog, sir"' (vi, 325).

Although Warton did not question the authenticity of Ossian in print, there is some suggestion in the manner of his references to the poems in the Dissertation that their authenticity is not beyond all doubt. And among the Trinity College MSS. is a fragment headed 'Doubts &c. about Ossian'. Under this heading are arranged the following items: '1. That there should be no religious Idea or Image – 2. That there should be such Sentiments of Humanity – 3. Such Taste of Beauty. – 4. Similes – 5. General imagery. 6. Savages are not so struck with their wild scenes – . . . as to describe them [MS. in part indecipherable] and to think them strange – To persons accustomed to politer life they are only *strange*. 7. Tradition in *all* Countries imperfect.' Professor Wellek judged the comments on Ossian in the Dissertation to be an unfortunate lapse on Warton's part, but the MS. goes a long way to supporting Walpole's assumption that Warton was here being merely civil – probably to Blair whose Dissertation in defence of the poems had appeared in 1763.

XVII

Warton's *History* was edited twice in the nineteenth century; by Price in 1824 and by William Carew Hazlitt, the grandson of the essayist and critic in 1871. His editors find the *History* deficient not only in its lack of plan, but in its omission of authors who should have been included, and in its textual inaccuracies: Carew Hazlitt remarks: 'From a careful comparison of many of Warton's quotations with the very originals to which he refers, one can only draw the conclusion that he considered the faithful representation of texts as a matter of very subordinate consequence' (pp. x–xi). The books which Warton has conveniently seen in the library of 'the late Mr. William Collins' have 'been dispersed' – never to be located more. The account of a Christmas feast given by Queen Mary and King Philip of Spain for Princess Elizabeth which enlivened Warton's *Life of Sir Thomas Pope* was probably a more serious lapse from scholarly standards, as it seems possible that Warton forged the document from which he is supposed to have derived the information or that he took its authenticity too easily for granted.[10] But as Warton's methods of work were spasmodic and slovenly – as his brother found when seeking material for the completion of the *History* after his death – errors both trivial and serious were likely to have occurred when Warton was dealing with such areas of material.

The structural weaknesses in the *History* reach their climax in the third volume. Here a dissertation on the *Gesta Romanorum* as the origin of many of the tales and legends of English romance fiction heralds consideration of the work of Surrey. An account of More is interrupted for a twenty-five-page quotation from the romance of *Ywain and Gawain*; and Warton seems to find a certain relief in quoting at length the drinking song from *Gammer Gurton's Needle* at the conclusion of a section on the versifying of the Psalms. The allegorical effectiveness of Sackville's *Induction* to the *Mirror for Magistrates* is dwelt on at some length. The *History* ends with a general view of the reign of Elizabeth 'as the most POETICAL age of these annals' (p. 490), stressing the abundance of fable, fiction and fancy not only in native literature but also in translation from the classical and Italian writers: these are related to the spirit and manners of the times. Learning was beginning to advance, so that:

> On the whole, we were now arrived at that period,
> propitious to the operations of original and true poetry,
> when the coyness of fancy was not always proof against
> the approaches of reason, when genius was rather
> directed than governed by judgment, and when taste
> and learning had so far only disciplined imagination,
> as to suffer its excesses to pass without censure or
> control, for the sake of the beauties to which they were
> allied. (p. 501)

It is a conventional enough ending, and its tone is more final than Warton's plan, 'a conspectus of poetry from the Conquest to the Revolution', would have implied. Warton had appeared to Percy to be fatigued with his researches in the 'sixties, and the various undertakings, classical, antiquarian and local historical, find their place in the *History* itself, accounting for some at least of the otherwise irresponsibly digressive pattern of the work. Indeed parts of the *Life of Bathurst* were to be used to eke out the notes on Milton's minor poems. Passages in the third volume of the *History* are taken, often word for word and quite irrelevantly, from the text of the *Life of Sir Thomas Pope*.

XVIII

But against these weaknesses in Warton's *History* must be set its status as a pioneering work in taste and criticism, and one which bears the authenticity of a sensitively apprehended view of poetry. He shows himself aware of treading much of the ground for the first time, and, as he supposed, the last. Of the *Pricke of Conscience* he remarked, 'I prophecy that I am its last transcriber' (i, 256). Conscious of his too frequent and copious use of quotation he wrote:

> It is neither my inclination nor intention to write a catalogue, or compile a miscellany. It is not to be expected that this work should be a general repository of our ancient poetry: I cannot, however, help observing, that English literature and English poetry suffer, while so many pieces of this kind [he is referring to *Sir Bevys*] still remain concealed and forgotten in our manuscript libraries. (i, 207–8)

He was reading many of the manuscripts for the first time for centuries: it is no wonder that his treatment of them was unequal. Ker pointed out that Warton had unfortunately missed the *Gawain* and *Pearl* MSS; but in fact, although *Gawain* is not dealt with in the *History*, an extract from *Pearl* is quoted as if it had been transcribed and inserted from the catalogue description (iii, 107n). Errors in transcription might be numerous, and glossing faulty, but when one looks at his appreciation of Gavin Douglas's prologue to the sixth book of his translation of the *Aeneid*, one sees in his selection a critical attitude of permanent value. 'The several books', he says, 'are introduced with metrical prologues, which are often highly poetical; and shew that Douglas's proper walk was original poetry' (p. 282). He quotes for nearly seven pages the charming description of May, and observes:

> The poetical beauties of this specimen will be relished by every reader who is fond of lively touches of fancy, and rural imagery. But the verses will have another merit with those critics who love to contemplate the progress of composition, and to mark the original workings of genuine nature; as they are the effusion of a mind not overlaid by the descriptions of other poets, but operating, by its own force and bias, in the delineation of a vernal landscape, on such subjects as really occurred.

So he renders the passage into modern English. Again, there is the admiration for Sackville's *Induction*:

> These shadowy inhabitants of hell-gate are conceived with the vigour of a creative imagination, and described with great force of expression. They are delineated with that fulness of proportion, that invention of picturesque attributes, distinctness, animation, and amplitude, of which Spenser is commonly supposed to have given the first specimens in our language, and which are characteristical of his poetry. (p. 233)

The influence of Dante, hitherto generally regarded as a 'Gothic' poet, is seen in the greater licence given to extravagances of description; comparing Dante with Virgil:

> It must be allowed, that the scenes of Virgil's sixth book have many fine strokes of the terrible. But Dante's colouring is of a more gloomy temperature. There is a sombrous cast in his imagination: and he has given new shades of horror to the classical hell. We may say of Dante, that
>
>   Hell
>   Grows DARKER at his FROWN. –

The sensations of fear impressed by the Roman poet are
less harrassing to the repose of the mind: they have a
more equable and placid effect. The terror of Virgil's
tremendous objects is diminished by correctness of
composition and elegance of style. We are reconciled
to his Gorgons and Hydras, by the grace of expression,
and the charms of versification. (p. 254)

The repudiation of formal statement as in itself a desirable end
for the artist to perfect is here given concrete expression in
criticism; the responsiveness of reader and poet alike is roused
more by Dante than Virgil: 'the Charms which we so much
admire in Dante, do not belong to the Greeks and Romans. They
are derived from another origin and must be traced back to a
different stock' (p. 255). So the characters over the gate of brass
in the Inferno, quoted and translated by Warton, impress by the
'severe solemnity in these abrupt and comprehensive sentences,
and they are a striking preparation to the scenes that follow. But
the idea of such an inscription on the brazen portal of hell, was
suggested to Dante by books of chivalry; in which the gate of an
impregnable enchanted castle, is often inscribed with words
importing the dangers or wonders to be found within' (p. 239).

XIX

The ease and breadth of reference, the absence of any prejudice
and preconception to impede the responsiveness of the writer to
the poetry he is discovering to his public, remain Warton's major
contribution to the writing of literary history. As Chalmers
observed, the magnitude of the undertaking exceeded the
original idea. He praised the digressions for the wealth of information they contained. Warton, he wrote:

was the first who taught the true method of acquiring
a taste for the excellencies of our ancient poets, and of
rescuing their writings from obscurity and oblivion. Of
Warton it may be said as of Addison; 'he is now
despised by some who perhaps would never have seen
his defects, but by the lights which he afforded them'.

His erudition was extensive, and his industry must have been at one time incessant. The references in his History of Poetry only, indicate a course of varied reading, collation, and transcription, to which the common life of man seems insufficient. He was one of those scholars who have happily rescued the study of antiquities from the reproaches of the frivolous or indolent. Amidst the most rugged tracks of ancient lore, he produces cultivated spots, flowery paths, and gay prospects. (p. 85)

His successor, Courthope, deplored that Warton set about his work in the spirit of an antiquary, though he allowed that 'his reading was wide, his scholarship sound, his taste fine and discriminating; and though he had no pretensions to be called a great poet, his verse is at least marked by genuine poetic sensibility' (ix, xii). But these qualities enabled Warton to keep the relationship between the reader and the writer paramount when discussing poetry, and to widen the historical approach and the perspectives of the imagination accordingly in opening up tracts of early literature and manners to his contemporaries. And when Eliot could write, not so very long ago, about alliteration 'as primitive as that of *Piers Plowman*', Warton's subtler approach to medieval literature retains an intrinsic importance even in the twentieth century.

XX

Of all the attempts which have been made to express the essential character of Warton's achievement, that which regards him as a precursor of Romanticism is plainly inadequate, as, indeed, is that which sees him, conversely, as an essentially Augustan figure. Nichol Smith's suggestion that Warton found in the romances a relief from the classics fails to explain why Warton was so preoccupied with early literature, and, more important, the critical standpoint which dominated the greater part of his writings. R. D. Havens saw Warton as a transitional figure of purely historical significance:[11]

The truth of Warton's opinions does not matter but
their inconsistencies and other limitations do. We read
the *Observations* and the 'Verses on Reynolds's
Window', not for light on the *Faerie Queene* or on Gothic
architecture, but on a subject about which we know
much less, – the mid eighteenth century. If we are
ever to understand this period, it will be through a
careful study of such typical figures as Thomas Warton,
a study, not only of their successes, but of their failures,
a study which does not overlook their conventionality
and conservatism in its search for originality and
liberalism. Such a study will convince us of the
impossibility of tagging the writers of the time as
'romantic' or 'classic'.

The statement is a just one, but in the assumption on which it
rests it defeats the true end of studying literary history – the only
one which makes it of living interest – that, namely, to attempt,
however imperfectly, to interpret the spirit in which the Wartons
approached the problems and responsibilities of interpreting and
assessing their literary inheritance.

In his last work, that on Milton's minor poems, Warton wrote
of his subject:

Smit with the deplorable polemics of puritanism, he
suddenly ceased to gaze on *such sights as youthful poets
dream* . . . instead of embellishing original tales of
chivalry, of cloathing the fabulous atchievements of
the early British kings and champions in the gorgeous
trappings of epic attire, he wrote SMECTYMNUUS and
TETRACHORDON, apologies for fanatical preachers and
the doctrine of divorce. . . . Yet in this chaos of
controversy . . . he sometimes seems to have heaved a
sigh for the peaceable enjoyments of lettered solitude,
for his congenial pursuits, and the more mild and
ingenuous exercises of the muse. In one of his prose
tracts, he says, 'I may one day hope to have ye again
in a still time, when there shall be no Chiding. . . .'
When Milton wrote these poems Romances and
fabulous narratives were still in fashion, and not yet
driven away by puritans and usurpers. . . . Milton, at

least in these poems, may be reckoned an old English
poet; and therefore here requires that illustration,
without which no old English poet can be well
illustrated. (Preface, pp. xi–xii and xx–xxi)

These early poems of Milton seem to Warton the last emanation
of those flights of fancy which had figuratively and inventively
bodied forth the experiences of life itself, to transmute mundane
existence into an artificial but poetical ideal. This faculty has
departed with the new insistence on the importance of everyday
life and manners. He illustrates his point with reference to
Elizabethan love poetry. When the Elizabethan lover praises
his mistress;

> She is complimented in strains neither polite nor
> pathetic, without elegance, and without affection: she
> is described, not in the address of intelligible yet artful
> panegyric, not in the real colours, and with the genuine
> accomplishments of nature, but as an eccentric ideal
> being of another system, and as inspiring sentiments
> equally unmeaning, hyperbolical and unnatural. (iii,
> 501)

All or most of these circumstances contributed to give a
descriptive, a picturesque, and a figurative cast to the poetical
language. This effect appears even in the prose compositions of
the reign of Elizabeth I. In the subsequent age, prose became the
language of poetry.

Thomas Warton does not localise the problems of the poets of
his time merely in terms of a reaction against Pope, but attempts
with reference to a rich diversity of literary contexts to ascertain
the nature of the experience offered by true poetry. In so far as
his particular concern is with English poetry he locates its origins
in the highly fictionalised renderings of past modes and bygone
ideals of that allegorical and romance tradition which flowered
in the natural genius of Spenser, Shakespeare and Milton.

Notes

1 *The Gothic Revival* (Pelican; London, 1962), 21–2, 33, 16.
2 Arthur Johnston, *Enchanted Ground* (London, 1964), 79–80.

3 The Percy Letters, *The Correspondence of Thomas Percy and Thomas Warton*, ed. M. G. Robinson and Leah Dennis (Louisiana State U.P., 1951), 69–70.

4 *The Poems of Gray, Collins and Goldsmith*, ed. Roger Lonsdale (London, 1969), p. xvii.

5 Thomas Warton's Inaugural Lecture as Professor of Poetry, delivered 1757; unpublished MS., translated by Professor W. S. Watt.

6 *The Correspondence of Thomas Percy and Thomas Warton*, pp. xxii, 123, 130, 133.

7 *Mant*, i, lviii–lxi.

8 W. J. Courthope, *A History of English Poetry*, 6 vols (London, 1926), i, x–xi.

9 Mason to Walpole, 1772, in *Horace Walpole's Correspondence with William Mason*, ed. W. S. Lewis, G. Cronin Jr., and C. H. Bennett (Yale ed. *Walpole's Correspondence*, vols 28–9; London, 1955), i, 148; 'Thomas Warton', *D.N.B.*, ed. Sir Leslie Stephen and Sidney Lee, 63 vols (London 1899), lix; cf. Chalmers, 'Life of Thomas Warton', in *The Works of the English Poets*.

10 See H. E. D. Blakiston, 'Thomas Warton and Machyn's Diary', *E.H.R.*, xi (1896), 282–300.

11 R. D. Havens, 'Thomas Warton and the Eighteenth Century Dilemma', *S.P.*, xxv (1928), 50.

Postscript

The Question of Pre-Romanticism

I

The entry on Gerard in the *Dictionary of National Biography* (1890) cites Gerard's definition of taste:

'Taste consists chiefly in the improvement of those principles, which are commonly called the powers of imagination', including the senses of novelty, sublimity, beauty, imitation, harmony, ridicule, and virtue.

The author comments: 'The word has a much wider scope than that which, according to modern ideas, belongs to the subject of taste.'

I have tried to show how in its 'wider scope' the concept of taste acts as a focal point for the extension of old cultural meanings and values and the development of new. (That as a term it should be polysemous, used in connection with the trivial and the evanescent as well as the weightily philosophical, is itself a sign of its distinctive importance in the mid-eighteenth century.) The new recognition of the importance of an emotional response to art or nature, and the association of such a response with the cultivation of sensibility through reflection and sentiment, is intimately bound up with the idea of taste as a faculty in terms of which certain connections of thought and feeling can be made. But acceptance of this involved first – as Hume saw – the identification of the individual sensibility as the locus of value and second, the need to establish a consensus of educated or trained taste for the safeguarding of socially ratified standards of artistic achievement.

The concept of taste, in fact, already contained within itself that unresolved tension between the individual and the social which we meet later in the Arnoldian conception of culture and in much of the educational thinking associated with that conception. Even the ideas of G. E. Moore, which had so significant an influence on the Bloomsbury group, involve a similar attempt to combine the response of the individual sensibility with an ethical absolute. Of course these later phases of the tension (as one can see in the history of the term 'culture') were exacerbated by the decay of that Christian belief which had provided society with the guarantee that standards were divinely authorised.

II

For Wordsworth and Coleridge, however, the word 'taste' has lost most of its philosophical significance. This arises in part from an unwarranted association of its metaphorical vehicle with a passivity of response. Wordsworth writes:[1]

> it is a metaphor, taken from a *passive* sense of the
> human body, and transferred to things which are in
> their essence *not* passive – to intellectual *acts* and
> *operations*. . . . But the profound and the exquisite in
> feeling, the lofty and universal in thought and
> imagination . . . are neither of them, accurately
> speaking, objects of a faculty which could ever
> without a sinking in the spirit of Nations have been
> designated by the metaphor *Taste*. And why? Because
> without the exertion of a cooperating *power* in the mind
> of the Reader, there can be no adequate sympathy
> with either of these emotions: without this auxiliary
> impulse, elevated or profound passion cannot exist.

It is significant, too, that Wordsworth saw the social training of taste as of doubtful value precisely because it was regarded as a special faculty (falsely, he thought) and not the response of the whole living man:[2]

> If a man attaches much interest to the faculty of taste
> as it exists in himself, and employs much time in those
> studies of which this faculty (I use the word 'taste' in
> its comprehensive though most unjustifiable sense) is
> reckoned the arbiter, certain it is his moral notions and
> dispositions must either be purified and strengthened
> or corrupted and impaired. How can it be otherwise,

when his ability to enter into the spirit of works in
literature, must depend upon his feelings, his
imagination, and his understanding, that is upon his
recipient, upon his creative or active and upon his
judging powers, and upon the accuracy and compass
of his knowledge, in fine upon all that makes up the
moral and intellectual man.

Again, whatever complexity the concept of taste may have in
the abstract it was inevitably associated with what was felt as the
socially limited aesthetic cultivation of the previous age. The
essential process is described by Coleridge:[3]

> It is a painful truth that not only individuals, but even
> whole nations, are oft times so enslaved to the habits of
> their education and immediate circumstances, as not to
> judge disinterestedly even on those subjects, the very
> pleasure arising from which consists in its
> disinterestedness, namely, on subjects of taste and
> polite literature. Instead of deciding concerning their
> own modes and customs by any rule of reason, nothing
> appears rational, becoming, or beautiful to them, but
> what coincides with the peculiarities of their education.
> In this narrow circle individuals may attain to
> exquisite discrimination, as the French critics have
> done in their own literature; but a true critic can no
> more be such without placing himself on some central
> point, from which he may command the whole.

Although as it is used here 'taste' is notionally independent of the
limited response of a particular age or culture, it is clearly on the
way to being identified with these limitations.

The Romantics of course saw themselves extending the concept
of the possible on the widest fronts, both individually and socially:
political radicalism has from the beginning a central significance
in the movement. This certainly led to injustice towards the
achievements of the previous age. In *The Spirit of the Age* Hazlitt
conveys both the largeness of aim of the Romantics and the
unfairness which it entailed; the poetry of Wordsworth:[4]

> is founded on setting up an opposition (and pushing
> it to the utmost length) between the natural and

artificial; between the spirit of humanity, and the
spirit of fashion and of the world!

It is one of the innovations of the time. It partakes
of, and is carried along with, the revolutionary
movement of our age: the political changes of the day
were the model on which he formed and conducted his
poetical experiments.

III

But if the Romantics tended to see their aims too antithetically in
relation to those of the previous age, the subsequent view of the
mid-eighteenth century as merely its precursor – pre-Romantic –
represents a corresponding distortion. The assimilation was made
possible by taking certain interests and emphases in the literature
and criticism of the previous age in isolation and relating them to
similar interests and emphases in the Romantic movement itself –
primitivism, the response to natural scenery, the love of the
Gothic, the reaction against the poetry of Pope, and so on. But
even when these fragmented elements are examined it is clear
that often they can be associated on only a superficial or inessential
level. If, for example, we look at Thomas Warton's use of Gothic
architecture as a setting in his 'Grave of King Arthur', and
compare it with Scott's in the opening of the second canto of 'The
Lay of the Last Minstrel', we shall find in the first a predominant
concern with the mood evoked by the associations of the past
which certain features of the architecture (not looked at too
closely) have prompted. In Scott's poem, however, the detail of
the description seems almost to be an attempted reconstruction
of the medieval building as an authentic historical setting. The
themes and moods employed or expressed by writers from
Thomson and Young onwards were used to very different effect
and different ends by the later generation of poets.

In his article 'Towards defining an Age of Sensibility' Northrop
Frye suggested that the decades preceding the publication of the
Lyrical Ballads should be called 'The Age of Sensibility', because:[5]

roughly the second half of the eighteenth century is one
which has always suffered from not having a clear

historical or functional label applied to it. I call it here
the age of sensibility, which is not intended to be
anything but a label. This period has the 'Augustan'
age on one side of it and the 'Romantic' movement on
the other, and it is usually approached transitionally,
as a period of reaction against Pope and anticipation of
Wordsworth. . . . What we do is to set up, as the logical
expression of Augustanism, some impossibly pedantic
view of following rules and repressing feelings, which
nobody could ever have held, and then treat any
symptom of freedom or emotion as a departure from
this. Our students are thus graduated with a vague
notion that the age of sensibility was the time when
poetry moved from a reptilian Classicism, all cold and
dry reason, to a mammalian Romanticism, all warm and
wet feeling.

This is a fair enough generalisation, and one which is persuasively
succinct, but Professor Frye relates the term chiefly to experiments
in the poetic expression of moods, leaving out of account the
reflections and sentiments associated with these.

IV

I have assumed in my attempts to chart the literary preoccupations of the mid-eighteenth century that the poets, novelists,
critics and philosophers are held together in a common and
distinctive endeavour. Theirs is a conscious attempt to explore the
significance of new ways of seeing, feeling and judging. The idea
of conscious control is seldom abandoned. A new valuation is
placed on the individual sensibility: there is a new concern with
the basic emotional attributes of the individual human being, not
with their acceptable social manifestation. This new consciousness
is accompanied, too, by a growth of self-awareness, a tendency
which is observable in the beginnings of the growth of historical
relativism in criticism, and an increased sense of the complexity
of individual and social psychology and their relation to history.
In Adam Ferguson after all one finds an early sociologist.[6]
In the work of Joseph and Thomas Warton the criteria of taste –

genius, sublimity, pathos, and picturesqueness – find their most consistent expression. I have tried to consider their achievement in the context of the problems which faced them and the assumptions about literature which were available to them. Their work exhibits an authentic freshness of response and a desire to open up new areas of poetic delight. Joseph Warton's insistence on the importance of the feelings in experiencing true poetry and Thomas's investigations into the past conditions from which poetry had flowered give them a place of central importance in this period of the ascendancy of taste.

Notes

1 Quoted by Raymond Williams, *Culture and Society* (London, 1958), 41.
2 *The Prose Works of William Wordsworth*, ed. A. B. Grosart, 3 vols (London, 1876), ii, 54.
3 *Lectures on Shakespeare* (Penguin anthology), 237.
4 *The English Poets and the Spirit of the Age* (Everyman; London, 1951), 252–3.
5 *English Literary History*, xxiii (1956), 144–52, p. 144.
6 See, for example, his *Civil Society* (1767).

Select Bibliography

(a) Joseph and Thomas Warton

WARTON JOSEPH, *Odes on Various Subjects*, 1746; Warton edited *The Works of Virgil in Latin and English*, 4 vols, 1753, translating the Eclogues and Georgics into verse (2nd edn 1763; 3rd edn 1778); *Adventurer*, nos. 49, 51, 57, 63, 71, 76, 80, 83, 87, 89, 93, 97, 101, 105, 109, 113, 116, 122, 127, 133, 139; *World*, no. 26.
An Essay on The Writings and Genius of Pope, 1 volume, 1756; 2nd edn 1762 re-titled *An Essay on the Genius and Writings of Pope*; 3rd edn 1772; 4th edn 1782 issued with second volume completing the survey of Pope's works. Gregg International Publishers reprint of the 1782 4th edn corrected 1970.
The works of Alexander Pope edited in 9 volumes, 1797.

WARTON, THOMAS, *Observations on the Faerie Queene of Spenser* in 1 volume, 1754, 2nd enlarged edn in 2 vols, 1762 (Gregg International Publishers Reprint, 1970).
Life and Literary Remains of Ralph Bathurst, Dean of Wells, 2 vols, 1761; edited *Theocriti Syracusii quae supersunt*, 2 vols, 1770; *Life of Sir Thomas Pope*, 1772, 2nd enlarged edn 1784; *A History of English Poetry* published in three volumes, vol. I, 1774, vol. II, 1778; vol. III, 1781. The fragmentary fourth volume (88 pages) was issued in 1789, and an index to the whole work in 1806. The fourth revised edition compiled by W. Carew Hazlitt, 1871. Gregg International Reprint of the first edition, 1969.
An Enquiry into the Authenticity of the Poems attributed to Thomas Rowley, 1782 (2nd corrected edn).
Poems upon Several Occasions by John Milton, 1785; 2nd edn enlarged, 1791.

JOHN WOOLL: *Biographical Memoirs of the Revd. Joseph Warton, D.D.*, London, 1806, Richard Mant's *The Poetical Works of The Late Thomas Warton, B.D.* 5th edn, corrected and enlarged, *Together with Memoirs of his Life and Writings*, 2 vols, Oxford, 1802; and Clarissa Rinaker: 'Thomas Warton. A Biographical and Critical Study', *University of Illinois Studies in Language and Literature*, ii, 1916, are the only available full-length studies of the Wartons. Among several useful articles on their work are those by R. D. Havens: 'Thomas Warton and the Eighteenth

Century Dilemma', *S.P.*, xxv, 1928, 36–50; Paul F. Leedy: 'Genres Criticism and the Significance of Warton's *Essay on Pope*, *J.E.G.P.*, xlv, 1946, 140–6; L. C. Martin: 'Thomas Warton and the Early Poems of Milton', *Proceedings of the British Academy*, xx, 1934, 25–43; David Nichol Smith: 'Warton's *History of English Poetry*', *Proceedings of the British Academy*, xv, 1929, 501–4; and Hoyt Trowbridge: 'Joseph Warton's Classification of the English Poets', *M.L.N.*, li, 515–18, 'Joseph Warton on the Imagination', *M.P.* xxxv, 1937–9, 73–87.

W. D. MacClintock: *Joseph Warton's 'Essay on Pope'. A History of the Five Editions*, Chapel Hill, 1933, gives a close analysis of alterations made by Warton to his most important work.

The Correspondence of Thomas Percy and Thomas Warton, ed. Leah Dennis and M. G. Robinson, Louisiana, 1951, and Arthur Johnston: *Enchanted Ground. The Study of Medieval Romance in the Eighteenth Century*, London, 1964, illuminate the achievement of Thomas Warton.

British Museum Add. MSS. 42560 and 42561; Bodleian MS. Don c. 75, and the Warton MSS. in Winchester College and Trinity College, Oxford, contain much valuable material as yet unpublished. Still inaccessible to scholars are the MSS. owned by the Swann family from which Burns Martin published a selection in *S.P.*, 1936, 53–67.

(b) General

I. PRIMARY MATERIAL

ALISON, ARCHIBALD, *Essays on the Nature and Principles of Taste* (1790), 2 vols, 1817.

BAILLIE, JOHN, *On the Sublime* (1747), Augustan Reprint Society Publication no. 43, Los Angeles, 1953.

BEATTIE, JAMES, *Dissertations Moral and Critical*, London and Edinburgh, 1783.

BLACKWELL, THOMAS, *An Enquiry into the Life and Writings of Homer* (1735), London, 1824.

BLAIR, HUGH, *A Critical Dissertation upon the Poems of Ossian* (1763).

BLAIR, HUGH (ed.), *The Poems of Ossian Translated by James Macpherson, Esq., with Dissertations on the Era and Poems of Ossian and Dr Blair's Critical Dissertation*, 2 vols, Glasgow, 1821.

BOSWELL, JAMES, *Life of Johnson*, ed. R. W. Chapman (Oxford Standard Authors), London, 1965.

BOSWELL, JAMES, *Journal of a Tour to the Hebrides*, ed. R. W. Chapman, Oxford, 1951.

Select Bibliography

BROWN, JOHN, *History of the Rise and Progress of Poetry*, London, 1764.

BURKE, EDMUND, *A Philosophical Inquiry into the Origins of our Ideas of the Sublime and Beautiful*, (1756), ed. J. T. Boulton, London, 1958.

COLERIDGE, SAMUEL, *Biographia Literaria*, ed. J. Shawcross, 2 vols, Oxford, 1907.

COOPER, JOHN GILBERT, *Letters Concerning Taste*, (1755) Augustan Reprint Society Publication no. 30, Los Angeles, 1951.

DENNIS, JOHN, *Critical Works*, ed. E. N. Hooker, 2 vols, Baltimore, 1939.

DODD, WILLIAM, *The Beauties of Shakespeare*, 2 vols, London, 1752.

DUFF, WILLIAM, *An Essay on Original Genius*, London, 1767.

GERARD, ALEXANDER, *An Essay on Taste* (1758), Edinburgh, 1780.

GOLDSMITH, OLIVER, *Collected Works of Oliver Goldsmith*, ed. Arthur Friedman, 5 vols, Oxford, 1966.

HOGARTH, WILLIAM, *An Analysis of Beauty*, 1753.

HUME, DAVID, *Essays Moral, Political and Literary*, ed. T. H. Green and T. H. Grose, 2 vols, London, 1875.

HURD, RICHARD, *Works*, 8 vols, London, 1811.

HUTCHESON, FRANCIS, *Essays on the Nature and Conduct of the Passions And Affections*, 1728.

JOHNSON, SAMUEL, *Works*, ed. Arthur Murphy, 12 vols, London, 1806.

JOHNSON, SAMUEL, *Lives of the English Poets*, ed. G. Birkbeck Hill, 3 vols, Oxford, 1935.

KAMES, HENRY HUME, LORD, *Elements of Criticism* (1762) 2 vols, Edinburgh, 1788.

LOWTH, ROBERT, *Lectures on the Sacred Poetry of the Hebrews* (1753), trans. G. Gregory, London, 1847.

MORGANN, MAURICE, *An Essay on the Character of Falstaff* (1777).

NICHOLS, JOHN, *Literary Anecdotes of the Eighteenth Century*, 9 vols, 1812–15.

NICHOLS, JOHN, *Illustrations of the Literary History of the Eighteenth Century*, 8 vols, 1817–58.

PERCY, THOMAS, *Reliques of Ancient English Poetry* (1765).

PERCY, THOMAS, *The Percy Letters*, General Editors D. Nichol Smith and Cleanth Brooks, 5 vols, Louisiana, 1944–57.

REYNOLDS, SIR JOSHUA, *Discourses* (1769–90), (Everyman), 1928.

SHAFTESBURY, ANTONY ASHLEY COOPER, EARL OF, *Characteristics of Men, Manners, Opinions, Times* (1708–14), 3 vols, London, 1773.

SPENCE, JOSEPH, *Polymetis*, 1747.

SPENCE, JOSEPH, *Observations, Anecdotes and characters of books and men,* ed. James M. Osborn, 2 vols, Oxford, 1966.

WEBB, DANIEL, *Remarks on the Beauties of Poetry* (1762), ed. Hans Hecht, Hamburg, 1920.

WOOD, ROBERT, *An Essay on the Original Genius and Writings of Homer* (1769), London, 1824.

YOUNG, EDWARD, *Conjectures on Original Composition* (1759).

II. SECONDARY MATERIAL

ALTICK, RICHARD, *The English Common Reader, a Social History of the Mass Reading Public,* Illinois, 1957.

ABRAMS, M. H., *The Mirror and the Lamp, Romantic Theory and the Critical Tradition,* New York, 1953.

BATE, WALTER J., *From Classic to Romantic,* Harvard, 1949.

BELJAME, ALEXANDER, *Men of Letters and the English Public in the Eighteenth Century, 1660–1744,* ed. Bonamy Dobrée, trans. E. O. Lorimer, London, 1948.

CASSIRER, ERNST, *The Philosophy of the Enlightenment,* Princeton, 1951.

CHAPIN, CHESTER F., *Personification in Eighteenth Century English Poetry,* New York, 1955.

CLARK, SIR KENNETH, *The Gothic Revival* (Pelican), London, 1962.

CLIFFORD, JAMES L., *Man versus Society in Eighteenth Century Britain,* Cambridge, 1968.

COHEN, RALPH, *The Art of Discrimination,* London, 1964.

COLLINGWOOD, R. G., *The Idea of Nature,* Oxford, 1945.

CONGLETON, J. M., *Theories of Pastoral Poetry in England, 1684–1798,* Gainsville, 1952.

CRANE, RONALD S., 'English Neo-classical Criticism: an Outline Sketch', *Critics and Criticism, Ancient and Modern,* Chicago. 1952.

CRANE, RONALD S., 'On Writing the History of English Criticism, 1650–1800', *University of Toronto Quarterly,* xxii, 1952, 376–91.

DAVIE, DONALD, *Purity of Diction in English Verse,* London, 1952.

DEANE, C. V., *Aspects of Eighteenth Century Nature Poetry,* London, 1967.

DRAPER, J. W., *The Funeral Elegy and English Romanticism,* New York, 1929.

EMPSON, WILLIAM, *Some Versions of Pastoral* (Peregrine), London, 1966.

FAIRCHILD, HOXEY N., *Religious Trends in English Poetry,* vol. i, New York, 1939.

Select Bibliography

FLETCHER, ANGUS, *Allegory: the Theory of a Symbolic Mode*, Cornell, 1964.

FUSSELL, PAUL, *The Rhetorical World of Augustan Humanism*, Oxford, 1965.

GEORGE, M. DOROTHY, *London Life in the Eighteenth Century* (Pelican), London, 1965.

HIPPLE, WALTER J., *The Beautiful, the Sublime and the Picturesque in Eighteenth-Century British Aesthetic Theory*, Carbondale, 1957.

HOOKER, E. N., 'The Discussion of Taste from 1750–1770, and the New Trends in Literary Criticism', *P.M.L.A.*, xlix, 1934, 577–92.

HOOKER, E. N., 'The Reviewers and the New Criticism, 1754–70', *P.Q.*, xiii, 1934, 189–202.

JACK, IAN, *Augustan Satire. Intention and Idiom in English Poetry, 1660–1750*, Oxford, 1952.

LOVEJOY, A. O., 'On the Discrimination of Romanticisms', *P.M.L.A.*, 1924, 229–53.

MACDONALD, W. L., *Pope and his Critics*, London, 1951.

MACLEAN, KENNETH, *John Locke and English Literature of the Eighteenth Century*, Yale, 1936.

MCKILLOP, A. D., *The Background of Thomson's 'Seasons'*, Hamden, Conn., 1961.

MAYO, ROBERT D., *The Novel in the Magazines, 1740–1815*, Evanston, Illinois, 1962.

MONK, SAMUEL HOLT, *The Sublime, A Study of Critical Theories in Eighteenth Century England*, New York, 1935.

MUELLER, WILLIAM B., *Spenser's Critics: Changing Current in Literary Taste*, Syracuse, 1959.

PANOFSKY, ERWIN, *Meaning in the Visual Arts* (Peregrine), 1970.

PLUMB, J. H., *England in the Eighteenth Century* (Pelican), 1951.

RICHARDS, I. A., *The Philosophy of Rhetoric*, New York, 1936.

RICHARDS, I. A., *Principles of Literary Criticism*, London, 1948.

ROBERTSON, T. G., *Studies in the Genesis of Romantic Theory in Europe*, Cambridge, 1923.

ROSTON, MURRAY, *Prophet and Poet, The Bible and the growth of Romanticism*, London, 1965.

SMITH, LOGAN PEARSALL, *Words and Idioms*, London, 1925.

SOFEN-RØSTVIG, MARIE, *The Happy Man: Studies in the Metamorphoses of a Classical Ideal*, vol. 1 (1600–1706) 1954, vol. 2 (1700–1766) 1958.

SPACKS, PATRICIA MEYER, *The Insistence of horror: Aspects of the supernatural in eighteenth century poetry*, Cambridge, Mass., 1962.

STEPHEN, SIR LESLIE, *English Literature and Society in the Eighteenth Century* (University paperback), 1963.

STRAUS, RALPH, *Robert Dodsley, Poet, Publisher and Playwright*, London, 1910.

SUTHERLAND, J., *A Preface to Eighteenth Century Poetry*, Oxford, 1948.

TUCKER, SUSIE, *Protean Shapes*, London, 1967.

TUVESON, ERNEST, *The Imagination as a Means of Grace, Locke and the Aesthetics of Romanticism*, Berkeley, 1960.

VAN TIEGHEM, PAUL, *L'ère romantisme: le romantisme dans la littérature européenne*, Paris, 1948.

VAN TIEGHEM, PAUL, 'La notion de vraie poésie dans le préromantisme européen', *Révue de la Littérature Comparée*, i, 1921, 215–51.

VEREKER, CHARLES, *Eighteenth Century Optimism. A Study of the Inter-relations of Moral and Social Theory in English and French Thought between 1689 and 1789*, Liverpool, 1967.

WEARMOUTH, ROBERT F., *Methodism and the common people of the eighteenth century*, London, 1957.

WELLEK, RENE, *The Rise of English Literary History*, Chapel Hill, 1941.

WHITNEY, LOIS, *Primitivism and the Idea of Progress in English Popular Literature of the Eighteenth Century*, Baltimore, 1934.

WILES, R. M., *Freshest Advices, Early Provincial Newspapers in England*, Ohio State U.P., Columbus, 1965.

WOODHOUSE, A. S. P., *Collins and the Creative Imagination*, Toronto, 1931.

WURTSBAUGH, JEWEL, *Two Centuries of Spenserian Scholarship, 1609–1805*, Baltimore, 1936.

I have in general omitted novels, poetry, drama, essays and magazines of the eighteenth century from the above lists. Certain editions and anthologies have been particularly helpful. Among these are Roger Lonsdale, *The Poems of Gray, Collins and Goldsmith*, London, 1969; E. F. Carritt, *A Calendar of British Taste, 1600–1800*, London, 1948; James Clifford, *Eighteenth Century English Literature. Modern Essays in Criticism* (Galaxy), 1959; W. H. Durham, *Critical Essays of the Eighteenth Century*, New Haven, 1915; E. D. Jones, *English Critical Essays (Sixteenth, Seventeenth and Eighteenth Centuries)* (World's Classics), London, 1947; and Alexander Chalmers, *The Works of English Poets from Chaucer to Cowper*, 21 vols, London, 1810.

Index

227

Index

Index